Urban America Reconsidered

URBAN AMERICA RECONSIDERED

Alternatives for Governance and Policy

DAVID IMBROSCIO

CORNELL UNIVERSITY PRESS
ITHACA AND LONDON

First published 2010 by Cornell University Press
First printing, Cornell Paperbacks, 2010
Printed in the United States of America

Library of Congress Cataloging-in-Publication Data

Imbroscio, David L.
    Urban America reconsidered : alternatives for governance and policy /
David Imbroscio.
        p. cm.
    Includes bibliographical references and index.
    ISBN 978-0-8014-4852-2 (cloth : alk. paper) — ISBN 978-0-8014-7565-8
(pbk. : alk. paper)
    1. Urban policy—United States. 2. Municipal government—United
States. 3. Community development, Urban—United States.
4. Liberalism—United States. I. Title.
    HT123.I434   2010
    320.8'50973—dc22   2009041331

Cornell University Press strives to use environmentally responsible
suppliers and materials to the fullest extent possible in the publishing
of its books. Such materials include vegetable-based, low-VOC inks
and acid-free papers that are recycled, totally chlorine-free, or partly
composed of nonwood fibers. For further information, visit our website
at www.cornellpress.cornell.edu.

Cloth printing   10 9 8 7 6 5 4 3 2 1
Paperback printing   10 9 8 7 6 5 4 3 2 1

To Amanda

CONTENTS

PREFACE

Beyond Liberalism

I write this book as an American, as an urbanist, and as a critical scholar—one who cares deeply about the ailing of his nation and its cities and believes deeply in the potential of critical urban research to contribute to a healing. I conceived this project and wrote many of its chapters while haunted and enraged—haunted by the television pictures from New Orleans following Hurricane Katrina and enraged that such a horrible thing could happen here, in my country, with its fabulous wealth and profoundly democratic pretensions.

Over several years of study and consideration I have come to believe that only part of the blame for the urban ills of America lies with those who resist democracy and reject justice in favor of inequality and injustice. Equally at fault are those who care deeply about the ends of justice and democracy in cities but are misguided as to means. These persons, who embrace the philosophical framework and programmatic agenda of liberalism, fail to understand—and face up to—what is required to achieve such ends (cf. Alperovitz 2005). And the costs of this failure have been enormous. For over half a century, misguided liberal policies and strategies have more often than not been as destructive to cities and their people and institutions as they have been ameliorative.[1] As a result, human suffering has intensified and urban democracy has remained emasculated.

A first key aim of this book is thus to critique this liberalism—both in its philosophical and programmatic manifestations. Although much recent critical urban scholarship has focused on liberalism's *neo* form, especially the rollback of the activist and interventionist centralized state over the past three decades (see, e.g., the work of progressive geographer Jason Hackworth, 2007), it is my contention that the real problem lies with liberalism itself, in all its forms,[2] including its more appealing social democratic/New Deal variety (cf. Greider 2009; Hess 2009).

A recent insight offered by another progressive geographer, Mark Purcell, nicely captures the inspiration behind a second key aim of this book. Although recognizing that such a characterization "slightly overdraws the picture," Purcell (2004, 764–65) points out, perceptively, that "the urban policy debate in the US is dominated by liberals and neoliberals," while critical[3] scholars only "observe and critique." In light of this reality, he suggests it is "imperative" for critical scholarship "to leave the audience and enter the debate." An "effective way to do so," adds Purcell, is to proffer

> policy proposals that both critique and offer concrete alternatives to the liberal and neoliberal visions. Whether or not such policy proposals are actually realized, they would at least begin to nudge the debate off its current liberal/neoliberal axis. What is more, they can introduce alternatives to the contemporary capitalist city into a discourse that sorely needs them.

In line with this exhortation, I attempt to introduce such alternatives into this discourse by offering the kinds of concrete, but critical, policy proposals that can rival those of liberalism and neoliberalism (also see Hess 2009). For too long, as Purcell notes, critical urban scholars have been mere audience members in the urban policy debate, with—I would add—devastating consequences for cities and their citizens. In this book, I attempt to take some small steps toward changing that, with the goal of enhancing democracy, equality, and social justice in America's cities.

As I write these words in the spring of 2009, there is again a renewed optimism (or hope) in the possibility that liberalism can save America's cities.

My analysis, however, suggests that this optimism is again misguided—as it was in the late 1940s, the mid-1960s, the late 1970s, and the mid-1990s. During each of those eras, liberalism produced its rather predictable results—and hopes for a rebirth of urban democracy and a significant amelioration of urban problems were quickly dashed. Of course only the unfolding of history will judge whether I am indeed correct in this assessment. If I am, it is my hope this book will help forge a new way forward.

Forging this new way forward seems at this moment as imperative as ever. Again, as I currently write, the larger-order economic and financial institutions in the United States—constructed, defended, and propped up by political liberals as much as neoliberals and conservatives—have revealed themselves to be even more corrupt, more rotted, and more enfeebled than almost anyone imagined. Contrary to the beliefs of most liberals, we seem to stand on the precipice of what political economist and social theorist Gar Alperovitz (2005, 3) aptly identifies as a "*systemic* crisis"—an historical era where "the political-economic system must slowly lose legitimacy because the realities it produces contradict the values it proclaims" (emphasis in original). Solving such a crisis, Alperovitz adds, ultimately requires—by definition—the "development of a new system."

While my analysis in this book focuses more narrowly on developing alternatives for cities, rather than on comprehensive political-economic system change, it does nevertheless hint at what such a new system in the broader sense might look like. Inspired by Alperovitz's vision, that new system would be one that is decentralized, egalitarian, community-oriented, republican, and entrepreneurial—and where property ownership and control—"the locus of real power in most systems," as Alperovitz (2005, 5) reminds us—would be structured in an altogether different manner. It is thus my hope that this book can, in some small way, contribute to the larger-order, long-term project of replacing the current dysfunctional political-economic system in the United States with one that better fulfills the aspirations of its citizens to build a more just, democratic, and prosperous nation.

—David Imbroscio

Louisville, Kentucky

Acknowledgments

No book is produced individually, as you know.
—George Orwell, *1984*

I read Orwell's observation so many years ago, and have been moved by it ever since. As I tallied the many debts I have accumulated to complete this project, it became especially poignant. Yes, indeed, no book is ever produced individually, and this one is most certainly no exception.

Numerous friends and colleagues read and commented on parts of the manuscript in its many earlier forms and/or offered much appreciated support and encouragement along the rather long journey. I thank Gar Alperovitz, Victoria Basolo, Bob Beauregard, Yasminah Beebeejaun, Larry Bennett, Julie-Anne Boudreau, Susan Clarke, Jonathan Davies, James DeFilippis, John Dryzek, Judy Garber, Ed Goetz, Susan Greenbaum, Dennis Judd, Loren King, Avery Kolers, Bob Lake, Marc Levine, Karen Mossberger, Kathe Newman, Marion Orr, Michael Leo Owens, Mike Pagano, Joel Rast, Adolph Reed, Laura Reese, Susan Saegert, Hank Savitch, Mara Sidney, Janet Smith, Jeff Spinner-Halev, Clarence Stone, Todd Swanstrom, Phil Thompson, Thad Williamson, Hal Wolman, Elvin Wyly, and Jordan Yin. The rather lengthy nature of this list should not in any way diminish the gratitude I feel to each. I am immensely thankful and fortunate to have such a wonderful community of friends and colleagues from which to draw intellectual and emotional sustenance.

Larry Bennett and James DeFilippis also undertook the heroic task of closely and thoroughly reading the entire manuscript, offering copious criticisms and suggestions for improvement. There is little doubt that this book is much stronger due to their insightful comments. Both Larry and James pushed me to write a sharper and, frankly, a better book. For assistance with the initial stages of putting together the bibliography, I thank my graduate assistant Amy Shelton. My former chair at the University of Louisville, Chuck Ziegler, provided years of support for my work, without which this book could not have been written. Steve Elkin and Clarence Stone, my graduate school mentors, remain after all these years a source of great inspiration and support. Special thanks also go to Ron Vogel, a source of steadfast encouragement and sage advice over the last decade and a half, and a much appreciated and valued combination of friend and colleague. As my current chair, Ron also ensured that my teaching and service obligations were compatible with the time commitment required in the final stages of this project. I also wish to thank Preston Quesenberry for his many years of close friendship and unconditional support. I remain marveled by Preston's intellect and humanity. Through our thousands of hours of intense conversation over the past decade, I have learned more from him than perhaps anyone I have ever known.

My deepest thanks go to Amanda LeDuke. In many ways, this book is as much hers as mine. Most certainly, anyone who knows me well knows I could not have written it without her love and the almost superhuman level of emotional support she has provided over the years. Her multiple close reads of the manuscript in its various forms produced untold editorial changes, both stylistic and substantive. It is only because of her remarkable insightfulness and significant editorial talents—and her generosity in sharing them selflessly—that this book is what it is. Without them, the book would be considerably less readable and most definitely less coherent. She also worked diligently to ensure that all of the more mundane details regarding references and aberrant spaces were in good order. And she was willing to celebrate with great zest each time I finished yet another stage in the long process of bringing the book to completion. For all of this, and more, it is to her that I dedicate this book.

Some of the material appearing in this book has been adapted from previously published work. I gratefully acknowledge the permission of each publisher to reprint the relevant passages. Chapter 1 draws on "Reformulating Urban Regime Theory: The Division of Labor between State and Market Reconsidered," *Journal of Urban Affairs* 20, no. 3 (1998): 233–48. Copyright © Urban Affairs Association. Chapter 2 draws on "Overcoming the Neglect of Economics in Urban Regime Theory," *Journal of Urban Affairs* 25, no. 3 (2003): 271–84. Copyright © Urban Affairs Association. Chapter 3 draws on "Shaming the Inside Game: A Critique of the Liberal Expansionist Approach to Addressing Urban Problems," *Urban Affairs Review* 42, no. 2 (2006): 224–48. Copyright © Sage Publications. Chapter 4 draws on "United and Actuated by Some Common Impulse of Passion: Challenging the Dispersal Consensus in American Housing Policy Research," *Journal of Urban Affairs* 30, no. 2 (2008): 111–30. Copyright © Urban Affairs Association. Chapter 5 draws on "The Local Public Balance Sheet: An Alternative Evaluation Methodology for Local Economic Development," in *Critical Evaluations of Economic Development Policies,* edited by Laura Reese and David Fasenfest (Detroit: Wayne State University Press, 2004), 77–100. Reprinted with the permission of Wayne State University Press. Copyright © 2004 Wayne State University Press.

Introduction

RECONSIDERING URBAN AMERICA

Over the past two decades two related but distinct orthodoxies have taken hold within the academic study of urban America. Both are grounded in elements of philosophical liberalism. And both are deeply misguided. The first, *urban regime theory,* concerns *urban governance* in American cities; the second, what I call *liberal expansionism,* concerns *urban policy* for addressing the problems faced by American cities. It is the central argument of this book that both of these orthodoxies need to be challenged, reconsidered, and, ultimately reformulated with or replaced by superior alternatives.

Although these two orthodoxies consume and adversely affect the academic realm, they also have significant deleterious impacts on real world political practice. Regarding urban regime theory, as conventionally understood it offers primarily an empirical-explanatory account of the political dynamics in cities. In contrast, in this book I demonstrate that, if properly reformulated, it can elucidate a prescriptive guide (or a "road map" of sorts) to how inegalitarian urban governing regimes can be progressively reconstructed. Thus, urban regime theory, which now is of limited practical use, can instead aid the tens of thousands of progressive leaders and activists tire-lessly working throughout the United States to enhance democratic equal-ity in cities. The second academic orthodoxy, liberal expansionism, tends to delude real world policymakers into thinking that a preponderance of careful social-science research conclusively proves the case for adopting its regional policies for confronting America's myriad urban problems. How-ever, as I also demonstrate in this book, when one examines liberal expan-sionism more closely and with less ideological bias, it turns out that this ostensibly conclusive case is largely illusionary. This examination, in turn, can create a political opening for the pursuit of an alternative (and poten-tially superior) set of urban policies to address these problems.

Thus, the ultimate goal of advancing the central argument in this book is an eminently practical one. The state of governance in urban America, a nation professing to democratic and egalitarian ideals, is dismal; the de-gree of human suffering resulting from America's entrenched urban prob-lems, severe. My intent and hope is that the ideas presented within might help alleviate this suffering and advance both democracy and equality in America's cities.

Urban Regime Theory

First conceived by scholars in the early to mid-1980s (see Fainstein and Fainstein 1983; Elkin 1985c), *urban regime theory* soon became the domi-nant mode of urban political analysis (see Stone 1987, 1989). By the 1990s, urban scholarship witnessed an explosion of analyses using regime theory as the lens to understand governance in cities,[1] a trend continuing in the new century.[2] As a result, urban regime theory, while not without its share of sympathetic critics (see chapter 1), has today achieved the status of or-thodoxy (Davies, forthcoming).

The strong analytic appeal of urban regime theory led to its rapid and commanding rise as the central theory for understanding urban gov-ernance. Particularly important was its ability to "dispense...with the stalled debates" between pluralist and elitist accounts of urban politics from the 1960s and 1970s, by rejecting both approaches in favor of a *politi-cal economy* perspective (Lauria 1997a, 1; also see Vogel 1992). However, while regime theory adopted the central tenet of political economy—that economic forces play a strong role in shaping urban governance—it also avoided economic determinism by appreciating how "politics [also] matters" in shaping that governance (Stone 1987, 17).

The roots of urban regime theory can be traced to the seminal work of Yale political economist Charles Lindblom in explicating the dynamics of comparative (national-level) political economies. Lindblom, a towering figure in twentieth-century social science, is rightfully thought of as the godfather of regime analysis. His magnum opus, *Politics and Markets: The World's Political-Economic Systems,* published in 1977, set forth all of the basic tenets of the approach that subsequently became *urban* regime theory (see, especially, Elkin 1982 and Stone 1980). Most important among these tenets was the idea that urban political processes are "largely a consequence of the division of labor between state and market as that is manifest in cities" of capitalist democracies such as the United States (Elkin 1987, 18; also see Stone 1989). On one side of this division is the state (or, in the case of urban politics, the local state), which provides the city with a range of collective goods and is popularly controlled via elections. On the other side is the market, which provides economic investment and development for the city and is controlled privately by businesspersons.

Urban regime theory centrally holds that, because this division of labor estranges public power from economic activity, the local state is left too weak to accomplish the complex policy tasks required to govern the city effectively. Therefore, local public officials need to form cooperative arrangements with nongovernmental (private) actors to create a capacity for effective governance. These largely informal arrangements between public officials and private actors are called "urban regimes" or, more concretely, "governing coalitions" (Stone 1989, 5). In forming governing coalitions, public officials seek to meld their limited resources with resources held by extrastate organizations and actors. And, because members of the city's corporate-oriented business community are likely to hold a concentration of resources useful for accomplishing complex governing tasks, they appear as especially attractive governing partners. Hence, the regime formation process privileges business interests and, as a result, most urban regimes revolve around a cooperative arrangement between local public officials and corporate-oriented elites (Stone 1989; also see Elkin 1987). Regime theory also holds that the power wielded by these regimes stems largely from their ability to accomplish these complex governing tasks,

not from their ability to dominate and subordinate oppositional political forces. It thus understands political power in social production rather
than social control terms—a matter of possessing the "power to, not power
over" (Stone 1989, 229).

Urban regime theory clearly represented an advance over the earlier
pluralist and elitist theories of urban governance.[3] Moreover, it offered a
generally attractive and compelling empirical account of contemporary political dynamics in market-oriented democracies (see Elkin 1985a, 1985b,
2006). One powerful way to appreciate this attractiveness is to understand
the superiority of regime theory in comparison with much of the scholarly
work produced by the broader discipline of political science (cf. Stone 2008).
For example, while urban regime theory long ago transcended the largely
discredited pluralist theory of political power, this theory still dominates
mainstream political science (see Gunnell 2004). Such dominance continues in spite of pluralism's well-understood limitations (see Elkin 1985b).
Along these same lines, although regime theory remains deeply grounded
in liberal theory (Davies 2002), it developed by gleaning crucial insights
from the best of neo-Marxian scholarship of the 1970s (such as the endemic
tensions between capitalism and democracy). In contrast, mainstream political science has largely eschewed this scholarship (Sapotichne, Jones, and
Wolfe 2007), at its analytic peril (Lindblom 1982; Imbroscio, forthcoming).
Regime theory also largely avoids the two research traditions embraced
with a fervor by mainstream political science, behavioralism and rational
choice—both of which have been shown to be highly problematic (see, for
example, Dryzek 1988; Green and Shapiro 1994, 2005). Finally, whereas
regime theory maintains a more critically oriented value stance, giving
it heightened analytic capacity and insight (see Imbroscio, forthcoming),
mainstream political science tends to be underlain by values that largely
celebrate the status quo (Stone 2008; Lindblom 1982).[4]

Nevertheless, despite urban regime theory's numerous attributes—
especially in comparison with mainstream political science—in its conventional form it remains hampered by some deep deficiencies that significantly
weaken its explanatory and prescriptive potential. Regarding that unrealized potential, what I find most significant is that, as currently formulated,
urban regime theory can offer no prescriptive guide to how urban regimes
can be progressively reconstructed to advance both democracy and equality in America's cities. As the urban governance scholar Timothy Collins

(2008, 1183) has astutely reminded us, if the current undemocratic and in-egalitarian nature of urban regimes is to be altered, "it is incumbent upon regime analysts to identify the factors that help create viable, socially equi-table, coalitions" (also see Gendron 2006). The critique and reformulation of urban regime theory developed in this book, then, is thus not offered merely to sharpen our explanatory account of how American governance functions. Rather, I seek to critique and reformulate urban regime theory because, by doing so in appropriate ways, the approach potentially holds the key to revealing a guide (or "road map") to how significant progressive changes (or reconstructions) in that governance might be brought about.

Liberal Expansionism

Throughout the past half century urbanists have struggled with the Hercu-lean task of ameliorating the multiple problems of America's central cities. Various policy approaches have become fashionable over the years, captur-ing the attention (and imagination) of hopeful scholars desperately seek-ing solutions to these multiple and deep-rooted problems. The expansion of social services via the War on Poverty/Great Society, the reorientation of city development policy in progressive directions, the rapid proliferation and growth of community development corporations, and the enhance-ment of human-capital investment, especially urban school reform, have all had their (urban) moment.[5]

Of late the dominant, indeed almost hegemonic, policy approach em-braced by American urbanists has been what I term *liberal expansionism*.[6] This approach combines a liberal political philosophy (in the contempo-rary, American sense) with the idea that the social and economic problems of America's central cities can only be solved by—to use the metaphors of two well-known works by liberal expansionists—"crossing the city line" (Dreier, Mollenkopf, and Swanstrom 2001, 230) or "playing the out-side game" (Rusk 1999, 11). Central cities are failing, according to this perspective, because they and their poorer residents are too *isolated*—governmentally, politically, socially, fiscally, and economically—especially from their wider metropolitan regions (i.e., from the suburbs that surround them) as well as from the resources of other extracity institutions such as higher-level governments and large philanthropic foundations. The antidote to this multifaceted isolation is *expansion*[7]—creating governmental, political, social, fiscal, and economic linkages between the central city, its population, and institutions and resources existing beyond its boundaries. In the archetypical contemporary liberal vein, the vehicle for fostering these expansionist linkages is usually the activist state (especially operating on a centralized level). This activist state promotes the classic (and venerable) liberal goals of enhancing educational and economic opportunity for individuals, class and racial residential integration, and the modest reduction of economic inequality via government-directed redistribution.

To date, the most comprehensive—and perhaps quintessential—liberal expansionist tract is *Place Matters: Metropolitics for the Twenty-First Century*, authored by three prominent American urbanists, Peter Dreier, John Mollenkopf, and Todd Swanstrom. By highlighting the "outpouring of 'new metropolitan thinking'" that has occurred from the mid-1990s onward, Dreier, Mollenkopf, and Swanstrom (2004, 305) nicely capture the pervasiveness of expansionist ideas. This outpouring included the "acclaimed books" by politicians-turned-scholars Myron Orfield and David Rusk, the "lucid syndicated columns" of journalist Neal Peirce, the "prescient arguments" adduced by the National League of Cities under William Barnes, the "careful policy assessments" made by the National Academy of Science, the "provocative ideas" proffered by legal scholar john powell, and the "compelling studies" by the Bruce Katz-led Brookings Institution Center for Urban and Metropolitan Policy (which recently changed its name to the Metropolitan Policy Program, dropping the *Urban* tag altogether).[8] The Brookings Institution has been particularly important in promoting liberal expansionist ideas, publishing many of the books by Orfield and Rusk, as well as producing scores of studies like those mentioned above. Liberal expansionist thinking also has been aggressively promulgated by another Washington, D.C.-based liberal think tank, the Urban Institute, especially in the area of housing policy.[9] Major liberal foundations have gotten into the act as well, supporting liberal expansionist policy initiatives with generous funding. Last but certainly not least was the Clinton administration, whose Housing and Urban Development Secretary Henry Cisneros "promoted and funded regional initiatives, conferences, and reports" (Dreier, Mollenkopf, and Swanstrom 2004, 305), and whose Vice President Al Gore penned the foreword to a major Brookings book on liberal expansionism (see Katz 2000). These liberal expansionist ideas, while somewhat dormant doing the George W. Bush presidency, are potentially poised to rise to prominence once again in the new Democratic administration of Barack Obama (see, for example, Angotti 2008).

The upshot of this outpouring of research and writing, as Dreier, Mollenkopf, and Swanstrom (2004, 305) conclude, is that "new metropolitan approaches" (most of which are thoroughly in the liberal vein) have been placed "squarely on the agenda" of America's "policy intellectuals." In addition to the promotion of greater metropolitan regionalism in urban policymaking (the so-called *new regionalism*), the expansionist impulse currently in vogue runs deeper. It also includes the need for cities to create linkages with the global economy, tap extraregional labor pools, and draw down additional intergovernmental (especially federal) resources in the form of an enlargement of the social welfare state.[10]

Liberal expansionism thus decidedly looks beyond the local to solve urban problems. The local scale is, as Dreier, Mollenkopf, and Swanstrom (2004) argue in *Place Matters,* much too limited to do much good; thus the only alternative is to search elsewhere for solutions. This stance shifts the focus of energy and effort from that which is internal and nearby to that which is external and distant. More generally, it greatly deemphasizes *place-oriented* strategies, which are rooted in a community development approach that attempts to confront urban problems where they spatially exist, in favor of *people-oriented* strategies, which frequently seek to relocate persons far from the places where they now reside.

As with urban regime theory's account of urban governance, there is much that is attractive about liberal expansionism's account of urban problems. For instance, a clear—even compelling—logic links liberal expansionism's empirical diagnosis of the causes of such problems to its attendant policy solutions. Even more basically, this approach exudes a certain commonsensical quality; as such, its proponents often characterize the approach as the *natural* policy response to urban problems (see chapter 3). Finally, liberal expansionism comes wrapped in a seemingly compelling normative sheen, one that appropriately exacts a sense of rough justice among the haves, the have-nots, and those in between.

Despite having some clearly attractive features, I believe the liberal expansionist approach is deeply flawed on both normative and practical grounds. The driving force propelling this critique is an aspiration to reshape current institutional practices and policies designed to address urban problems. In essence, then, as in the case of urban regime theory, the ultimate goal of my critique of liberal expansionism is constructive (or *re*constructive) and practical: demonstrating how the dominant policy approach to addressing such problems—liberal expansionism—is misguided can help open the door politically to the serious consideration of other viable, and potentially superior, approaches.

The Philosophical Root of Failure

Unfolding in the chapters to follow is an analysis of the root cause of the failures of both conventional urban regime theory and liberal expansionism. Such failures, I argue, are largely attributable to elements of a *deep philosophical liberalism* lying at the heart of both. The element of philosophical liberalism most damaging to urban regime theory is the liberal conception of institutions, especially its embrace of a clear and strict institutional separation between matters deemed public and those deemed private, the so-called public-private distinction (see Frug 1980). This stance causes conventional versions of the theory to misconceptualize state-market dynamics and be remiss in its investigation and understanding of crucial economic processes.

The philosophical liberalism of liberal expansionism runs even deeper. Salient here is not only the institutional public-private distinction but also ontological, operational, and instrumental elements of philosophical liberalism. In an ontological sense, we see liberalism's excessive individualism, which privileges the individual in comparison with any collectivity. Liberal expansionism values such collectivities (e.g., cultural groups or place-based communities) primarily in terms of the aggregation of individual utilities rather than as entities with inherent value. Operationally, we see liberalism's excessive materialism, where measurement of this individual utility and achievement is done almost exclusively in a material sense, with income being especially important. Here, liberal expansionism devalues utility derived from nonmaterial sources, such as the psychological benefits of group solidarity, cultural expression, or community control.[11] And, perhaps most important, in an instrumental sense we see liberalism's excessive focus on individual mobility, as liberal expansionism involves the significant movement of people through regional space. Reflecting on this last and most crucial aspect of philosophical liberalism, the eminent political theorist Michael Walzer (1990, 12) reminds us that "liberalism is, most simply, the theoretical endorsement and justification of this movement." In the liberal view, then, mobility represents "the enactment of liberty, and the pursuit of (private or personal) happiness."

On Alternatives

If a deep philosophical liberalism lies at the heart of the failure of both conventional urban regime theory and liberal expansionism, remedying this failure requires developing an alternative approach that moves away from such a philosophy. In several of the chapters to follow, I offer such an approach.

At the approach's core lies an array of (what I identify as) *local economic alternative development strategies* (or LEADS for short).[12] These strategies avoid the most troubling philosophical aspects of liberalism: the institutional mix between public and private is more fluid and contingent; there is a clear ontological recognition of the value of collectivities (in fact, many such strategies are explicitly collectivist in nature); success is operationalized less materially; and the instrument for achieving efficacy deemphasizes movement in favor of rootedness. Notable examples of LEADS include efforts to build community-based development institutions, worker-owned firms, publicly controlled businesses, and webs of interdependent (locally networked) entrepreneurial enterprises. Equally notable is the innovative use of economic development tools to generate indigenous, stable, and balanced economic growth in local economies.

One useful way to understand the theoretical underpinning of such strategies is through the familiar lens of equality and efficiency, the two key values that many public policy and institutional design efforts hope to realize (see, for example, Elkin 1987; Bluestone, Stevenson, and Williams 2008; Okun 1975). Although these two values are often considered to be locked in a trade-off with one another, where the realization of a greater degree of one diminishes the realization of the other,[13] the beginning premise animating the LEADS is that currently employed local economic development policies are, in practice, realizing *neither.* From the LEADS perspective, the benefits generated by currently employed approaches flow mostly to those already advantaged, exacerbating inequity, while at the same time such approaches operate with considerable wastefulness and inefficiency (see, for example, Levine 2000; Eisinger 2000).

Inversely, the theory buttressing the LEADS holds that these alternative strategies embody the potential to realize *both* equality and efficiency. This dual potential springs primarily from three key attributes:

- *Broadening Ownership.* The LEADS commonly transform the way productive economic resources and institutions are owned. In the typical model of ownership in the U.S. economy, represented most notably by the traditional private business corporation, the scope of ownership is largely narrowed to a wealthy group of private investors. The LEADS, in contrast, operate with an ownership structure much broader in nature, so that capital and, at times, land, are held by various collectivities (workers, community members, citizens) or an array of small, independent entrepreneurs. Such a structure potentially facilitates greater equality, as the fruits of ownership are more widely shared, and greater efficiency, as broad-based ownership mitigates free-riding behavior and the resulting collective action problems (see Dahl 1985).

- *Democratizing Control.* The LEADS commonly transform the way productive economic resources and institutions are controlled. In the current economic system, democratic control over these resources and institutions is now either indirect at best, coming via limited governmental regulations, or severely compromised by processes that blatantly violate key democratic principles—such as the one-person, one-vote criterion (see Alperovitz 2005). In contrast, the LEADS extend democratic control to a greater proportion of a local economy, either by internally democratizing economic institutions (usually in a community-based form) or by bringing economic resources directly under the purview of democratic public authority. Such democratization potentially yields more equitable outcomes, given the equalization of power that democratic control enables, and enhances efficiency, since democratic processes bring with them a certain *intelligence* (Lindblom 1965) that allows for more effective *social problem solving* (Elkin 1987; also see Stone 1989).

- *Valuing Place and Community.* The LEADS commonly transform the way the economic problem is understood. In the conventional view of economics, little inherent value is accorded to particular local places and the sense of community in them (see Bolton 1992). In contrast, the LEADS focus explicitly on the goal of developing established local places and building community. The valuing of community, and the communitarian ethos flowing from it, potentially engenders increased equality, as there is a greater concern for the well-being of all community members (see Euchner and McGovern 2003), and greater efficiency, as the valuing of local places facilitates the usage of existing local economic resources in more productive ways (see Williamson, Imbroscio, and Alperovitz 2002).

It is my most central claim that the LEADS hold the key to both strengthening the explanatory and, especially, the prescriptive elements of urban regime theory, while providing a means to address urban problems that is superior to liberal expansionism.

An Overview of the Book

Part 1 offers a reconsideration of the current understanding of urban governance in America. At the core of that understanding is the orthodoxy of urban regime theory. Although urban regime theory has in many ways been a fruitful innovation, it is also plagued by some significant deficiencies that make it less theoretically compelling and practically useful. Chapters 1 and 2 explicate these deficiencies. The former explains how urban regime theory misconceptualizes the *division of labor between state and market* as overly rigid and largely static, while the latter demonstrates that urban regime theory has, at its peril, largely neglected the *study of the economic (or market) side* of that division.

Part 2 moves the discussion from a reconsideration of urban governance to a reconsideration of the policies needed to address America's urban problems. Liberal expansionism as a policy approach to address these problems parallels what regime theory is as an understanding of urban governance—a conventional wisdom or orthodoxy that needs to be challenged. Chapter 3 mounts this challenge by demonstrating that liberal expansionists have no solid evidentiary base on which to *shame the inside game,* and instead only do so because of their liberal value commitments or ideology. Without such empirical evidence, liberal expansionism loses its ostensibly compelling appeal, since its "shaming of the inside game"—that is, its critique of both community development efforts and the viability of central cities—provides much of the basis for such appeal. Chapter 4 challenges the consensus that strongly endorses one key element of liberal expansionism: efforts to deconcentrate or disperse the urban poor into the suburbs. This challenge reveals many fundamental weaknesses in the key tenets and policy positions of what I call the *dispersal consensus.* The existence of such weaknesses, in turn, strongly suggests that the normative desirability and policy efficacy of such efforts is questionable at best.

The analyses in parts 1 and 2 point to the idea that the key to strengthening urban regime theory and supplanting liberal expansionism lies in the reconstructive potential of a number of local economic alternative development strategies (or LEADS). Regarding the strengthening of urban regime theory, most important is the potential embodied by the LEADS to endow it with a prescriptive guide (or road map) for understanding how alternative political coalitions and institutional arrangements can be engendered. These local economic alternative development strategies, in essence, have the potential to facilitate the progressive reconstruction of urban regimes, allowing for the current corporate domination of urban regimes to give way to governing arrangements more egalitarian and democratic in nature. Moreover, these same strategies have the additional potential to serve as a vehicle for addressing urban problems that is superior to liberal expansionism. On this score, they offer a potential means to achieve a significant reduction of both poverty/inequality and the degree of uneven development in urban America.

In light of this potential, part 3 is dedicated to a further exploration of these local economic alternative development strategies. Chapter 5 focuses on the salutary contributions of the *local public balance sheet,* an alternative methodology for assessing and practicing local economic development rooted in the LEADS approach. Chapter 6 examines how the LEADS can enhance *community economic stability,* a condition where communities possess the job base and general level of economic vibrancy to afford their populations a decent standard of living over time. If the LEADS are to deliver on their constructive potential to facilitate both the progressive reconstruction of urban regimes and the significant amelioration of urban problems, then it is imperative that such community economic stability be realized.

The concluding section, part 4, turns to a consideration of political matters. It examines what is politically desirable (from a normative standpoint) and what is politically feasible (from a practical standpoint). Employing these criteria, chapter 7 develops an extended *critique of the liberal politics* undergirding both conventional urban regime theory and liberal expansionism. This liberal politics is found to be both normatively undesirable and, in practical terms, politically infeasible. Chapter 8 explicates the fundamentals of the *new alternative politics* of the LEADS. It demonstrates the normative superiority of this politics vis-à-vis its liberal rivals, while engaging the more complex question of whether—and, if so, how—such a politics can be feasibly practiced in America's cities.

The ultimate objective of this book is to initiate a *conversation*—a conversation that *reconsiders* orthodoxies at the same time it *considers* alternatives to those orthodoxies. Thus I appeal to readers, both those sympathetic to my perspective and those who might be skeptical or even antagonistic, to engage the content of this book for what it is—a voice in a broad and complex conversation about how best to build a more democratic, a more equitable, and a more just urban America.

Part I

Reconsidering Urban Governance

The Critique of Regime Theory

1

RECONCEIVING THE STATE-MARKET DIVISION

By the mid-1990s, urban regime theory emerged as the dominant, even orthodox, way to understand the nature of governance in urban America. Urban regime theory's dominance did not immunize it against criticism, however. In fact, over the past decade and a half, scholars have proffered a number of sympathetic critiques of it. Such critiques have pointed to conceptual limitations and weaknesses inherent in the approach. To correct for these limitations and weaknesses, these sympathetic critics frequently have suggested modifications to its original formulation.

In accordance with this trend, I offer my own sympathetic critique and modification to urban regime theory. The basis for this critique is the theory's erroneous conceptualization of the division of labor between state and market within cities. This conceptualization tends to be overly rigid and largely static. Urban regime theory therefore must be reformulated to overcome this significant deficiency. At the heart of this reformulation lies the potential contribution from what I introduced above as the LEADS (or local economic alternative development strategies). The reformulation of urban regime theory made possible by the LEADS is of crucial importance for its *practical* implications. Namely, such a reformulation not only enhances our capacity to explain the nature of urban governance; it also reveals how American urban regimes might be progressively reconstructed to advance both democracy and equality in cities (cf. Collins, 2008; Gendron, 2006).

Critiques of Regime Theory

The virtual avalanche of critiques of urban regime theory began in earnest with the publication of an entire book of essays devoted to this enterprise. This book, *Reconstructing Urban Regime Theory: Regulating Urban Politics in a Global Economy* edited by the progressive geographer Mickey Lauria (1997b), stands as the most prominent and systematic among the early critiques of the theory. Setting out the basic framework of the book's critical project, Lauria (1997a, 2) criticized urban regime theory for its failure to move beyond "middle-level abstractions." Its heavy reliance on such abstractions, he argued, left urban regime theory too focused on the internal political dynamics of the city. Specifically, regime theory misguidedly focused an excessive degree of attention on the political management and maintenance of internal governing coalitions. Because of this limitation, Lauria suggested that urban regime theory be reformulated by wedding it to regulation theory (which offers an account of the larger-order dynamics of capitalism).[1] Regulation theory, he noted, provides "higher-level abstractions" that link the local (i.e., internal) politics of the city understood so well by regime theory with an understanding of external (i.e., national and global) structural forces (Lauria 1997a, 2).

In another provocative essay in the same book, British geographer Joe Painter offered a related critique of urban regime theory and, similar to Lauria, suggested a possible conceptual reformulation. Responding to Lauria's proposed marriage of urban regime theory with regulation theory, Painter (1997) criticized leading regime theorist Clarence Stone's notion that *selective incentives* provide the glue bonding the regime's governing coalition together (see Stone 1989). Painter instead argued that the intentionalist, rational-choice perspective underlying the selective incentive concept is incompatible with the methodological stance of regulation theory. A "reworking" of regime theory is therefore in order, he urged, to "remove its rationalist assumptions" (Painter 1997, 142). In particular, Painter recommended the use of the acclaimed French sociologist Pierre Bourdieu's concept of *habitus* as the vehicle for this reworking (see, for example, Bourdieu 1990). This idea of habitus sees social actors' dispositions or socialization, generated and regenerated by social structures, as constituting the practices of everyday life. For Painter, an understanding of how such everyday practices come about through actors' habitus offers a more compelling account of the dynamics of urban regime formation.

Additional scholarship followed Lauria's basic critique faulting urban regime theory for its supposed *localist* orientation, that is, its preoccupation with theorizing the city's internal political dynamics to the exclusion of the external environment. Because of this negligence, regime theory purportedly (1) exaggerates the importance of agency compared to structure in explaining local policy choices (Kantor, Savitch, and Haddock 1997); (2) underestimates the obstacles facing progressive local politics (Sites 1997); and (3) remains limited as a vehicle for cross-national comparison (Stoker 1995; Davies 2003).

Still other scholars proffered a more eclectic array of critiques. Scholars claimed that urban regime theory neglects the variation in civic cultures across cities (Reese and Rosenfeld 2002); wrongly downplays the role of identity politics in urban regimes (Bailey 1999); exhibits normatively problematic features (Davies 2002), and fails to adequately theorize the politics of race (Horan 2002; Kraus 2004). Moreover, such critiques continue to be proffered of late. Notably, urban regime theory has been depicted as undertheorizing the importance of cultural factors in city politics (Sharp 2007); unable or willing to question the underlying ideological frameworks shaping city politics (Bennett and Spirou 2006); and, in a more general sense, as theoretically stagnant (Sapotichne, Jones, and Wolfe 2007). Other prominent recent critiques have come from urban geographer Jason Hackworth (2007), who hits again on the localist theme, and sociologists Richard Gendron and William Domhoff (2009), who argue that urban regime theory misunderstands the nature of political power and conflict over land use. In short, such critiques clearly remain a prominent and robust feature of the urban studies literature well into the twenty-first century (see also, for example, Keiser 2009; McGovern 2009; Collins 2008).[2]

Thus, sympathetic critiques of urban regime theory have been a near preoccupation of empirically minded urban theorists almost continuously for well over a decade. Yet, what is most surprising given the volume of, and variation in, such critiques is that so little attention has been paid to the theory's most foundational and arguably most important element—the division of labor between state and market. Conventional urban regime theory's conceptualization of that division is, in fact, deeply flawed. Exposing this flaw is of crucial importance because it holds the key to illuminating paths for constructing more progressive urban regimes, hence greatly bolstering the theory's potential salutary contribution to urban political practice.

Conventional urban regime theory conceptualizes the division of labor in overly rigid and largely static terms. Such conceptual *rigidity* stems most notably from regime theory's understanding of the nature of economic development and wealth creation (i.e., accumulation) in cities. In particular, and reflecting its deep philosophical liberalism, urban regime theory posits a strict "public-private split," as the creation of wealth and economic development is portrayed as inevitably dominated by the activities of the traditional, for-profit private sector (Berk and Swanstrom 1994, 8). This conceptualization is, in turn, *static* because regime theory views the institutional structures for economic development and wealth creation as beyond the reach of the political process. Highlighting the static nature of this conceptualization, political economists Gerald Berk and Todd Swanstrom (1995, 2; 1994, 13) point out, perceptively, that urban regime theory fails to take its own "politics matters" slogan "far enough" because it regards the current division of labor "as fact...[rather than] as the object of struggle."

Recognizing that the division of labor between state and market sets the context for understanding governance in cities is the great strength of urban regime theory. Conceptualizing that division in an unyielding way is its great deficiency. This erroneous conceptualization not only distorts the empirical understanding of regime dynamics; more crucially, it biases the normative understanding of political practice by blinding urban scholars and activists alike to the possibilities for building alternative urban regimes based on modifications in the state-market division. On this score, scholars are left less able to perceive and properly assess evidence of emerging trends supportive of these possibilities, while activists miss potential opportunities for engaging in strategic actions to begin to bring these possibilities about.

The State-Market Division

To better grasp how urban regime theory misconceptualizes the division of labor between state and market, it is useful to examine the work of the most influential of regime theorists, political scientist Clarence Stone (see especially Stone 1989).[3] In one of his earliest expressions of urban regime theory, Stone (1987, 15) pointed to the unbending nature of the state-market division. It is a "durable" feature of the context of urban politics, one unlikely to be subject to much variation. In a series of later works that more fully develop the theory, Stone consistently posited the division in a rigid manner: following the above-identified conceptualization, the task of providing economic development and wealth creation (i.e., accumulation) for the city was seen by Stone as almost exclusively falling on the traditional, for-profit private sector. The "private ownership of business enterprise," Stone recognized, "is less than universal, as governments do own and operate various auxiliary enterprises from mass transit to convention centers." Nevertheless, "the economic arena [is] dominated by private ownership" (Stone 1989, 7). Similarly, responding to a critique of urban regime theory, Stone restates the specifics of his theoretical commitments surrounding this issue, unambiguously asserting that "I take a profit-based economy *as a given*" (Stone 1991, 294, emphasis added). This conceptualization also appears in the secondary literature on Stone's work. For example, in a comprehensive overview and assessment of regime theory informed largely by Stone's work, political scientist Gerry Stoker (1995, 56) made a parallel point using similar language, noting that regime theory "takes *as given*...an economy guided mainly but not exclusively by privately controlled investment decisions" (emphasis added).

   This inflexible conceptualization of the division of labor is surprising for Stone, since he is otherwise committed to a metatheoretical approach emphasizing agency, fluidity, and contingency.[4] Stone (1997, 2) maintains that the key analytic task of regime analysis is not "to assume the dominance and immutability of some structures in order to deduce the consequences of their dominance"; rather, it is "to treat structures as largely contingent and therefore in need of ongoing examination." More recently, Stone (2009, 262) argued for "rejecting functional necessity as an overriding cause," because "the contingent nature of [historical] development reveals important variations and alternative paths of [that] development."

In this regard, Stone frequently cites as a chief influence the work of historical sociologist Philip Abrams. Particularly compelling for Stone is Abrams's notion of "structur*ing,* the reciprocal flow of action and structure" (Abrams 1982, 192, emphasis added; see Stone 1989, 1991, 1997, 2006, 2009).[5] Structuring, Stone (1997, 2) writes, "rests on the formula that, while agents act through structures, agents nevertheless can shape the structures through which they operate." However, the rigid and nondynamic nature of his conceptualization of the division of labor seems to be more in line with something generally anathema to Stone—a heavy-handed structuralist approach, with its accompanying determinism. In short, while Stone allows for and even accentuates the potential for substantial agent-driven structural modification, this potential does not extend to the structures constituting the division of labor itself. Instead, to repeat, regime theory accepts these structures *as a given.*[6]

This empirical stance in turn shapes Stone's normative vision for remedying the current deficiencies of urban political practice. Rather than systematically addressing the possibilities for remaking the division of labor, Stone's constructive work has focused primarily on how the institutions of urban public education and some related social services might be reformed (see Stone, Orr, and Worgs 2006). Hence, for Stone, the key to improving political practice lies less within the economic development arena (although education may have indirect implications for development), and more within the realm of the social welfare state; less in the structures of accumulation, and more in those of collective consumption. It is here that the deep philosophical liberalism of conventional urban regime theory manifests itself programmatically as well: education is, of course, the quintessential liberal remedy for nearly all societal ills.

Stone's thinking on these matters undoubtedly was influenced by his decades of studying the governance of Atlanta (see Stone 1976, 1989, 2001, 2005, 2006). Yet, another keen observer of that experience, sociologist Floyd Hunter, came to quite a different judgment. It was Hunter's (1953) account of the governance of Atlanta, which he called Regional City, that sparked the famous community power debate of the 1950s, 1960s, and 1970s. In the revised version of his classic study published just as that debate was ending, Hunter (1980, 164), in contrast to Stone, stressed the need for a reconstruction in the state-market division or, in his words, for "exercising broader and deeper rights of direct democracy than have been exercised in the American scheme of capital accumulation and distribution to date" (also see Gendron 2006; Gendron and Domhoff 2009). Thus, while Stone acknowledges "a considerable debt to [Hunter's] analysis of the importance of the close but informal link between Atlanta's governmental and economic sectors" (Stone 1989, xi; Stone, 1988b), he nevertheless largely eschews Hunter's *solution* for reducing the systematic bias in governance generated by that link.[7] It is tempting to trace this choice of focus to strategic pragmatism on Stone's part—and, indeed, efforts at pragmatism are generally admirable. However, the task of thoroughly reforming urban education systems seems almost as daunting as remaking the state-market division and, on the payoff side of the equation, less likely to bring about a fundamental progressive change in political practice (see Fitzgerald 1993; Imbroscio 1998).

Three Alternative Conceptions

Understanding that urban regime theory conceptualizes the division of labor between state and market in an overly rigid and static manner logically implies that the division can be alternatively constituted. There exist at least three such possibilities, or three possible *reconstructions* of this division. At the heart of these reconstructions is the notion that the urban economic development and wealth creation (i.e., accumulation) process can be driven in a manner differing from how that process is normally understood. Most notably, a significant driver of urban accumulation can be the (1) local public sector itself; (2) a community-based (third) sector, neither truly public nor private; or (3) an agglomeration of small-scale, entrepreneurial enterprises.

The Local State as Urban Accumulator

The first reconstruction of the division of labor involves *breaching* it. To reiterate, the key defect in urban regime theory's conceptualization of the division stems from its understanding of the nature of economic development and wealth creation (i.e., accumulation) in cities. Specifically, because of its deep philosophical liberalism, urban regime theory accepts as inevitable the so-called public-private distinction (Frug 1980), whereby each sector occupies a separate and distinct domain (also see Garber 1990). Although, according to conventional urban regime theory, the local state has an ancillary role in facilitating economic development and wealth creation by performing basic regulatory functions and providing necessary public goods (see Stone 1989), actual property ownership/control and profit making is understood as falling within the private sector's domain.

This deep philosophically liberal standpoint misses the potential for the local state to play an expanded and more direct role in the city's accumulation process. As conventional regime theory recognizes, cities have traditionally owned (and, at times, made profits from) various public-goods-like "auxiliary enterprises," including airports, sports stadiums, public utilities, convention centers, and mass transit systems (Stone 1989, 7). What has not been adequately appreciated, however, is that—even in this era of privatization—public ownership and profit-making opportunities are widely available to cities in other more conventional areas of economic activity where the traditional private sector has historically been dominant.

These public ownership and profit-making opportunities represent one key thrust of (what I have identified as) the LEADS (local economic alternative development strategies). Along these lines, over the past three decades, cities and other local governments have gained public ownership of a variety of businesses. These range from minor league sports teams, telecommunication systems, a variety of retail activities, training and consultancy businesses, motels, auto-towing companies, bottled water sales, fertilizer and soil enhancer production, and the ownership of an amusement park.[8]

Also in the LEADS mode, cities have often played the role of being a direct real estate investor—purchasing land and buildings and selling them at a profit or retaining public ownership and profitably leasing them to private enterprises. Along these same lines, many cities have obtained an equity stake (partial ownership and profit-making opportunities) in downtown malls, hotels, and office buildings by providing public financing for urban redevelopment projects. Cities even have cast themselves as venture capitalists, making equity investments in local enterprises with considerable potential for growth.[9]

The Community as Urban Accumulator

Thus, conventional urban regime theory's conceptualization of the division of labor between state and market, with its strict public-private distinction, fails to comprehend the potential for the local state to play an expanded and more direct role in the local economic development and wealth creation process. An even more significant lacuna in conventional urban regime theory is its failure to look past the duality of this distinction and see the potential for a *third* sector—neither truly public nor private—to play a significant role in accumulation. The second reconstruction of the division of labor hence involves moving *beyond* it altogether.

The "community economics movement" lies at the heart of this third sector (Soifer 1990, 240). This movement, which represents another key element of the LEADS, has generated a variety of community-based and community-oriented economic institutions and businesses in cities. Often nonprofit in form and democratic in governance, these institutions and businesses differ from the two common modes of economic organization, the private-corporate model and the public-enterprise model. Hence, they have been described as vehicles for developing a model of accumulation that goes *beyond the market and the state*.[10] Community development corporations (CDCs) are the most prevalent example of these community economic institutions. Over the past forty years, thousands of CDCs have become notable players in the urban real estate market, especially in the area of housing, but also in commercial/industrial property development. More recently, cities have seen the rapid proliferation of community finance institutions such as community development banks and community credit unions. There are also thousands of urban-based consumer cooperatives operating in the United States today.[11]

Worker-owned firms—whether structured as an ESOP (employee stock ownership plan) or a worker (producer) cooperative—represent another organizational form comprising this LEADS *third way* (Shavelson 1990; Dahl 1985). By extending ownership and control of capital beyond an individual entrepreneur or the traditional business corporation, these forms of organization root firms more broadly in the local community, giving businesses a community base. Like CDCs and consumer cooperatives, worker-owned firms in the United States number in the thousands and often operate in the nation's urban areas (see Williamson, Imbroscio, and Alperovitz 2002; Alperovitz 2005).

Searching for innovative paths to urban regeneration, community groups in cities have, over the years, explored other ways to create community-owned economic enterprises. These include such eclectic examples as an employment agency, an auto insurance company, and a variety of retail establishments.[12] Similarly, many local officials—fearful of losing their major league sports teams to the enticements of rival cities—became interested in adopting a community-ownership structure modeled on the Green Bay Packers National Football League franchise. The Packers are owned by a nonprofit corporation with nearly 112,000 shareholders, most of whom reside within the Green Bay, Wisconsin, area (see Shuman 2006, 1999). Their corporate by-laws prevent any individual shareholder from gaining more than a small portion of total ownership; these by-laws also make it next to impossible for the team to be moved or sold to outsiders. On the minor league level, especially in baseball, there are already several examples of teams owned by their fans via community corporations.[13]

Small-Scale Entrepreneurs as Urban Accumulator

Urban regime theory's narrow understanding of economic development and wealth creation causes it to not only fail to recognize the potential role played by the local state and community-based organizations in the accumulation process. The theory is even further narrowed by the conception that only a particular *version* of the for-profit private sector necessarily drives that process (Berk and Swanstrom 1994). In this version of the for-profit private sector, two central principles stand out. First, the private sector is seen as dominated by "large, multilocational corporations" that inevitably play "a commanding role" in organizing the local economy. These multilocational corporations "are distinguished from ordinary business firms by their large size, their multiple administrative and operational units, and their location in scattered business sites" (Kantor 1995, 90). Second, the private sector is seen as composed primarily of capital that is relatively mobile. On this second point, which flows from the first, Berk and Swanstrom (1995) cite the work of regime theorist Stephen Elkin. As Elkin (1994, 135) notes, it is because "capital can move in and out of local boundaries at will" that we find the kind of urban governance patterns depicted by urban regime theory.

What conventional urban regime theory fails to grasp is that the traditional, for-profit private sector operating in cities need not be characterized by these two principles. This sector could instead be organized along different lines. Such an organizational pattern represents yet another key thrust of the LEADS.

For instance, rather than being dominated by large multilocational corporations, the city's private sector might be more diversified—driven to a greater extent by an array of small, independent businesses. Small businesses require a variety of support services and more general economic links to other enterprises (Shuman 2006; Fisher 1988). Hence, the resulting local economic base would be marked by a considerable degree of market interdependence, with many highly networked small firms. Consequently, business investment becomes more rooted geographically as firms require close spatial (agglomerative) relationships with one another. This phenomenon, in turn, lessens the intensity of capital mobility in local economies (Berk and Swanstrom 1994). Hence a third reconstruction of the division of labor seeks to make it more *bound* to these local economies.

As the economy continues to develop into a postindustrial (or post-Fordist) model, these smaller enterprises emerge as increasingly vital actors. In the current economic landscape, mass production has declined relative to more flexible production systems. This change amplifies the importance of smaller firms in the production process because they tend to embody the necessary flexibility to respond to new demands for rapid product innovation.[14] The economic importance of smaller firms also expands with the developing postindustrial economy's tendency toward vertical disintegration rather than vertical integration. The vertically integrated firms of the industrial era established economic clout by controlling a larger scope of production internally within the firm. In contrast, vertically disintegrated firms enhance their flexibility by depending heavily on external firms (via subcontracting) to provide needed materials and corporate services. This *externalization* creates fertile market opportunities for numerous other (often small) businesses. Such enterprises often cluster together in urbanized space to reduce the transaction costs of subcontracting (Scott 1988).

Expanding Regime Typologies

There is no reason to conceptualize the division of labor between state and market in a rigid and static manner. Drawing on the possibilities embodied in the LEADS, at least three alternative reconstructions of this division can be readily identified. A corollary to this conclusion is that it is possible to expand the existing typologies of possible urban regimes (cf. Berk and Swanstrom 1994).

Several urban political scientists have developed well-known regime typologies frequently surveyed in the literature.[15] For example, Stephen Elkin (1987) identified pluralist, federalist, and entrepreneurial regimes, while Clarence Stone (1993) classified regimes as maintenance, developmental, middle-class progressive, and lower-class opportunity expansion (also see Fainstein and Fainstein 1983; Savitch and Thomas 1991). The last of these four relates closely to Marion Orr and Gerry Stoker's (1994) conception of a human-capital regime—a type of regime associated with Stone's own collaborative multicity study of urban education reform (Stone et al. 2001).

Yet, the plethora of regime types generated by each of these theorists share one common feature—they all remain rooted in an unyielding conceptualization of the division of labor between state and market.

The three potential reconstructions of the division of labor identified above produce three additions to the established typologies. I label these urban regime types community-based, petty-bourgeois, and local-statist. Not surprisingly, myriad difficulties confront the formation and maintenance of these regimes. Perhaps the most formidable difficulty stems from the current structure of the division of labor between the state and the market itself. Although the division of labor should be seen as the key object of political struggle, this struggle is not easily won. Understanding that the structures of the division of labor themselves can be the subject of agent-driven modification does not mean that the efforts of agents will be successful. Therefore, not unlike Stone's extension of his typology to include a lower-class opportunity expansion regime, these three alternative regimes also are, in Stone's (1993, 20) words, "largely hypothetical." Nevertheless, we do find nascent empirical manifestations of these three regimes in contemporary and historical city politics, just as Stone observed "hints" of his opportunity expansion regime in select cities.

Community-Based Regimes

The first of the three additions to the typology is the community-based regime. The building blocks of this regime are the institutions and enterprises of the community economics movement. These third-sector institutions and enterprises, as noted above, reconstruct the division of labor in ways that move it beyond the simple duality of state and market. Community-based regimes would be centered around a governing coalition dominated by two sets of actors: the leaders of community-based groups, rooted largely in the city's neighborhoods, and their allies who have captured the public power of city government via the electoral process.

Chicago presented a nascent version of such an urban regime in the mid-1980s. During that period, progressives captured public power and worked closely with the city's strong corps of community-based organizations to pursue alternative economic ideas and some notable albeit limited third-sector development efforts (Giloth 1991; Clavel and Wiewel 1991). However, this regime was never fully instituted and could not be maintained after the premature death of its charismatic leader, Mayor Harold Washington (see Ferman 1996). Nevertheless, the potential embodied in the Chicago experience under Washington is now legendary in the urban literature, and continues to inspire analysis and evaluation and serve as a model for potentially emergent progressive regimes (see Alexander 2007; Giloth 2007a).

As Stone's work suggests, the key ingredient for the longer term viability of any urban regime lies in its ability to tap a base of resources needed for effective urban governance. Because under current conditions "governmental authority, standing alone, is inadequate" to provide this governance (Stone 1993, 22), public officials must meld their limited resources with those of nongovernmental actors. Because the corporate business sector holds a concentration of the necessary resources, it appears as an attractive governing partner. Thus, the familiar corporate regime emerges in city after city (Stone 1989). On the other hand, a reconstruction of the division of labor in which the community economics movement plays a significant role in the city's accumulation process alters this dynamic. Such a reconstruction—if it can indeed be brought about—would furnish the community-based, neighborhood-oriented sector with its *own* concentration of resources garnered from their ownership and control of economic institutions and enterprises. These resources would, in turn, make the community-based regime—with its governing alliance between community groups and progressive public officials—a potentially viable governing arrangement.

Petty-Bourgeois Regimes

Another addition to the typology is the petty-bourgeois regime. The building blocks of this urban regime are the small private (i.e., petty-bourgeois) businesses rooted or bound spatially in a city economy marked by a high degree of economic agglomeration. These petty-bourgeois regimes would have a decidedly republican flavor,[16] as public officials would share power in the city's governing coalition with a collection of independent producers. Given the existing weaknesses of the local state and its resulting inability—acting alone—to govern the city effectively, the key to a regime's long-term viability lies in its capacity to tap extrastate resources. In petty-bourgeois regimes, the crucial societal resource base would be held by what Stone (1989, 228) calls a "resource-rich but noncorporate middle class," in this case composed of the owners and operators of small enterprises. A reconstruction of the division of labor that greatly augmented the importance of small business to a local economy—again, if such a reconstruction can indeed be brought about—would enable this class to create and sustain strong political organizations independent of the city's corporate elite.

During the late 1980s and early 1990s, political scientist Richard De-Leon (1992) found evidence of the potential emergence of a variant of such a regime in San Francisco. His perceptive work outlined the possibilities for a transformation in that city's governance from an *anti-regime,* which simply blocks the exercise of power by any political coalition, to an activist urban regime built on a governing alliance between progressive forces in control of local government and the city's extensive, densely networked small business community. However, before such an alliance could solidify, progressives lost electoral control of city hall, undermining one of the key pillars of this nascent regime type. More recently, in his survey of equity-oriented economic development initiatives in American cities, Robert Giloth (2007a, 4) reports that progressive regimes in Austin, Seattle, as well as San Francisco have drawn upon "the independent resources of professionals and small business...[to] shift governing relationships away from a narrow focus on urban growth."

Local-Statist Regimes

The final addition to the typology is the local-statist regime. This regime would be built on a significant enlargement of the local state's role in the city's accumulation process. Such an enlargement reconstructs the division of labor between state and market by breaching the strict public-private distinction this division assumes.

In local-statist regimes, public officials would be able to govern the city more autonomously. The significant expansion of the public sector into the accumulation process—once again, if it can indeed be bought about—would greatly augment the resources under the city's control. Such a process, in turn, creates something analogous to the notion of a "strong state" (Krasner 1978) on the local level. Therefore, in contrast to the previous two alternative regimes, the viability of this regime type would not depend on garnering extrastate resources to govern the city. Under these conditions, such resources would already be available via the fruits of state-controlled accumulation efforts.

Examples of this urban regime type, even in a nascent stage of development, remain elusive. Thus far, contemporary local governments have made only limited forays into the property ownership and profit-making realm (Williamson, Imbroscio, and Alperovitz 2002). To find an analogue of these regimes, some scholars instead point to the historical experience of American cities in the colonial period and the early nineteenth century. During this era, municipal corporations undertook a variety of public enterprise and public profit-making activities.[17] If they could once again engage in these activities on a large scale, cities would begin becoming "powerful, independent bodies" (Frug 1980, 1150), laying the foundation for a viable local-statist regime.

Legitimating Accumulation

A foundational tenet of urban regime theory is that the institutionally divided public and private sectors of capitalist democracies—the state and the market—exist in an uneasy relation to one another (Elkin 1987; Stone 1987). In Charles Lindblom's (1977, 190) seminal account, the demands made by private businesses on government as a prerequisite for their continued economic investment are "often in conflict with the demands that the electorate makes." Simply put, the dynamics of democracy clash with the dynamics of capitalism, resulting in an *enduring tension* (Judd and Swanstrom 1988)—or in Marxian language, a profound *contradiction*—between the processes of capital accumulation and democratic legitimation.[18]

Conventional urban regime theory holds that the key task of an urban regime is to "accommodate" or "bridge" or "hold in check" this tension between accumulation and legitimation as it arises in cities (Stone 1987, 15; 1989, 6; 1993, 2). And the effective accommodation (or bridging or checking) of this tension is the *best* that urban regimes can hope for. Such conditions merely allow a highly partial and constrained version of democratic legitimation in cities to coexist with a reasonably healthy process of economic accumulation (cf. Shefter 1985). Hence, within conventional regime theory, the basic, underlying tension itself can never be directly challenged. It is a condition responsive to treatment and capable of amelioration, yet ultimately incurable.

Liberating urban regime theory from its strict conceptualization of the division of labor reveals the prospect for unburdening city politics from this nagging tension. It is possible, perhaps, to have a healthy process of accumulation that also is conspicuously more legitimate.[19]

Along such lines, the three regime types described above all embody the potential to provide the city with a more legitimate form of accumulation. For example, in community-based regimes, organizations affiliated with the city's community-based, neighborhood-oriented sector carry out a substantial portion of local accumulation functions. This arrangement potentially subjects accumulation to enhanced grassroots, democratic control (DeFilippis 2004; Boyte 1980). Likewise, in petty-bourgeois regimes, accumulation functions—while still under private control—are shared more equally by a whole host of smaller businesses rather than a handful of larger ones. This arrangement gives petty-bourgeois regimes their republican character, approximating the political ideal identified by Berk and Swanstrom (1995, 28) as a "commonwealth of independent producers" (also see Alperovitz 2005; Lasch 1991). Under these conditions, the potential exists for accumulation to achieve a greater measure of democratic legitimacy because economic power extends more broadly throughout the city. Finally, local-statist regimes hold much of the same promise. In this case, many accumulation functions are put under the control of the democratically elected local government, presumably enhancing the legitimacy of these functions (cf. Frug 1980). This path to enhanced legitimacy has, however, remained unrealized at the national level of government, as various programs of *nationalization* in the second half of the twentieth century largely failed to achieve this goal (Lindblom 1977; Nove 1983). Yet, with the locus of public ownership and control situated at a decentralized level of government, there is a greater potential that democratic control over accumulation can be more fully achieved and maintained (Alperovitz 2005; Lynd 1987a; Goodman 1972).[20]

In its current deep philosophically liberal formulation, conventional urban regime theory's acceptance of a rigid and static conceptualization of the division of labor between state and market is a significant deficiency. Most crucially, it impedes the theory's ability to understand and appreciate the potential possibilities for building regimes founded on alternative constructions of that division—(re)constructions potentially made possible by the pursuit of the LEADS. Because of the capacity of these regimes to enhance political legitimacy in cities, their identification as potentially viable governing arrangements is especially salient for advancing a key practical goal of this book: to reveal a prescriptive guide to how significant progressive changes advancing local democracy and equality might be brought about in urban America. A crucial remaining question, of course, is whether these alternative regimes can be feasibly built and maintained, especially in light of current political conditions in cities where corporate business power is so very dominant.

2

REENGAGING ECONOMICS

Conventional urban regime theory's deep philosophical liberalism, which posits a strict distinction between the public and private, causes the theory to conceptualize the division of labor between market and state in ways overly rigid and largely static. This misconceptualization arises from regime theory's current lacuna that prevents it from seeing the possibilities for alternative wealth creation and economic development in cities. The root of these missteps lies in conventional urban regime theory's failure to engage economic questions in a sustained and systematic way. This failure has left it with deep deficiencies. These deficiencies once again weaken urban regime theory not only as an explanatory theory but as a prescriptive one as well. In this regard, conventional urban regime theory can offer no prescriptive guide (or "road map") for understanding how urban regimes can be progressively reconstructed to advance both democracy and equality in urban governance.

This neglect of economics by urban regime theory is at first glance quite surprising. Regime theory conceptualizes significant interdependencies between the market and the state, making it a theory of political *economy* rather than merely one of political *process* (see Elkin 1985b). Along these same lines, regime theory's transcendence of the discredited pluralist theory of power is rooted in its embrace of this political economy perspective (see Imbroscio, forthcoming). Especially important here was that the initial formulation of regime theory drew heavily upon neo-Marxist theory of the 1970s,[1] with its strong focus on the political-economic dynamics of the capitalist system (see Stone 1987; Elkin 1985b).

Nonetheless, despite these political-economy attributes, conventional urban regime theory remains deeply grounded in philosophical liberalism, which posits a strict distinction between the public and the private (also see Davies 2002). And, as we saw in the last chapter, the static conceptualization of the market-state division that results from this public-private distinction treats the market (or economic) side of the division *as a given* (Stone 1991; Stoker 1995). Thus, with the market side taken as given, it becomes less surprising to find that urban regime theory neglects a systematic analysis of economic matters.

This neglect of economics in urban regime theory can be traced to other factors as well. Most notable among these is the sociology of knowledge from which the theory emerged. Namely, most of its theoreticians and practitioners have been political scientists—scholars trained in the analysis of the polity and instinctively drawn to examine politics most intensely. So, again, perhaps it should not be that surprising to find the analysis of economics neglected in urban regime theory.

The Lingering Specter of *City Limits*

The deleterious consequences of urban regime theory's neglect of economics can be best understood by revisiting its longstanding debate with the economic determinist perspective developed in political scientist Paul Peterson's now-classic book, *City Limits* (1981). Peterson's book—tightly argued, theoretically sophisticated, and empirically grounded—aspired in one salvo to define virtually the entire field of urban politics out of existence. It purported to demonstrate that, as a force shaping local policy-making, city politics was mostly irrelevant, and therefore not worthy of close study by serious scholars.

To reach this provocative and (at the time) counterintuitive conclusion, Peterson argued that the mobility of economic resources (resulting from the nature of capitalism), combined with the intergovernmental (subnational) competition for investment (resulting from the nature of American federalism), left American cities almost completely constrained by economic pressures. In Peterson's view, these constraints are powerfully determinative of local political choice. Specifically, cities are compelled, by necessity, to pursue developmental policies (that enhance the economic position of the city) while eschewing policies to redistribute wealth (that harm this economic position). Because developmental policies enhance the economic position of the city, Peterson argued that their pursuit is in what he called the *unitary interest* of the city (considered as whole), and therefore, largely beyond the scope of local political struggle.

Not surprisingly, Peterson's argument greatly disturbed those who had committed their professional careers to the study of city politics. The uproar that followed among political scientists in the urban field was—by normally staid academic standards—raucous; the response, swift and intense. Leading the counterattack were urban regime theorists, who responded in two principal ways to Peterson's economic determinist argument. Yet both of these responses ultimately proved to be inadequate.

The first response was to sidestep the economic considerations so central to Peterson and simply analyze more closely developmental policymaking in cities. In doing so, they found it to be marked by more conflict and more pursuit of particular interests—which is to say, marked by more *politics*—than allowed for in Peterson's unitary interest model (Sanders and Stone 1987). Peterson (1987, 541) answered this critique by pointing to the core arguments in *City Limits* regarding the privileged place occupied by development policy on local agendas: "a critique that ignores four-fifths of the supporting evidence has conceded most of the argument." For Peterson, despite the appearance of conflict and the pursuit of particularistic agendas, developmental policymaking is still overwhelmingly in the unitary interest of city. He closed his response by reminding readers of the powerful economic constraints faced by cities: intercity rivalries, he wrote, are "more intense than ever. Anyone who suggests to local politicians that they avoid...[development policy] will be giving advice that will most likely be ignored" (Peterson 1987, 546).

This retort provoked a second response by regime theorists, one that did lead them to consider the economic side of the urban political-economy dynamic in a much more direct, albeit ultimately unsystematic and limited, way. In their engagement of economics, urban regime theorists and their allies challenged Peterson by contending that the economic constraints so crucial to his model were not nearly as intense as he claimed. Political scientist Todd Swanstrom (1988, 88–89), for example, pointed to the existence of "slack in the intergovernmental marketplace." Whereas "Peterson portrays the intergovernmental marketplace as taut," Swanstrom pointed to empirical research demonstrating that "there is more slack than [Peterson's] market theory [of politics] acknowledges." To demonstrate the existence of such slack, Swanstrom adduced evidence showing that "local taxes and incentives have very little effect on [business] location decisions." Therefore, he surmised, if what intergovernmental actors (localities and states) do fails to affect business location, these actors are not tightly locked into competition for mobile investment. Cities hence have the economic space to maneuver. Leading regime theorist Clarence Stone's work challenged Peterson's model in a similar way, arguing that the existence of many place-specific business opportunities available only in cities slows the degree of capital mobility in urban economies (and therefore mitigates the economic constraints). Along these same lines, Stone also noted that many established city businesses have large sunk investments from which they cannot easily walk away (see, for example, Stone 1988a, 1988b).

This early foray into the realm of economics by regime theorists, while not without some validity, also proved to be inadequate. Failing to fully appreciate the intensity of the economic constraints on the city left regime theory empirically vulnerable and prescriptively irrelevant. Regime theory, in short, seemed to be in a state of denial. By merely pointing to the complexities of business location and the fact that *all* capital is not immediately mobile, it embraced a tenuous empirical claim that seemingly flew in the face of obvious urban economic dependencies (see Jones and Bachelor 1986; Kantor 1988; Shefter 1985). By the 1980s it had become abundantly clear that in most cities there is *enough* mobile investment (actually or prospectively) to significantly affect the city's economic vitality.[2]

On the prescriptive side, regime theory's denial of the empirically obvious exposed it to Peterson's taunting (quoted above) where he condescendingly concluded that the theory generated policymaking advice likely to "be ignored" (Peterson 1987, 546). Such irrelevance is especially acute when moving *beyond policy* and into the deeper realm of institutional design (see

Elkin 1993). It is in this realm that the institutional prescriptions necessary to bring about progressive urban regime reconstruction—the key constructive goal of my project—are considered. Therefore, conventional urban regime theory stands as especially deficient in prescriptive terms.

Urban regime theory's denial of the economic determinist challenge has continued through the present. Much subsequent regime scholarship simply assumed away this powerful theoretical challenge without ever debunking its central tenets (see Mossberger 2009; Stone 2005). Other scholarship acknowledged urban regime theory's weakness vis-à-vis economic determinism, but failed to offer its own debunking of Petersonian-type economic determinism (see Davies 2002; Sites 1997).

Yet, until this Petersonian-type economic determinism is convincingly debunked in both theory and—especially—practice, there is little hope that the creation and maintenance of progressive urban regimes can be realized. For as long as a Petersonian-type view is seen to be valid, it is improbable that the political momentum for progressive change can ever be generated (see Frug and Barron 2008; Swanstrom 1988). Such momentum inevitably will be stymied by what the progressive writer and activist Michael Shuman (2006), borrowing Maggie Thatcher's famous catch phrase, calls the logic of TINA: There Is No Alternative to corporate-dominated urban regimes and their regressive policy agendas. As I have shown thus far, conventional urban regime theory, despite its many attributes, has hitherto been unable to demonstrate the fallaciousness of this logic. It therefore fails to help advance the struggle to transform urban governance to better realize democratic and egalitarian ideals. Of course social-science research can, in and of itself, do little to realize these ideals. Yet, under the right political conditions, such research can inform and aid the work of progressive leaders and activists engaged in such a struggle. It can help to alter the prevailing discourse, while at the same offering an alternative vision to which such leadership and activism can aspire.

Exorcising Economic Determinism

How might a reformulated urban regime theory exorcise the TINA-infused, economic determinism of the Petersonian perspective? The first step is simply to confront the economic reality faced by cities squarely and soberly. Specifically, the key to developing an empirically and prescriptively powerful theoretical alternative to economic determinism is to not gainsay the force of the city's economic dependency. Second, rather than undervaluing the intensity of the economic constraints on the city, regime theory instead needs to demonstrate that city officials *respond* to these pressures in the wrong way—by pursuing misguided economic development strategies. If this cannot be convincingly demonstrated, then the Petersonian model largely holds: cities must do mainstream, corporate economic development given the economic constraints they face. And, as Peterson (1981) showed, this is indeed much of what cities *actually* do.

In an early development of regime theory, Elkin (1987) perceptively captured the essence of what is required to jettison economic determinism. First, he clearly acknowledged the centrality and weight of the economic constraints facing cities: cities, he wrote, face the "necessity of earning [their] keep." Therefore, "virtually all issues dealt with by cities are deeply involved with economic development" and, as a result, citizens and officials "can hardly avoid considering the commercial well-being of the city." In short, he concluded, cities "*must* adopt certain policies to promote economic vitality—and that, being rational, they do" (Elkin 1987, 99, 174, 179).

Yet, Elkin (1987, 99) added a second, and crucial, point: the "roots of the city's failures," he noted, lay not in the existence of these constraints but instead in how cities' "impulse" to act in response to them "gets translated into action." Most crucially, certain "*interpretations* of how to meet the problem of earning the city's keep"—that is, certain economic development strategies—get pursued largely for political reasons, but these strategies generally fail to work well (Elkin 1987, 179; also see Mier and Fitzgerald 1991). Elkin's argument thus pointed to the fundamental flaw in the Petersonian perspective. Peterson was right in claiming that most cities must pursue development policies. He was also correct to claim that a unitary interest exists and that development policy can conceivably fulfill that interest (what Elkin referred to as the *commercial public interest*). However, Peterson wrongly assumed that what cities *actually do* in the name of development policy *fulfills* that interest.

Elkin's (1987, 179) work also pointed to two interrelated bodies of knowledge that must be accumulated to sustain this powerful argument: (1) a systematic critique of "presently employed growth strategies"—that is, so-called corporate-center or mainstream[3] strategies, and (2) the corresponding development of alternative ideas about how city economies function and how best to promote local economic vitality. Stone and his colleague Hayward Sanders (Sanders and Stone 1987, 523) made a similar but weaker claim regarding the first of these issues in their critique of Peterson's economic determinism: "many [urban development] projects," they wrote, "have mixed consequences so that the net effect is often open to *some* doubt and debate" (emphasis added). Yet, the tentativeness of this claim—a tentativeness that stems from their failure to engage in a systematic evaluation of the economic outcomes of urban development policy— leaves regime theory's position vis-à-vis economic determinism much less tenable and, as I suggested above, much more open to criticism.

Thus, the work of Elkin (1987) provides the best guide for how to overcome Petersonian-type economic determinism. Yet, despite its perspicacity, Elkin's broadly sweeping theoretical book only gestured at contributing to the production of the necessary knowledge. For example, to critique economic development strategies, Elkin (1987, 97) merely sketched the case of Detroit's failure with the corporate-center strategy. Given the strategy's obsessive focus on bricks-and-mortar approaches to development, he quipped, "Detroit is like nothing so much as a third-world country that equates wealth with physical structures." Likewise, regarding the formulation of alternative economic ideas for generating economic vitality, Elkin (1987, 179) only briefly questioned whether the conventional approach to urban economic development (emphasizing the export of goods and services to other communities) should be eschewed in favor of an alternative strategy (of import replacement): "A great deal depends on whether exporting is the fundamental process by which cities prosper or whether import replacement is also crucial. Import replacement strongly points to other than a [corporate-center] strategy."

It thus has fallen to later generations of urbanists to pursue this twofold research agenda. With the knowledge derived from it—the nascent fruits of which are sketched below—urban regime theory can be reformulated in ways that, finally, exorcise the economic determinism of the Petersonian perspective and transcend its TINA logic. Such an exorcism and transcendence can help open the door for the development of more progressive urban regimes by demonstrating that another political-economic future for American cities is indeed possible.

What Is to Be Done?

Urban regime theory must engage economic questions in a sustained and serious manner if it is to be strengthened both in explanatory and prescriptive terms. Following the course plotted by Elkin (1987), two central research tasks that respond to this charge are thus in order.

Critiquing Corporate-Center Strategies

Regime theory must first demonstrate empirically that presently employed development policies largely fail to meet standards of economic rationality. By exposing this economic *ir*rationality, regime theory in turn demonstrates the fallaciousness inherent in Peterson's economic determinism because the policies cities are ostensibly compelled to pursue are, in reality, *not* in the economic interests of the city.

The major thrust of these presently employed development policies finds its root in a *corporate-center* strategy. Although cities also pursue a variety of other policies on a lesser scale, they channel a preponderance of resources and energies toward urban development in this corporate-center form (see, for example, Judd 2003; Hackworth 2007; Sanders 2005). The corporate-center strategy emphasizes remaking cities' downtowns "into modern 'corporate centers' of offices, up-scale commercial establishments and residences, hotels, and other tourism and convention [and entertainment] facilities" (Levine 1988, 119). It involves the conspicuous use of an array of generous financial subsidies to attract investment, and primarily physical development initiatives, often entailing large-scale changes in established patterns of land use (see Eisinger 2000; Bennett and Spirou 2006; Staley 2001; Levine 2000). Philosophically, its roots lie in the cultural tradition of privatism (Warner 1968), which strongly weds the economic interests and fates of cities to the vibrancy of their private businesses, while relying heavily on private institutions (rather than public controls and planning) to generate and regulate local economic development (Barnekov and Rich 1989). Corporate-center strategies thus embody the essence of the "neo-liberal city" (Hackworth 2007).

Clearly, there is a general sense that this effort and related strategies are failing to produce the desired results. The literature on urban economic development is replete with studies suggestive of this conclusion.[4]

Urban political economist and historian Marc Levine's (1987, 2000) ongo-ing work on Baltimore provides a more comprehensive and long-term examination of the issue. Spurred by mainstream urban analysts' herald-ing of Baltimore as an urban renaissance, Levine cut through the hype and the boosterism surrounding that city's redevelopment effort with a careful and systemic evaluation of its consequences. What he found is that, despite the outward appearance of economic vitality and regeneration, the city's pursuit of the corporate-center strategy produced rather dismal re-sults. This strategy produced only limited spin-off development, created jobs of mostly poor quality, raised questions of fiscal unsustainability given the exorbitant implementation costs incurred, yielded few public benefits, and failed to generate trickle-down redevelopment to distressed urban neighborhoods.

These existing studies—especially in the mode of Levine's economically grounded, contextually and historically sensitive, and critically evaluative work—represent a good first step to developing a full-blown and compel-ling critique of presently employed (corporate center) urban development strategies. If urban regime theory is to be strengthened to debunk the Petersonian perspective and the logic of TINA, additional research in this vein must be undertaken.

Such additional research is indeed beginning to emerge. In a notable re-cent example, urban geographer Timothy Collins (2008, 1192–93), drawing on my earlier work (see Imbroscio 2003), specifies that his recent analysis of sport stadium building and downtown redevelopment in Phoenix heeds the "call for empirical case studies to destabilize the hegemonic ideology of corporate-centered development that guides local government decision-making." Similar to Levine's work on Baltimore, Collins demonstrated that the Phoenix efforts failed to meet the standards of economic rational-ity "defined either in terms of the city's unitary interest or in terms of the goal of downtown redevelopment."

Building an Alternative Economic Paradigm

The second body of knowledge that research must generate to strengthen urban regime theory involves the development of alternative ideas about the nature of city economies and how to promote their vitality. Not only are these ideas important in their own right, they also form a complement to the above-discussed effort to critique corporate-center development. This is because such alternative ideas provide a useful theoretical underpinning for that critique, while concurrently prescribing an altogether different policy agenda.

Like the critique of corporate-center development, the advance of alternative economic ideas also contributes to the reevaluation of Peterson-type economic determinism. Whereas the critical analysis of corporate-center development demonstrates the economic failure of what is *currently practiced* by cities, this second body of knowledge demonstrates the possibility of a *superior substitute*. If it can be demonstrated that such a substitute exists, then it becomes even clearer that cities are not, as the Petersonian TINA logic insists, compelled by economic reasons to pursue their current (corporate-centered) economic development agendas.

Urban regime theory's neglect of economics essentially leaves it with a tacit (and unexamined) embrace of conventional economic theory, since it takes economic processes *as a given*. Such a posture also betrays urban regime theory's deep philosophical liberalism that weds it to a strict public-private distinction. This distinction greatly limits its ability to inquire into the market (or economic) side of the state-market division of labor. In essence, the market side is deemed largely *private* and hence not the proper subject of study for a body of scholarship concerned with political matters (or *public* policy).

In contrast, as I have argued, it is imperative that urban regime theory intensely engage economics. This intense engagement is necessary if regime theory is to be strengthened both in an explanatory sense and—most crucial for my project—in a prescriptive sense so that it might offer a road map for progressive regime reconstruction. Key here is the effort to build a new alternative economic paradigm, elements of which are sketched below. This new paradigm is firmly rooted in and inspired by the theoretical underpinnings of the local economic alternative development strategies introduced in earlier chapters. As such, it challenges many of the tenets of conventional economic theory.

Community Economic Stability   A first building block is to further refine and develop the concept of community economic stability. Community economic stability refers to a condition where localities "possess job opportunities and a general level of economic activity…adequate to provide a decent standard of living for their populations over a sustained period of time" (Williamson, Imbroscio, and Alperovitz 2002, xiv).

Whereas conventional economics focuses obsessively on the benefits of market *dynamism,* with its uninhibited flow of economic resources to ostensibly more productive uses, the new alternative economic paradigm needs to specify systematically the benefits flowing from community economic *stability.* For example, when the economic instability generated by capital mobility and disinvestment devastates whole communities, multiple inefficiencies and social costs arise. Trillions of dollars in physical infrastructure (such as transportation systems, housing, and a host of industrial facilities) are literally thrown away, invaluable social infrastructure (or social capital) is lost, wrenching emotional costs are imposed on individuals and families, the public sector must shoulder significant fiscal burdens, and the quality of political citizenship declines.[5]

By measuring the myriad costs and inefficiencies engendered due to the lack of community economic stability, the new alternative economic paradigm can provide a different lens through which to assess competing local economic development strategies. For example, an adequate appreciation of the economic value of community stability would redirect public subsidies for development to strategies that root business investment in place. These strategies might entail many of the alternatives introduced in the last chapter, such as community-based economic institutions and the development of indigenous (often small and highly networked) businesses (Williamson, Imbroscio, and Alperovitz 2002).

Public Balance Sheets   To provide a proper accounting of the myriad costs and inefficiencies generated by community instability, as well as other important costs and benefits of local development neglected by conventional economics, the new alternative economic paradigm can employ an analytical tool known as the local public (or community) balance sheet.[6] The public balance sheet tallies the social costs and benefits of local policies and private sector development and disinvestment decisions, evaluating the "tangible, measurable, quantifiable costs" being imposed on citizens and their communities from such actions, while comparing "the *total* taxpayer and public benefits from direct intervention to maintain local employment against the *total* costs" (Alperovitz and Faux 1979, iii).

Whereas conventional economics treats the costs imposed on citizens and communities from development and disinvestment as negative externalities and assumes them to be minimal (Buss and Yancer 1999), the public balance sheet methodology embodies a much more expansive conception of such externalities. This conception, in turn, allows for the inclusion of the kinds of infrastructural, human, fiscal, social, and political costs cited above. Moreover, the public balance sheet approach also moves beyond the framework of conventional economics by rejecting "the narrow considerations of private profit and loss that are typically used to evaluate public action," thereby providing a "more comprehensive and rational guide" for local policymaking (Alperovitz and Faux 1979, iii).

As a result, the public balance sheet can inspire a range of innovative and socially transformative policy prescriptions. Such prescriptions emerge as the true costs and benefits of private sector development decisions are included in the analysis of competing development strategies. Notable examples include linkage (or linked development) policies, anti-big-box retail efforts, attempts to create a legally recognized community property right in industrial facilities, the use of eminent domain powers to prevent capital flight, local public ownership of productive assets, and antisprawl policies.[7]

Asset Specificities   In congruence with the notion that community instability can destroy wealth-producing social capital, the work of Swanstrom emphasizes that successful economic development largely springs from the strength of rooted social relationships (also see Granovetter 1985). As Swanstrom (1993, 73) explains,

> social relations are not simply drags on economic growth, but, properly understood, are essential for a well-functioning economy. Capital is not some "thing," that can be moved about the globe willy-nilly in search of higher profits. Capital is a complex social relation that exists in a fragile [and embedded] relationship with its social environment.

In a subsequent refinement of this work, Swanstrom and his colleague Gerald Berk (Berk and Swanstrom 1995, 2) argue for the need to emphasize the importance of capital *im*mobility for vibrant local economic development, or what they refer to as "asset specificities" or "productive assets grounded in specific times and places." Understanding the importance of these asset specificities provides yet another element in the construction of an alternative economic paradigm.

As Berk and Swanstrom (1995, 9) demonstrate, conventional economics fails to conceptualize these values adequately because they flow from the use (as opposed to exchange) value of capital. As such, these values are rooted in social relations of trust and cooperation, experiential knowledge of specific production systems, and even conceptions of identity and the idiosyncrasies of specific actors. Asset specificities, therefore, are "so particular to a given setting... that they cannot be valued or sold in the open market," that is, they cannot be exchanged via normal market processes. And, if capital is moved, these values are lost, to be re-created in another place only at great cost. "If business followed the neo-classical market view of competition," Berk and Swanstrom (1995, 15) conclude, "it would find that the foundations of its productive power, its institutional fabric based on relations of trust, would soon be dissolved."

Once the economic value of asset specificities are properly understood as part of the new alternative economic paradigm, commonly employed urban development policies that seem economically rational can be exposed as being less so. Take, for example, the ubiquitous *growth machine*-type development schemes designed to intensify the exchange value of land through upscale commercial and residential development (see Logan and Molotch 1987; Molotch 1976). Because asset specificities are not fully reflected in relative land prices as expressed through the market, they can be easily destroyed by such policies. In essence, the economic pressures of land speculation "disrupt the rooted relationships of place," relationships "that are essential for capitalist growth" (Berk and Swanstrom 1995, 15). Similarly, as urban political economist Joel Rast (1999) insightfully demonstrated in his study of the political economy of Chicago, rising land prices driven by urban development policies displaced rooted, viable forms of industrial production that actually contributed more to the overall economic health of the city than the gentrified real estate development that replaced it (also see Frug and Barron 2008).

Economic Localism   An additional element of the new alternative economic paradigm is the understanding of the value of economic localism for urban economic development. This economic localism, or what the ecologically minded urban analyst David Morris (1982; also see Shuman

2006) terms *local economic self-reliance,* embodies two fundamental principles. First, rather than focusing heavily on export-oriented strategies, there
is an increased emphasis on augmenting local production efforts targeted
to meet local needs. This notion has affinity with the heterodox economic
thinker Jane Jacobs's (1969, 1984) highly influential concept of *import replacement* (replacing goods now imported into cities with those locally produced), or the more general idea of *import substitution.*[8] Second, rather than
undertaking a zealous effort to attract capital investment from external
sources, economic localism focuses more on economic development generated indigenously.

These two principles stand in contrast to the prescriptions of conventional economics, which stress the economic value of both exporting and
attracting business. This perspective is vivid in Peterson's *City Limits* (1981,
23, 27), as he "equate[s] the [economic] interests of cities with the interests of their export industries" and argues that to be "an economically productive territory," capital "must be attracted" to the city (also see Kantor
1995). Other work in economic development theory, informed by alter-
ative perspectives, questions and challenges this view. For example, the
export-oriented model of development has been characterized as "grossly
oversimplified" because it undervalues the significance of human capital,
entrepreneurship, and innovation. "Growth," it turns out "can come as easily from within as from without" (Vaughan 1988, 120). Likewise, many
export industries dominant in cities (e.g., the advanced service sector) are
only weakly connected to the rest of the city economy, causing such industries to generate only limited additional economic stimulation (Long 1987;
Stanback and Noyelle 1982).

Moreover, several economic advantages can flow from economic localism. For example, supporting indigenous development spares cities the
enormous costs usually incurred when investment needs to be attracted
from other places (Williamson, Imbroscio, and Alperovitz 2002). Additionally, import substitution policies targeting local production efforts to
meet local needs save city economies the considerable opportunity costs that
arise when available local resources remain underutilized (Persky, Ranney, and Wiewel 1993). Further, economic localism increases the degree of
interdependence among local economic actors, which in turn causes each
new activity to stimulate significantly more activity as it multiplies through
the local economy.

Alternative Institutions   A final but important element of this new alternative economic paradigm involves ways to alter the existing structure of business ownership from its common form to a more collective form. Worker-owned firms, business enterprises owned by community organizations (such as, but not limited to, community development corporations), community development finance institutions (such as community credit unions or community development banks), community land trusts, and even local-level public enterprises all meet this criteria by extending ownership (and control) of economic enterprises beyond either an individual owner or the traditional business corporation (Bruyn 1987; Alperovitz 2005).

Conventional economists view such collectivist forms of business ownership as mostly inefficient. The common claim is that such forms often fail to structure individual incentives properly, which leads to a variety of principal-agent problems, shirking behavior, and free riding. Others defend these ownership forms, noting that well-designed institutions can mitigate such problems (Dahl 1985; Shuman 1998). Concomitant to this defense lays a deeper critique of the model of human motivation that underlies conventional economists' claims. This model obsessively focuses on the role played by narrow, material self-interest in guiding human action (see Kelly 1977; Mansbridge 1990; Dryzek 1987).

From a local economic development standpoint, the most significant advantage of these alternative institutions for ownership is that they root economic activity more securely in communities. Increasing the degree of rooted investment limits capital flight and, in turn, enhances the community economic stability of cities (DeFilippis 2004; Williamson, Imbroscio, and Alperovitz 2002).

Reconstructing Urban Regimes

Thus, to sum up, conventional urban regime theory has largely neglected the examination of economic processes. This neglect has left it limited in both explanatory and prescriptive terms. These limitations are revealed most clearly by its inability to mount a decisive critique of the economic determinism of Peterson's *City Limits* perspective. Urban regime theory must therefore engage economic questions in a much more sustained and systematic way if it is to be strengthened. Specifically, it must demonstrate that cities often respond inappropriately to the economic pressures they face by pursuing misguided economic development strategies. Substantiating this claim necessitates both the construction of an effective critique of currently employed development strategies and, more significantly, the construction a new alternative economic paradigm rooted in the LEADS.

In addition, the theories and practices of this nascent alternative economics and their LEADS underpinnings can potentially facilitate the formation and viability of progressive (i.e., democratic and egalitarian) urban regimes. Otherwise put, and dovetailing with the discussion in chapter 1, this alternative economics can potentially point the way toward making economic development (or accumulation) processes more legitimate, hence overcoming the "enduring tension" (Judd and Swanstrom 1988, 3) that plagues American urban governance.

To understand this reconstructive dynamic recall that, as Stone (1989) demonstrates, urban regimes form as they do because the local state is too weak to govern autonomously and, therefore, must form alliances with resource-rich segments of civil society to create an effective capacity to govern. Because corporate interests usually are the only political force holding a concentration of such resources, public officials gravitate toward these interests to form urban regimes (Stone 1989). Therefore, institutionally, the regime reconstruction problem can be solved in one of two ways: (1) an alternative group in civil society can garner the necessary concentration of resources, or (2) the local state can be strengthened directly.

Key elements of the alternative economic paradigm detailed above can facilitate the required institutional change. To illustrate, consider Berk and Swanstrom's (1995) notion of asset specificities. Recognizing the economic value of asset specificities points to an economy of rooted, highly networked small businesses. This result occurs because such businesses thrive in environments that cultivate the use value of capital, such as the social relations of trust and cooperation and the experiential knowledge of specific production systems. In this sense, they diverge from growth-machine-type development policies designed to intensify the exchange value of land. Growth machine policies tend to enhance the resource base of land-oriented corporate interests, hence buttressing urban regimes with such interests at their center. In contrast, the rooted, networked small businesses (nurtured when asset specificities are properly valued) can form the basis of a new regime, akin to the *petty-bourgeois* form identified in the previous chapter. As these small businesses become an increasingly crucial part of the local economy, the interests controlling them can garner an enhanced resource base (making them therefore attractive regime partners for public officials). Such regimes also would be supported by another element of the alternative economic paradigm, economic localism, due to its emphasis on increased economic interdependence among local economic actors and its efforts to spur indigenously generated development.

Likewise, the effort to build alternative economic institutions, either in the community-based sector or via locally owned public enterprise, also can facilitate the necessary institutional change for regime reconstruction. Regarding the latter, expanding the local state's role in a city's economy augments significantly the resources under public control, creating something akin to a strong state (Krasner 1978) on the local level. With a stronger state structure, public officials possess the resource base necessary to govern more autonomously from civil society, thus freeing them from the need to form a governing coalition with corporate interests. This autonomy, in turn, provides the basis for a new regime akin to the *local-statist* model identified in chapter 1. Regarding the former, increased community ownership and control of economic production (via, for example, worker-owned firms, business enterprises owned by community development corporations, community finance institutions, and community land trusts) provides community-based, neighborhood-oriented interests with a solid base of resources. Holding such resources makes this group attractive as a governing partner for public officials looking for an alternative to corporate interests when forming an urban regime. Such regimes parallel the *community-based* form also identified in chapter 1.

Finally, other elements of the alternative economic paradigm can play an ancillary role in regime reconstruction. An appreciation of the economic value of community stability would encourage the reallocation of public development expenditures to strategies such as community-based economic institutions, local public enterprise, and indigenous (and networked) business development—all of which explicitly root and stabilize business investment in place. Similarly, the use of public balance sheets, with their focus on the true costs and benefits of development decisions, also would likely prescribe the same efforts to root investment as a means of mitigating the costs imposed on communities by mobile capital.

Part II

Reconsidering Urban Policy

The Critique of Liberal Expansionism

3

Reassessing the Shaming
of the Inside Game

Over the past decade the dominant—perhaps even hegemonic—policy approach embraced by urbanists to address America's urban problems has been what I term liberal expansionism. In this chapter I will build a critique of liberal expansionism by focusing on one key facet of it—namely, the spirited case made by liberal expansionists against what former Albuquerque mayor David Rusk (1999) calls *the inside game*. Rusk's experience as mayor of Albuquerque, a city that aggressively annexed its adjacent territory in the postwar period, led the politician turned scholar to strongly advocate that cities should be *without suburbs* (also see Rusk 1993). Rusk saw as imperative the need for cities to play the so-called *outside game* by expanding their boundaries to envelop or otherwise form expansive links with surrounding jurisdictions in the metropolitan region. The inside game, in contrast, is to be largely eschewed, argues Rusk (1999).

This inside game involves, most notably, the place-oriented, community development approach to addressing urban problems, as well as the internal policy actions and institutional capacities of central cities themselves (also see Dreier, Mollenkopf, and Swanstrom 2004). Basing his conclusions on "hard, cold facts on income and population," Rusk (1999, 13) argued that "playing only the 'inside game' is a losing strategy for even the most exemplary players. For both poverty-impacted cities and poverty-impacted neighborhoods, even the strongest inside game must be matched by a strong 'outside game' [that is, expansionist strategies of various stripes]."

It is this case against the inside game as a "losing strategy" for cities and urban neighborhoods—what I refer to as the *shaming of the inside game*—that provides the empirical basis behind the clarion call for expansionist urban policies. Hence, much of the critique of liberal expansionism necessarily questions whether this shaming of the inside game is, indeed, warranted.

It is my central contention that it is, in fact, not warranted. Instead, the shaming of the inside game relies more on the liberal value commitments of expansionists themselves rather than on careful empirical analysis. Although no social science truly can be value neutral (see, for example, Bernstein 1976), the shaming of the inside game is clearly ideologically biased in nature (cf. Kirby 2004). This bias is reflective of a subtle rather than blatant ideology—to employ economist and social theorist Robert Heilbroner's (1988) useful distinction. It involves such subtleties as the way issues are framed and conceptualized, the choices regarding research questions and, especially, how available evidence is interpreted. Moreover, not only is such ideological bias subtle in these ways, it also is largely unintentional (as researchers often fail to recognize how their own value commitments shape their research in ideological ways). Yet, while subtle and largely unintended, such ideological bias is unmistakably clear. Its exposure as the true basis upon which liberal expansionists shame the inside game should give urbanists good cause to question the current hegemony of liberal expansionism.

Seven Deadly Sins

Liberal expansionism's flawed, ideologically biased case against community development and the internal capacities of central cities—that is, its *shaming of the inside game*—revolves around seven different but related axes.

Greatest American Heroes?

To begin, consider again the work of Rusk, perhaps the quintessential liberal expansionist. Rusk (1999, 18) makes much of his case against the inside game by poignantly showing that, despite being engaged in a "truly heroic struggle," the thousands of urban-based community development corporations (CDCs) in America "are producing discouraging results" and, even more decisively, are "losing the war against poverty itself." Prominent liberal expansionists Peter Dreier, John Mollenkopf, and Todd Swanstrom (2001, 6) also approvingly reference this claim:

> Rusk found that between 1970 and 1990, the CDCs [in the South Bronx] were able to reverse population losses in their neighborhoods, but poverty rates continued to rise and buying power in the neighborhoods fell. Rusk concluded that if the outward movement to the suburbs continues in the New York region, the neighborhoods of the South Bronx will not be able to stem decay, *no matter how hard they work*.[1] (emphasis added)

Moreover, following Rusk, another prominent liberal expansionist and politician turned scholar, former Minnesota state senator Myron Orfield (1998, 77), expressed similar sentiments: "In a regional context," he writes, CDC-type development

> moves against the grain of a long-term strategy to establish access to opportunity for people and stability for core communities. After twenty years, even the largest and most successful…[CDC] initiatives in the country *have not changed the basic downward spiral* of poor, segregated neighborhoods. In the areas where the country's leading CDCs were operating, despite large CDC investment, family and individual poverty rates and median household income have moved further from metropolitan norms. (emphasis added)

There is, of course, little doubt that these conclusions are empirically correct. CDCs have clearly failed to win "the war against poverty itself" (Rusk), "stem decay" (Dreier, Mollenkopf, and Swanstrom) or change "the basic downward spiral of poor, segregated neighborhoods" (Orfield). The basic evidence is overwhelming (that is, Rusk's "hard, cold facts on income and population"). The pro-expansionist ideological bias rears its head, however, in the *analysis of the cause* of these failures. Namely, rather than engaging in careful empirical analysis, it is simply assumed that CDCs' failure to fight poverty effectively is due largely to one overriding factor: their *isolation* from external economic and social processes. They fail, that is, because they play "the inside game" (Rusk), because of the "outward movement to the suburbs" (Dreier, Mollenkopf, and Swanstrom), and because their work "moves against the grain" of broader regional dynamics (Orfield). Yet nowhere is this causal relationship confirmed with empirical data. It is, instead, merely (and speculatively) asserted, a product of the ideological biases of the liberal expansionists themselves.

This bias becomes more fully revealed when one considers that there exist other plausible reasons for CDCs' failure. Viewing the empirical evidence from a progressive place-oriented perspective rather than a liberal expansionist one leads geographer James DeFilippis, for example, to a different causal explanation. In his excellent book, *Unmaking Goliath: Community Control in the Face of Global Capital,* DeFilippis (2004, 56) concurs with the liberal expansionist account of the empirical results of CDCs: "all too often," he notes, "the reality has been that community-development efforts have failed to visibly or measurably improve the larger communities in which they are located." However, in strong opposition to liberal expansionists, he argues that a major cause of such failure has been the "neo-liberal communitarian" framework driving CDC theory and practice. This framework is marked by a commitment to free-market capitalism as the vehicle for urban development, coupled with the belief that inner-city communities operate as unified wholes that are largely absent of internal conflict. This neoliberal communitarianism, DeFilippis (2004, 55, 58) points out, "represents the fruition of the *depoliticization* of community development that came from its split from community organizing in the late 1960s" (emphasis added). And, he adds, "the current problems of CDCs stem from the flaws of...[this] framework." This conclusion, it should be added, has been reached by several other keen observers of community development efforts. These observers have developed causal explanations of CDCs' failure broadly consistent with DeFilippis's analysis.[2]

Did the Feds Ever Really Care?

A related claim is that past federal efforts to redevelop poor communities in central cities have been an abysmal failure. Although liberal expansionists—given both their liberal and expansionist proclivities—advocate deep federal involvement in urban policy, many previous antipoverty community development initiatives of the federal government are now seen as discredited because they were insufficiently expansionist.

Again, Rusk's (1999, 12–13) work nicely illustrates this sentiment. Recounting how cities "got into their present and sad state" and the failed efforts to counter decline, he writes that "for three decades the federal government has *targeted poor areas* with a succession of antipoverty initiatives." Prominent among such initiatives have been "community action programs, model cities programs, community development block grants [CDBGs], urban development actions grants [UDAGs], empowerment community and enterprise zone funds and tax credits—all," in Rusk's view, "variations on...the 'inside game'" (emphasis added). From this perspective, then, federal urban policy has failed because it has targeted poor places, that is, because of the pure folly of the inside game it has played.

The journalist Nicholas Lemann offered perhaps the most well-known statement in this vein. In the conclusion to his book on the Great Migration of African Americans from the rural South to the urban North during the mid-twentieth century, as well as in a widely read follow-up piece in the *New York Times Magazine,* Lemann reviewed the decades-long history of past federal efforts to redevelop poorer areas of central cities. Referring to these areas disparagingly as "ghettos" and "slums," Lemann (1991, 347) concluded that "the clear lesson of experience...is that ghetto development hasn't worked" (citing the failure of federal programs such as Urban Renewal, the War on Poverty, Model Cities, CDBGs, UDAGs, and enterprise zones). The reason for this abysmal failure has to do with the nature of the inside game and its isolation from "the social and economic mainstream of American society." Being isolated from the mainstream, such ghettos or slums provide an extremely inhospitable environment for both businesses and residences. "Ghettos aren't very attractive locations for businesses," he asserts. "Urban slums," he adds, "have never been home to many businesses except for sweatshops and minor neighborhood provisioners." Likewise, on the residential side, Lemann notes that "poor neighborhoods are usually transitional" or merely "temporary communities." "The standard model of progress for people living in urban slums," as seen from Lemann's liberal expansionist perspective, "...is to get a good job outside the neighborhood and then decamp for a nicer [and usually outlying] part of town" (Lemann 1994, 31, 28; 1991, 347–48).

Once again, we see the liberal expansionist value bias, as ideology is substituted for analysis. Liberal expansionists explain the failure of federal community development efforts by focusing almost solely on a single causal factor—isolation—sans much empirical evidence. Yet, also again, other plausible explanations for this failure are well documented by decades of urban scholarship. For example, some federal programs were based on a flawed development model (Urban Renewal, enterprise zones), were woefully underfunded (Model Cities), were directed toward downtown rather than neighborhood development (UDAGs), were not properly targeted to poorer areas (CDBGs) or, more commonly, had some substantial elements of all of the above. And, more generally, all of these place-oriented federal efforts have been, in historian Alice O'Connor's (1999, 79–80) apropos metaphor, "swimming against the tide" of an array of federal policies that have "encouraged the trends that impoverish communities in the first place." The feds then step in subsequently with only "modest and inadequate interventions" and then wonder "why community development so often 'fails.'"

Although liberal expansionists such as Rusk and Lemann use this frequent failure to shame the inside game and call for expansionism, the actual history of federal urban policy is more complicated. In the end, as Todd Swanstrom (1993, 74–75) points out in his earlier work critical of liberal expansionism:[3] "It is impossible to disprove Lemann's...assertion that 'ghetto development hasn't worked.'" Yet, Swanstrom notes, there are both empirical and normative reasons to be incredulous: "Lemann's idea that there is nothing to build on in poor black neighborhoods flies in the face of anthropological research on social order in the ghetto and smacks of the culture of poverty thesis."

Why *Not* Blame the Victim?

Turning from community development efforts to the evaluation of central cities themselves reveals a third way the inside game is shamed. Once again, we begin with a clear empirical fact: central cities have failed to address adequately an array of social and economic problems, especially concentrated poverty. But in order to shame the inside game, liberal expansionists blame this failure almost exclusively on the isolation of central cities from their surrounding metropolitan regions. No approach to urban governance, argue Dreier, Mollenkopf, and Swanstrom (2001, 17), "has made much progress on growing inequality, persistent poverty, and racial and economic segregation." Different types of "urban regimes [have] developed symbolic responses to these problems, but none can claim significant success." The reason for this failure, they conclude, is that "it is difficult for central cities by themselves to solve the problems generated by economic segregation and urban sprawl." Hence, such isolation leads, naturally, to a policy of expansionism: "It is only *natural,* therefore, for cities to reach out to suburban municipalities and attempt to forge regional solutions to their problems" (Dreier, Mollenkopf, and Swanstrom, 2001, 173; emphasis added).

Seeing expansionism as the "natural" reaction of cities attempting to address urban problems stands as a clear manifestation of the ideological biases exhibited by liberal expansionists. Faced with the "limits of localism" (Dreier, Mollenkopf, and Swanstrom, 2001, 171), the only way out conceivable to liberals is to expand—tapping extracity resources from surrounding regions as well as higher-level governments. Yet, this viewpoint once again assumes—without empirical evidence—that the *cause* of central cities' failure to solve their problems lies almost wholly in their isolation, rather than resulting from other, competing factors.

An alternative plausible explanation for central city failure is rooted in the internal governance of cities themselves. Cities may fail to solve problems not because they are isolated but because they are poorly governed. For example, as noted in the last chapter, governing regime after governing regime has zealously pursued a corporate-center urban development strategy. Many scholars suggest these efforts have been a grave mistake on both economic efficiency (costs vs. benefits) and equity (distributive) grounds.[4] If the massive amount of economic, political, and social resources dedicated to these flawed initiatives were redirected by urban regimes toward more productive development strategies (perhaps in the form of the local economic alternative development strategies, or LEADS), the exigency to capture the resources held by affluent but tightfisted suburbanites might be considerably abated. Lessening this exigency, in turn, might have the salutary effect of allowing cities to focus on their own indigenous strengths rather than exerting substantial political energy coveting their neighbors' wealth (who, it should be added, are not generally keen on sharing it; see Alperovitz 2005). In addition, because corporate center strategies *themselves* exacerbate urban social problems,[5] the pursuit of the LEADS might also lessen the acuteness of such problems and, once again, lessen the need to attract external resources via expansionism.

Rather than provide such an analysis, liberal expansionists simply *assume* that the preponderance of causality can be attributed to isolation. In fact, as pointed out in previous chapters, liberal ideology with its strict public-private distinction blinds expansionists *from even considering* the plausibility of any competing explanation. This affliction results because many of the alternative (or progressive) development strategies that might replace the corporate-center approach question the efficiency of, and seek to restructure, the current division of labor between the market and the state in American corporate capitalism. Yet, this division is from the liberal perspective assumed to be largely immutable and fixed (i.e., structurally determined), and therefore beyond reform.

Is There Any "There, There"?

Broad-minded liberal expansionists such as Dreier, Mollenkopf, and Swanstrom (2001, 157) understand the potential for progressive urban regimes, as such regimes "seek to challenge business domination of the urban development agenda" with alternative development strategies "emphasizing 'economic democracy' and 'equity planning.'" Illustratively, they highlight the mayoral experiences of Chicago under Harold Washington, Boston under Ray Flynn, and Cleveland under Dennis Kucinich, among others. However, their ultimate conclusion regarding this potential is, in a word, glum: "These experiences," Dreier, Mollenkopf, and Swanstrom (2001, 164) write, "show that even those cities with the most progressive local administrations cannot do much to correct economic segregation, concentrated poverty, and suburban sprawl."

Dreier, Mollenkopf, and Swanstrom (2001, 171) attribute the *cause* of this failure to the so-called limits of localism (also see Leitner and Garner 1993). This attribution is, once again, made without much empirical evidence, but it nonetheless fits nicely with the call for expansionism. There are, also once again, other plausible reasons to explain this failure. For example, the progressive measures examined by Dreier, Mollenkopf, and Swanstrom were almost always short lived—think, most notably, of Washington's premature death in Chicago (see Ferman 1996) or Kucinich's early electoral defeat at the hands of corporate interests (see Swanstrom 1985). Moreover, the resources devoted to progressive measures were almost always dwarfed by those devoted to corporate-center development strategies (such as in Boston under Flynn; see, for example, Horan 1997). Therefore, because an urban regime is, by definition, somewhat enduring, and since even in many so-called progressive regimes most of the urban development agenda was mainstream and corporate-centered, the *very idea* of the existence of progressive regimes (in big cities, at least) can easily be called into question. It is—to say the least—problematic to assess something as being a failure that never really existed in the first place. Once again, liberal and expansionist ideological biases against progressivism and localism explain this assessment more than do careful and rigorous analyses.

Is the Enemy of My Enemy My Friend?

Ironically, this "limits of localism" perspective causes liberal expansionists to embrace Paul Peterson's (1981) economically determinist *City Limits* argument with its TINA—"there is no alternative"—logic. Embracing the Petersonian perspective, Dreier, Mollenkopf, and Swanstrom (2001, 134–35), for example, assert that "local officials must make their cities attractive places to do business and retain middle-class residents." And progressive policies to help the poor and near poor, such as "living wage ordinances, housing 'linkage' policies, business taxes, clean air laws, plant closing laws, rent control, and lower utility rates," all present a Petersonian-type "dilemma" because such policies often spark capital flight. Although suggesting that it "may be a bluff when corporations threaten to leave," Dreier, Mollenkopf, and Swanstrom (2001, 135) nonetheless firmly and resolutely caution that "business warnings are not always empty threats."[6]

Coming from sophisticated urban political economists this statement is nothing less than jarring. Perhaps, to paraphrase the famous line about Keynes, "we are all Petersonians now." But perhaps not. Clearly, embracing the Petersonian perspective in this way flies in the face of decades of urban research finding this economic determinist market model of city politics to be deeply flawed.[7] Many such studies suggest, for example, that progressive policies—such as, to repeat the Dreier, Mollenkopf, and Swanstrom litany, "living wage ordinances, housing 'linkage' policies, business taxes, clean air laws, plant closing laws, rent control, and lower utility rates"—actually enhance local business climates because they lessen uneven development (and concomitant social problems), stabilize neighborhoods and local economies, and improve the quality of urban life more generally. In addition, as pointed out in the last chapter, the Petersonian perspective is also flawed because cities, in practice, *actually do* many things in the name of urban development that run contrary to their own economic interests. Yet, being driven by the ideology of expansionism with its need to shame the inside game's localism, such urban research debunking the Petersonian perspective goes blithely ignored by liberal expansionists.

Depends on the Ox Gored?

What is perhaps most remarkable about the ideological bias in the analyses of liberal expansionists is that, although they are thorough in tallying the failures of the inside game, the evidence presented that compellingly demonstrates the efficacy of the outside game is remarkably scarce. The inside game is most derided because of its failure to address concentrated poverty and economic (and, to a lesser extent, racial) segregation. But the outside game has not addressed those problems particularly well either and, as a result, liberal expansionists have yet to adduce any solid evidence in support of their claims. It is instead simply assumed based on value commitments (or faith) that outside game policies will *work,* that is, that they will significantly reduce the deep-rooted urban problems of concentrated poverty and segregation.

When evidence is presented in favor of expansionism it is usually speculative or shows improvement on the margins. Take the case of Minneapolis, a darling of liberal expansionists. Even under the most auspicious of conditions, little has been accomplished via outside game policies to address the city's problems with concentrated poverty and segregation (Goetz 2003). The other darling, Portland, Oregon, does have less concentrated poverty in its central city compared to most regions (Dreier, Mollenkopf, and Swanstrom, 2004, 239) but the region is also overwhelmingly white, and the white poor tend in general to be less spatially concentrated (Wilson 1996). In addition, Portland's regional governance structure has demonstrated considerable "shortcomings...with respect to taking up equity issues," such as providing affordable housing in its suburbs (Provo 2009, 379). Or, consider liberal expansionists' favorite program, the Gautreaux mobility program in Chicago (which helped public housing residents relocate from the inner city). Although often hyped by liberal expansionists, Gautreaux's results were marginal at best when considered vis-à-vis the massive scope of Chicago's poverty problem. After almost thirty years of operation, Gautreaux aided only a few thousand poor families and, while the improvements in their lives often have been real, these improvements are overall rather modest, even after the target population for the program was heavily creamed (selected in biased ways).[8] Yet, when the inside game shows similarly modest results—say, in the work accomplished by CDCs during the same period—such achievements are characterized as inadequate (Rusk 1999; Dreier, Mollenkopf, and Swanstrom 2001). In fact, the achievements of both games have been woefully inadequate given the massive scope of the problem, although liberal expansionists lionize the former while dismissing the latter.

On a Highway (or Mass Transit Line) to Hell?

A seventh way the inside game is shamed is by portraying central cities as social and economic basket cases. In order to justify expansionism, it is necessary to show that, in former long-time *Urban Affairs Review* editor Dennis Judd's useful phrase, "the city is always going to hell" (Judd 2005, 125), especially when compared to its more affluent suburbs.[9] There is no doubt that many central cities (and inner-ring suburbs) are experiencing multiple social and economic problems. Yet, it is far from clear that *isolation* is the key cause of such problems, or that the outside game would adequately address them. More to the point here, however, is that liberal expansionists tend to exaggerate central-city problems to justify their agenda.

Consider the well-known case of Louisville where the first city-county consolidation in almost three decades of a major metropolitan area was adopted in 2000. In order to justify this radical expansionist measure, advocates of "merger" (as it was known locally) portrayed the central city as "dying" from a "terminal illness," and hence needing to be saved by a merger with the suburban county (Savitch and Vogel 2000, 204–8).[10] Upon close empirical examination, however, this bleak picture of Louisville was revealed to be a gross distortion. A number of economic and fiscal measures indicated that the central city was "sound," with a degree of urban distress that, since 1970, "continued to improve." In fact, it was shown that "over the years, the city's fiscal picture had actually grown brighter than that of the county" (Savitch and Vogel 2004, 766). A broader look at the issue suggests a general trend in urban America toward increased central city vitality against a backdrop of suburban decline (Leinberger 2008). Although this trend is clearly uneven, it is also clearly significant.

Political Dimensions

The Louisville case also begins to reveal the political dimensions of the shaming of the inside game. When conceiving strategies to build a pro-urban political movement, liberal expansionists tend to eschew the politics of the inside game—with its strong potential for manifesting grassroots, populist, protest, and working-class/minority-empowerment orientations (see Thompson 1998)—in favor of an outside game politics that often tends to be corporate-driven, elite-oriented, middle-class/white-dominated, and more civil/consensus-oriented (see Kipfer 2004). Merger in Louisville brought such a change, as inside game politics was sacrificed for an outside game politics.[11]

Carefully studying the political effects of this institutional change, Louisville-based political scientists Hank Savitch and Ronald Vogel (2004) found that the augmented scale of the polity wrought by merger led to several key political changes. It made grassroots, populist challenges to the mayoral candidates of the corporate-liberal elite financially infeasible; it diluted the political influence of progressive and minority inner-city interests vis-à-vis suburbanites; and it centralized governing power in a strong executive. Yet this political restructuring (and its concomitant death knell for the politics of inside game) never much troubled liberal expansionists. Instead, liberal expansionists universally heralded the Louisville merger as enlightened, forward-thinking political reform (see Dreier, Mollenkopf, and Swanstrom 2001).[12]

Responding to the Savitch-Vogel critique in the second edition of *Place Matters,* Dreier, Mollenkopf, and Swanstrom (2004, 245) revised their take on the Louisville merger, this time offering a more nuanced assessment of it. "Clearly," they admitted, "urban [e.g., progressive, working class, and minority] interests that had a strong position in city government under the old system now have to share that power with suburbanites and Republicans."

Compare, however, this assessment to that of Savitch and Vogel (2004, 782), who view this political realignment as worthy of stern condemnation. "In Louisville," they concluded,

> city-county consolidation has enhanced the ability of affluent suburban-ites while reducing the political influence of blue-collar inner-city residents, particularly African-American residents.... [The realignment from the merger] has diluted the city's core constituency and weakened its ability to defend itself.... Consolidation was used to lodge a great deal of power in a "strong mayor," making it more difficult for poorly financed candidates to run for that office.... The major consequence of city-county consolidation in Louisville is likely to be a more internally cohesive [corporate] regime, coupled to weakened city neighborhoods that are less able to influence the development agenda and more rather than less urban sprawl.

In sharp contrast, Dreier, Mollenkopf, and Swanstrom (2004, 245), rather than condemn this new balance of political power, instead reveal their con-tinued lack of enthusiasm for inside game politics when they bloodlessly conclude: "Exactly how the Louisville case will play out in the coming years will be an interesting case study in the politics of regionalism."

We also see this spurning of inside game politics when examining Dreier, Mollenkopf, and Swanstrom's prescriptions for national-level po-litical reform. For example, in order to facilitate city-suburban political coalitions and help build a solid Democratic Party majority in the U.S. House of Representatives, they argue that congressional districts should be redrawn "by shifting population from overwhelming Democratic, often uncontested, central-city House seats toward suburban House districts" (Dreier, Mollenkopf, and Swanstrom 2001, 245). While there is no doubt such a shift might elect more Democratic representatives, those elected are more likely, however, to have suburban and white middle-class—that is, outside game—political orientations vis-à-vis the representatives they replaced.

The politics of the inside game is further shamed by liberal expansion-ists when they portray inner-city (often minority) leaders protecting their political power base as selfish, self-serving, or parochial. The liberal ex-pansionist Rusk (1999, 312–314), as a former mayor, claims he "know[s] the...feeling," when black mayors see regionalism as diluting mayoral political influence, adding that "it is easy for me to understand why many mayors approach regionalism skeptically and reluctantly." He, neverthe-less, castigates African American big city mayors for being "missing in (in)action" regarding their leadership role in building regional governing institutions. Likewise, Dreier, Mollenkopf, and Swanstrom (2001, 240) criticize many Democrats in Congress (presumably including many Afri-can Americans and Latinos who represent poor central-city constituencies) for being "so heavily invested in existing place-based programs that they are reluctant to consider metropolitan alternatives."

Often this criticism slips into liberal condescension. For example, ac-cording to Orfield (1998, 2002) a key lesson for regional coalition building is the need to "reach into the central cities to make sure the pro-expansionist message *is understood.*" Such didacticism is necessary because "central cities have a *volatile* political landscape" and "without *person-to-person contact* in the inner-city, the [regionalist] message *will be misunderstood.*" If regional-ism is *"misperceived"* in this way, it "threatens the power base of officials elected by poor, segregated constituencies," presumably causing them, however misguidedly, to resist expansionism (Orfield, 2002, 183; emphases added). A similar attitude regarding inner-city elected officials is exhibited by Dreier, Mollenkopf, and Swanstrom. Using the example of José Serrano, a Latino member of Congress who represents the South Bronx, they illus-trate their point that, somewhat counterintuitively, expansionist policies en-couraging the mobility of an inner-city congressperson's constituents to the suburbs do not militate against the political interests of poor districts. "In the long run," they explain, "Congressman Serrano *might realize*" this fact, "that increased residential choices would benefit not just those who move but also those who remain in the area." (2001, 249; emphasis added).[13]

Assessing the Political Dimensions

The question remains, however, does the politics of the inside game de-serve to be shamed? That is, is the shaming grounded in an empirically based and careful analysis of American urban politics in the twenty-first century; or, is it rather a product of the ideological biases of the liberal ex-pansionists themselves? In my view, it is much more the latter than the former.

The deepest problem with the liberal expansionists' shaming of inside game politics is that it is built upon a *biased analysis of political feasibility.*

Ultimately what liberal expansionists want most is equity-oriented regional policies (Bollens 2003, 1997) or, in a word, redistribution, which is broadly understood to include improved access to educational, employment, and housing/quality of life opportunities for the urban poor. From the liberal expansionist perspective, inside game politics as a means to achieve this redistribution is hopelessly infeasible—a certain dead end. Cities simply lack access to the necessary resources to advance the equity agenda very far.

This redistribution, however, obviously requires *two* conditions, both the necessary resources *and* the political will to redistribute those resources. Cities clearly have limited access to resources (what I will call *Type I* constraints on redistribution), and expansionism potentially links cities to greater resource pools upon which they can draw on the regional, state, and national levels. But such enhanced access to resources is useless unless a second constraint can be overcome. This second (*Type II*) constraint is the need to generate the necessary *political will* to engage in redistribution. It is not simply a question of having resources available to fund the equity agenda; the politics must also be supportive of redistributing these available funds.

Liberal expansionists shame inside game politics by treating Type I constraints as insurmountable, while characterizing Type II constraints as much less so. In reality, both types of constraints are quite formidable, and liberal expansionists have not provided any empirical basis to privilege Type II constraints over Type I. Instead, such privileging results chiefly from an ideological bias in favor of outside game politics over the politics of the inside game.

The constraints of the Type I variety are readily obvious: central cities are often home to a disproportionately poor population facing serious social problems, and such cities generally (but not always) have weaker fiscal and economic bases compared to many suburban jurisdictions and the national (or state) government as a whole. Moreover, as pointed out in. chapter 2, while the Petersonian perspective is flawed in its analysis of how cities must *respond* to heightened capital (and citizen) mobility, such mobility is indeed real and must be faced up to squarely and soberly (see Elkin 1987). With all else constant the smaller the geographic scale (such as that of individual cities), the more difficult it is to tap resources given the ease in which the resource rich can flee taxation and regulation.

But Type II constraints are also formidable. With expansionism comes a polity (or some governance or representative structure) that is, most saliently, more conservative politically and less likely to benefit (directly, at least) from redistribution. The solution that liberal expansionists have developed to lessen these constraints is to link certain suburban interests (those from the less affluent, inner-ring areas) together with central cities in political coalitions that fight for equity-oriented policies at the regional, state, and national levels (see Orfield 2002; Dreier, Mollenkopf, and Swanstrom 2004). Yet, like the lessening of Type I constraints, this too is problematic, and empirically there is not much evidence that the suburban dog can hunt.

The governance of the Clinton administration is the best case in point. Dreier, Mollenkopf, and Swanstrom (2001, 233), for example, see Clinton's electoral victories as cases where "the Democrats, in defiance of the conventional wisdom, successfully united central-city and suburban voters in two presidential elections." While admitting that "this coalition did not push the kinds of metropolitan reforms... [they] advocate," Dreier, Mollenkopf, and Swanstrom nonetheless argued that "its existence demonstrates that central-city and suburban electorates are not irrevocably divided." Yet, the reason *why* the kinds of metropolitan reforms they seek were not pushed for by President Clinton goes to the heart of the intensity of the Type II constraints. This reason is, ironically, nicely revealed earlier in their book. Discussing why Clinton's urban policy was, as they characterize it, "too little, too late," Dreier, Mollenkopf, and Swanstrom (2001, 130) point out that "in particular" Clinton did not push for their liberal expansionist agenda because he "did not want his urban policies to threaten suburban interests that were central to his electoral victories."[14] Thus, while central-city and suburban electorates may not be "irrevocably divided," such a coalition appears—given its inherent nature—unable to deliver much. A less ideological, more empirically driven analysis of political feasibility than that offered by liberal expansionists might conclude therefore that the real dead end politically for cities is the moderate, suburban-oriented corporate liberalism that dominates the mainstream of the Democratic Party.[15]

Much the same point can be made of Dreier, Mollenkopf, and Swanstrom's (2001, 245) proposal to redraw congressional districts so that the overwhelming Democratic populations of central-city districts are intermingled with suburban constituencies. Once again, this political strategy might elect more Democratic members of Congress, but most would likely be of the Clintonian variety, intensely concerned, as was Clinton, with not threatening the suburban interests central to their electoral victories. It is therefore an open question which political strategy is better to promote the feasibility of a pro-central-city urban policy—a Congress with a larger proportion of moderate Democrats who might modestly favor cities (an outside game politics), or one with a fewer number of progressives who intensely advocate for cities (an inside game politics). Both choices, frankly, offer only bleak prospects for a strong federal urban policy (cf. Barnes 2005). But the choice of one strategy over the other as *more* feasible reveals more about the ideological bias of liberal expansionists against inside game politics than it does about the realities of political feasibility.

Examining politics on the regional level also reveals the intensity of Type II constraints. The work of political scientist and housing expert Edward Goetz (2003) on Minneapolis, for example, compellingly shows that even under the most auspicious of circumstances outside game politics has produced only limited results addressing equity concerns. Likewise, a broader survey of regional equity policies shows that, when such policies do exist, they do not by and large result from the success of outside game politics on the regional level. Instead, such policies "commonly come in through the back door, as a result of federal and state programs that may or may not be concerned primarily with social equity" (Bollens 2003, 647; also see Kantor 2000).

Most interestingly, when liberal expansionists study this question *empirically,* they themselves also confirm the intensity of Type II constraints. For example, political scientist Margaret Weir and her colleagues Harold Wolman and Todd Swanstrom (2005, 757) examined the political feasibility of expansionism at the state level and found that "cities have less power within the Democratic Party caucuses in the state legislature, historically the main protector of city interest...[as]...the Democratic Party aims to please the swing districts in the suburbs." In addition, big city mayors—being too "preoccupied with [local] autonomy," as well as "the immediate fiscal condition of the city government"—remain "unlikely to lead the way" on the expansionist agenda in state politics. "Moreover," add Weir and her colleagues, "when mayors did reach out politically to suburbs, the suburbs were often reluctant to join for fear of being dominated by city interests." Concluding, they admit that their "research shows only inklings of city-suburban legislative coalitions based on objective common interests." As a result, although such coalitions are not "impossible," they are clearly "difficult" (also see Gainsborough 2001).

The other side of the liberal expansionist shaming of inside game politics is to assume that the Type I constraints afflicting this politics are immutable. But are they?

Certainly some extant evidence is suggestive of the possibility that the lessening of Type I constraints is at least no more difficult than lessening Type II constraints. As underscored in chapters 1 and 2, there currently exist thousands of local economic alternative development institutions capable of anchoring capital (such as worker-owned firms), generating alternative revenue streams for cities (such as municipal ownership), and augmenting the degree to which local economies benefit from local economic activity (via enhancing local multipliers). Such activity is, in its current state of development, small scale and largely marginal to local economies. Yet, if built upon and nurtured with effective leadership and a redirection of resources away from mainstream corporate center urban development schemes, it is plausible that the LEADS potentially could slow capital mobility and stabilize the local fiscal and economic bases of cities (Williamson, Imbroscio, and Alperovitz 2002). Such a slowing and stabilization in turn alters the structural context of city politics, effectively reducing the intensity of the Type I constraints. Along these lines, as discussed in chapters 1 and 2, at least three alternative urban regimes built from a lessening of Type I constraints can be readily identified and plausibly conceived.

Challenging Dominance, Constructing Democracy

The case for liberal expansionism finds its justification in the *shaming of the inside game*. Yet, much of this shaming is, in fact, unjustified by the available empirical evidence; it is, instead, more a product of the ideological biases of liberal expansionists themselves.

This conclusion strongly suggests that, when considering the social problems of American cities, the dominance—bordering on hegemony—currently enjoyed by liberal expansionist policies is largely unwarranted.

Moreover, as will be shown in part 4, the *politics* behind the practice of liberal expansionism also is normatively undesirable in significant ways. Thus, challenging this unwarranted dominance not only opens the door to more efficacious policies to address urban problems, but it also can facilitate the development of political practices that better realize the democratic and egalitarian aspirations for urban governance set out in earlier chapters.

4

RETHINKING THE DISPERSAL CONSENSUS

One salient element of liberal expansionism has garnered an especially orthodox hold on urban policy discourse: the idea that the amelioration of urban problems requires, almost above or prior to all else, that the central city's poor be deconcentrated—that is, dispersed—into wealthier, and usually suburban, neighborhoods. Thus, the general challenge to liberal expansionism demands that special critical analysis be devoted to what I refer to as the *dispersal consensus*.

Prelude to the Critique

Crisis and desperation can beget revelation. Such periods often expose, with remarkable clarity, the essence and strength of peoples' deeply held beliefs and value commitments, as well as the implications of such beliefs and values. It is during such periods, rather than with the falling of dusk, that the owl of Minerva spreads its wings most sumptuously.

In the world of American urban and housing policy experts, we saw such a revelation of beliefs and values during the crisis and desperation that was the city of New Orleans in the wake of Hurricane Katrina. In response to this crisis and desperation, more than two hundred social scientists—many quite prominent—quickly signed a petition endorsing the idea that "our goal...should be to create a 'move to opportunity'" for the thousands of low-income, displaced, and mostly African American former residents of New Orleans (Briggs et al. 2005). Rather than supporting polices that affirmatively facilitate the efforts of the displaced to reclaim their homes and communities, the petition advocated resettling the displaced in wealthier, often white, suburban neighborhoods in order to break up concentrations of poverty that existed before Katrina. The storm and its tragic aftermath hence could have a "silver lining," to quote the title of neoconservative David Brooks's *New York Times* column advocating such a resettlement plan. It provided policymakers with a relatively easy means (in fact, as the petition states, "an historic opportunity") to implement poverty deconcentration measures. Such measures address urban ills by dispersing the African American poor away from deprived areas of the inner city (in ways similar to the federal Moving to Opportunity [MTO] demonstration program or the well-known Gautreaux program in Chicago upon which MTO was modeled).

What such a strong academic endorsement of this controversial (and now strongly condemned) Katrina Move to Opportunity petition suggests, perhaps more than anything else, is how deeply and passionately many American urban experts hold beliefs and values impelling them to embrace deconcentration (or dispersal) policies. Although filled with caveats, nuance, and careful language, the petition's unequivocal advocacy of dispersal rather than "the right of return" (as championed by many grassroots, community-oriented groups) is nothing less than shocking, coming as it did from so many "well-intentioned, respectable scholars," most of whom happened to be left-of-center politically (Reed and Steinberg 2006, 6). Multiplying such shock is that the petition was dated just days after the ostensible Shining City on the Hill looked on as one of its great cities, and its citizens, suffered a catastrophe of near-biblical proportions.

Shock is further multiplied when one reads progressive scholars and activists Adolph Reed and Stephen Steinberg's brief but penetrating and trenchant attack on the Katrina petition's signatories. Disparagingly labeling these signatories "the Gang of 200," Reed and Steinberg (2006, 5–6) charged its members with "naiveté" and "hubris." This Gang of 200, they write, "rushed to tout their silly pet idea without a whit's thought of the social, political, and economic dynamics and tensions that might be at play in the debate over how to reconstruct New Orleans." Specifying, Reed and Steinberg added that the Gang of 200 "gave no thought that Republicans might link the city's repopulation to their desire to gut Democratic power in New Orleans and move Louisiana into the column of reliably Republican states." The Gang also failed "to consider the potential that their idée fixe would play into the hands of real estate development interests and others who relish any opportunity to dissipate New Orleans's black electoral majority." Reed and Steinberg further conveyed their astonishment that "the Gang of 200 [did] not see the expropriation of poor neighborhoods and the violation of human rights" that is justified by the population displacement via dispersal lying at the heart of their proposal, seeing the Gang of 200 as "strangely oblivious of their potential for playing into the hands of retrograde political forces." "Worst of all," the Gang of 200 provided, according to Reed and Steinberg, "liberal cover" for those implementing a resettlement plan in New Orleans "that is reactionary and racist at its core."

All of this is most jarring. It is somewhat puzzling as well because it is clear from the previous, pre-Katrina writings of some members of this so-called Gang that their more considered views about the problem of urban poverty are largely incongruent with the thrust of the petition. By signing it, then, it seems obvious that at least some of the signatories simply wished to express justifiable outrage over the staggering degree of human suffering laid bare by the storm and its aftermath. The intentions of these scholars were more likely to protest the decades of shameful government actions and inactions that allowed such deep-rooted poverty to exist within the borders of a lavishly wealthy nation.

Nevertheless, even if its membership fails to correspond exactly with the signatories of the petition, there is clearly a large group of American urban scholars (that is, a "Gang" in the Reed and Steinberg sense) who have coalesced around one central idea: that the only way to make a serious dent in ameliorating the plague of urban poverty and its associated social problems, not only in New Orleans but throughout urban America, is to disperse the poor into (usually) suburban neighborhoods. This coalescence is what I call the *dispersal consensus* (or DC for short). The DC is an element of liberal expansionism that has been especially hegemonic over the academic and quasi-academic discourse surrounding the amelioration of urban problems. As such, there has been little challenge to the DC's central premises, except among some elements of the place-oriented, progressive left and the market-oriented, reactionary right.[1]

Dispersal can be seen as an element of liberal expansionism because the key idea behind such efforts involves tapping extracity resources (expansionism) by using the (liberal) activist state (especially operating on a centralized level) to relocate people to different areas within the broader metropolitan region (usually beyond cities and their older suburbs). When relocated to such areas, the urban poor are ostensibly able to more easily access those extracity resources—especially employment and educational opportunities, as well as a host of public goods—that help lessen their economic disadvantages and the acuteness of urban problems more generally.

Six Crimes of Passion in Search of a Policy Agenda

The particular tack I take below to challenge the dispersal element of liberal expansionism is to demonstrate how the DC's zeal (or passion) to promote dispersal leads many of its members to engage in suspect and problematic practices, both in their research efforts and in their efforts to shape and prescribe public policy. Such practices point to the need to explore other paths for addressing urban problems, such as the local economic alternative development strategies (or LEADS) that have emerged so prominently in the previous chapters.

Eschewing Unflattering Questions

Much of what social scientists learn about the empirical world is driven by the questions they ask. In the classic case of this phenomenon—the study of revolution—scholars get a contrasting perspective on the same empirical observation by flipping the question from "why do people rebel?" to "why do people often remain quiescent even when living in the most appalling of social conditions?" (See Gaventa 1980).

In a similar way, the DC's passion for its dispersal agenda is first revealed by the research questions most choose to address when studying such policies. The exploration of these questions tends to bias and distort our understanding of dispersal efforts by projecting them in their most favorable light. This stands in contrast to other questions that might elucidate a more inconvenient truth. In his booklength study of deconcentration, *Clearing the Way: Deconcentrating the Poor in Urban America,* housing expert Edward Goetz (2003, 19–20) starkly exposed such a distortion in much of the extant research on dispersal. At a poignant moment in his book, he recounted:

> After giving a public talk on deconcentration in 1996, I was asked whether it was not simply overwhelmingly self-evident that the problems of America's central-city neighborhoods of poverty should be solved by deconcentration. The empirical evidence had, by then, shown quite convincingly that such concentrations are bad. Other empirical evidence (at that point, primarily the Gautreaux program) had shown that deconcentration benefits families that participate.

To which he noted that he "agreed then and still [does agree]…that *the logic* is compelling." However, what his excellent case study of Minneapolis provides is "an understanding of the difference between that *rather clean logic* of deconcentration on the one hand, and its *messy reality* on the other" (emphases added).

In its enthusiasm to push dispersal, the DC largely studies the clean and compelling logic of deconcentration rather than deconcentration's messiness in actual practice (a messiness that can include displacement and gentrification, minority political disempowerment, destruction of community, undermining of the legitimacy of community development, involuntary relocation, NIMBYism, and neighborhood destabilization).[2] The studies most commonly produced by the DC to show dispersal's logic use a clean experimental (or quasi-experimental) design to measure relocation benefits for the very limited number of families taking part in a dispersal program. The results of this plethora of research—especially the surfeit of studies of Gautreaux and the federal MTO demonstration[3]—are almost always favorable to the dispersal programs studied (or can be interpreted as such): "*All* mobility programs"—Dreier, Mollenkopf, and Swanstrom (2004, 392) note in their archetypical liberal expansionist tract, *Place Matters*—"report positive results." (emphasis added). These studies then are extolled by the DC. For example, Bruce Katz, director of the Brookings Institution's highly influential Metropolitan Policy Program and perhaps the DC's most prominent figure, enthusiastically declared the MTO evaluation to be a "'home run' in social science research" due to its clean experimental design (Goering 2003, 386). And, with such extolling comes the claim that such studies provide nearly conclusive scientific evidence demonstrating the desirability of deconcentration.

Recognizing the DC's strong tendency to avoid researching deconcentration's messiness, Goetz (2003, 20) pleads for a less biased research agenda. He urges researchers to, "at the very least," regard questions surrounding deconcentration's messy reality (especially its implementation and the resultant local socio-spatial dynamics) "as seriously as they regard its [compelling] logic." Such questions are clearly researchable; indeed, they have been thoroughly researched by Goetz himself, in his meticulously researched and intensely empirical book, as well as by others from outside the DC (see, for example, Bennett, Smith, and Wright 2006). When one, instead, does choose to study how deconcentration works in reality, one comes away with quite a different take on such efforts. Compared to the rather Panglossian view derived from research showing its clean logic, Goetz (2003), for example, is ambiguous about the desirability of large-scale deconcentration. Such ambiguity, in turn, opens the door for a fair-minded consideration of alternative strategies for fighting urban poverty (also see Goetz and Chapple, forthcoming).

Misconceiving Freedom of Choice

Even more striking is how the DC's perspective can effectively blind its members from seeing certain otherwise obvious realities. Most notable here is the ontological understanding of the crucial concept of *freedom of choice,* as it applies to one's decisions about where to live. In the ontology of the concept embraced by some leading dispersalists, the expansion of residential choices for the urban poor *only* exists when the ability to exit is enhanced. It does not include enhancing, to use the phrase of the venerable progressive scholar and long-time activist Chester Hartman (1984, 2002), "the right [or ability] to stay put."

Typical along these lines is the work of noted housing researcher Margery Turner of the Urban Institute. Discussing the policy problems faced by the Section 8 Voucher Program (now renamed the Housing Choice Voucher Program), she wrote: "The federal government can and should do more to ensure that all...voucher recipients have the opportunity to exercise real choice about where to live" (Turner 1998, 387). Yet, when considering how the exercise of choice might be made more "real," all of the policies she advocates involve expanding exit options, such as augmenting "the number and scale of assisted housing mobility initiatives" (that is, Gautreaux/MTO-type measures) and removing "regulatory and administrative barriers that now make it difficult for families to move between jurisdictions" (Turner 1998, 388; also see Katz and Turner 2001). In short, the drive to push dispersal seems to blind Turner to the reality that, in her words, exercising "real choice about where to live" also includes enhancing the choice to live in one's current neighborhood by making such neighborhoods more livable (see Imbroscio 2004b).

Such an unambiguous reality is clearly visible from outside the DC. Commenting on legal and policy scholar Owen Fiss's (2003) widely read proposal to disperse nearly all poor inner-city residents to low-poverty suburbs, Harvard political scientist Jennifer Hochschild (2003, 69), for example, made the straightforward and plain observation that "what ghetto residents really deserve is the right [that is, the choice] either to move *or* to stay in a community worth staying in" (emphasis added).

Turner's work (1998) is an especially stark example of how the DC's zealous pro-dispersal disposition leaves it with a distorted ontology of what constitutes freedom of choice for inner-city residents. However, this problem is endemic, in varying degrees, to much of the DC. The work of economist Anthony Downs of the Brookings Institution, a long-time and ardent supporter of dispersal (see, for example, Downs 1973), provides another representative example. Confronting the problems of the inner city, Downs (1994, 112–13), unlike Turner, did not exclusively advocate exit but rather endorsed a "mixed strategy" entailing that at least some effort be devoted to redeveloping distressed communities. Yet, he, like Turner, similarly fails to see that this redevelopment can be a strategy to *expand freedom of choice*. Instead, he justifies redevelopment only because it is politically expedient: "It is politically impossible," Downs writes, "to help residents...move out without trying to improve the areas themselves." City political leaders and local community development organizations, in particular, would be highly resistant to such a strategy, as they would see it as undermining their constituencies (Downs 1994, 103; also see Rusk 1999). Moreover, as a further justification for area redevelopment, Downs (1994, 113) notes the imperative to "improve the environment in inner cities for those who *will have to* remain living there" (emphasis added). The idea that some may *wish* to remain living there—and that buttressing this preference via efforts to make neighborhoods livable *enhances freedom of choice*—is not within the realm of reality, as that reality is understood by much of the DC.[4]

The DC's conception of the urban poor's freedom of choice is distorted in a second way: such *free* choices can be understood as such only because they are divorced from the context in which they are made. For example, the DC often points to the strong demand to participate in some dispersal programs, most notably Gautreaux in Chicago, as evidence for their central tenet that, if given the opportunity, inner-city residents will freely (and enthusiastically) choose low-poverty suburbs.[5] But the context in which these decisions were made—such as, most notably, while facing a difficult life in neglected, crime-ridden neighborhoods with substandard housing—is left out of the picture. Including this context transforms our understanding of the behavior of assisted mobility participants from an exercise of choice to a reaction to coercion.[6] Preferences for dispersal become nothing more than a desperate response to a set of desperate conditions, with little to do with any real notion of freedom of choice (Imbroscio 2004b).

Correcting for this distortion, Harvard law professor Gerald Frug (1999, 173) offers a more complete conception of the urban poor's freedom of choice. This conception, he writes, "supplements the freedom [of choice] to move with the freedom [of choice] to stay put—a freedom possible only if fear of violence and concern about bad schools no longer compel people to move, if they can, *whether they want to or not*" (emphasis added).

Illustrative of the DC's decontextualization distortion is housing researcher John Goering's evocative conclusion to his coedited book, *Choosing a Better Life,* which reports the interim findings of the MTO demonstration (Goering and Feins 2003). Addressing critics of dispersal programs, such as those who argue that attempts "to take minorities out of their traditional communities ... [are] racially perverse and politically and socially destructive," Goering (2003, 403) defiantly retorts: "In response we can only offer the voices and wishes of mothers and their children. Evidence from MTO families ... is that many mothers and children want and need to leave

behind dangerous inner-city projects for a different, better neighborhood."
This response—with its strong appeal to the moral authority evoked by
the "voices and wishes of [impoverished] mothers and their children"—
seems at first glance to be a powerful riposte to those critics suggesting
that dispersal efforts can have "perverse" and "destructive" effects socially,
politically, and culturally. This response, however, is largely emasculated
given the perilous context—that is, the "dangerous [environment of] inner
city projects"—under which those "voices and wishes" were expressed.
What else would one expect vulnerable mothers and children to voice and
wish for when facing such conditions?

Yet it is the selectivity of Goering's decontextualization that makes it
especially revealing as a strong expression of the DC's passion for dispersal. When needing to demonstrate the MTO study's scientific validity, specifically regarding potential validity threats from sample selection bias, the
context in which decisions about program participation were made cannot be avoided. In a rather remarkable understatement, Goering, Feins,
and Richardson (2003, 31) explain that "drive-by shootings, gang wars, and
drug-related violence were common in the neighborhoods where MTO
families were living. *This phenomenon likely may have made some people more
interested in joining the [MTO] demonstration*" (emphasis added). That surely
would seem to be the case—that is, the "voice" or "wish" to join MTO was
influenced by the dangerous environment in which the choice behavior occurred. But this simple fact, in the zeal to promote dispersal, is understood
highly selectively. The context is recognized when it is required for scientific reasoning, yet ignored when it undercuts pro-dispersal polemic.

Imputing Interests

At times this zeal leads the DC to adduce what are called *real* interest arguments in favor of dispersal. *Real* interest arguments—the most well known
of which is the Marxian notion of false consciousness—are those relying
on the imputation of an interest (or preference) of someone as being real
in absence of an empirically observable expression of that interest or preference (Elkin 1982). For obvious reasons such arguments remain highly
suspect; hence they require that a sophisticated methodological defense be
mounted on their behalf before they can be given serious consideration (see
Gaventa 1980).

Reed and Steinberg (2006, 6) allude to the proclivity of the DC to employ such arguments when they charge the "poverty research industry," of which the Gang of 200 is a key part, with being "predicated for decades on the premise that poor people are defective…[in ways that make them]…incapable of knowing their own best interests." To add specification to this charge, consider that what defines and unites the DC more than anything else is the deeply held belief that it is in the *interest* of the inner-city poor to, in the Katrina petition's words, "move to opportunity," almost always defined as outlying or low-poverty suburban areas. Fiss's (2003) eloquent plea for an aggressive, large-scale, and nationwide dispersal program captures the thrust of this belief well. He argues that, although "choosing to move [to outlying suburbs] entails a sacrifice," such moves should be facilitated because, for the families involved, "there is so much to be gained by [such] a move." The Katrina petition itself sees these moves by displaced residents of New Orleans as the way to "rebuild lives…[making] thousands of families…stronger than before [the storm]." Yet this belief flies in the face of evidence from previous dispersal programs strongly suggesting that, while many recipients desire to move from inner cities, many others desire to stay in or near them.[7]

For example, as noted above, the demand for the Gautreaux program in Chicago was robust (Rubinowitz and Rosenbaum 2000). However, in a profile of other Chicago public housing residents required to relocate following the demolition of their homes, "counselors…estimated that less than 1 percent of their clients opted for the suburbs" (Zaterman, Gross, and Kalenak 2001, 287). Likewise, Goetz (2003, 73) notes that research undertaken in Baltimore, San Francisco, Newport News, Virginia, and Kansas City, Missouri, showed that many displaced residents of public housing "wanted to remain in the community where they had been living." He points to other research indicating that the widely held "assumption that poor families *want* to move to outlying areas" is "questionable" (241, emphasis in original; also see Basolo and Nguyen 2005). For example, in Omaha many inner-city public housing residents, pushed to make outlying moves by a desegregation court order, instead waited out a 120-day restriction period preventing nonoutlying moves and stayed in inner-city areas. In New Haven, members of a plaintiff class that successfully sued to desegregate the city's public housing "did not want to move to the suburbs, away from friends and support groups" (Goetz 2003, 241; also see Gibson

2007; Kleit and Manzo 2006). More generally, Goetz (2003, 241) notes that in some cities housing authorities find it difficult to find enough applicants for their Gautreaux-type mobility programs, and "even those who move out may turn around and move back to impacted [i.e., poorer, inner-city] neighborhoods at a later date." (also see Briggs 1997a, 1997b).[8] These findings are consistent with Goetz's (2000) own intensive study of Minneapolis, where the overwhelming preference of residents displaced from public housing was to remain in the city (over 70 percent) and more specifically to remain in their immediate area (approaching 50 percent).

This disjunction between the DC's fervent advocacy of dispersal and the urban poor's ambivalence about being dispersed leaves the former with the burden of knowing what is best for the latter, that is, what is truly in their *real* interest. Such an interpretation of the urban poor's real interests is, however, at a minimum open to debate. As even a dispersalist as ardent as Fiss (2003, 6) acknowledges, moves to outlying areas impose "great human...costs." While, at the same time, preferences to stay in inner cities find their roots in many legitimate sources, such as feelings of ethnic group solidarity, a desire to stay connected to kinship or friendship networks and other community support systems (such as churches), political empowerment, or a need for access to public transportation or social services.[9] Moreover, as elaborated below, evidence demonstrating the effectiveness of dispersal programs is mixed at best, while other evidence suggests that, in many cities, just "moving a few blocks"—away from a distressed public housing development, for example—"can make a big difference" for improving the level of personal safety and the quality of housing conditions for families (Varady and Walker 2003, 378). In this light, then, even Reed and Steinberg's (2006, 5) rather harsh contention that the "Gang of 200's petition reproduces and reinforces...a disregard for the idea that poor people may have, or deserve to have, emotional attachments to a place they consider home" seems well warranted.

Goering's (2003) interpretation of the revealed preferences of the urban poor in *Choosing a Better Life* provides a stark example of the DC's proclivity to engage in *real* interest thinking. Goering treats the revealed preferences of the urban poor as true expressions of their real interests *only* as long as these preferences are for the *right* thinking. Such *right* thinking comes when the urban poor express preferences for, to quote the book's title, "choosing a better life" by moving from inner-city housing projects.[10]

When such moves are made, Goering (2003, 403) admonishes the critics of dispersal to heed and respect these preferences—"the voices and wishes of mothers and their children...[who] want and need to leave behind dangerous inner-city projects for a different, better neighborhood." However, when the urban poor fail to make the *right* choices by *not* expressing a strong desire to move to outlying, low-poverty neighborhoods, as is the case with many Housing Choice Voucher Program (Section 8) recipients, such revealed preferences are seen as perhaps not reflecting their real interests. Rather than being respected—even lionized—such preferences instead need to be unpacked and examined more closely. In such cases, notes Goering (2003, 404), "careful evaluation of the typical housing search process for Section 8 recipients may well suggest that 'voluntary' choices are deeply constrained by prior imprints of racial discrimination, fear, and lack of information." Although this conjecture "may well" (to quote Goering) in fact be true, the crucial point here is the double standard applied in the evaluation of preferences: the choices of the urban poor, when *not* made in the *right* ways, are no longer to be automatically respected or taken as representing the poor's real interests; instead, they are now considered to be deeply constrained and only "voluntary" in a set-off-in-quotation-marks way.

Countenancing Repression

Real interest arguments are not only empirically problematic; they also can be politically dangerous. Of particular concern is that such arguments can quite easily be used by some, in the name of knowing what is *best,* to justify repressing the human freedom and individual autonomy of others.[11] This danger is especially acute if there is great social and cultural distance between the parties,[12] or if those holding relational power are infused with a technocratic mind-set that overly values instrumental rationality (see Bobrow and Dryzek 1987).

In a great irony, their urgency to further dispersal goals leads elements of the DC to endorse policies that in subtle but conspicuous ways actively repress the freedom and autonomy of those whom they wish to liberate: the urban poor. Take, for example, Goering's (2003, 404) analysis of the "deeply constrained" choices exercised by Section 8 recipients. To make such choices *less* constrained, Goering—following this ironic pattern—recommends *more* constraints on these choices. What is needed in certain housing markets, he argues, is the utilization of more so-called restricted-use vouchers (that is, those that limit housing choice of the urban poor to more affluent and possibly predominately white neighborhoods). Such a repression of the urban poor's freedom to live where they choose is necessary, at least for a period of time, in order "to establish new 'norms' for housing search" (Goering 2003, 404). Hence, the revealed preferences of the poor are—conceivably—eventually respected as embodying their *real* interests, and they once again are allowed to freely choose their neighborhood. But this privilege comes only after a period of reeducation so that new norms can be inculcated by restricted-use vouchers. Such restricted-use vouchers—and the repression of residential freedom they engender (Imbroscio 2004a)—are of course the centerpiece of assisted mobility programs (such as Gautreaux and MTO) touted by the Gang of 200's Katrina petition and enthusiastically advocated for expansion by much of the DC.

Nonetheless, despite the general enthusiasm for expanding Gautreaux-type programs with restricted-use vouchers, dispersalists see this substantial degree of repression as politically and morally unpalatable if it were to be spread to the entire public housing program. "Outside an experimental context [such as Gautreaux or the MTO demonstration]," write G. Thomas Kingsley and Kathryn Pettit (2005, 131) of the Urban Institute, "this has never been done...[as] the final choice of where to move is always left to the family. All in all, it seems doubtful that this principle would [ever] be abrogated." Moreover, even Goering (2003, 398) recognizes that restricted voucher programs are "not suited for everyone."

Instead, most members of the dispersal consensus recommend what can be interpreted as more subtle forms of repression. Rather than using restricted vouchers to refashion the injudicious residential preferences of the urban poor, the preferred method of accomplishing this goal is to have housing bureaucrats or their agents provide information and counseling to Housing Choice Voucher Program (Section 8) recipients. This information-based counseling "about the benefits of being pioneers and moving to low-poverty neighborhoods" is commonly referred to as "mobility education" (Kingsley and Pettit 2005, 131). It is in turn buttressed by ancillary counseling efforts to provide "encouragement" (Turner 1998, 388) and "to motivate families" (Goering 2003, 399) to *do the right thing* by choosing to decamp for the vast low-poverty suburban frontier.

Although at first glance such efforts might seem innocuous, some housing experts from outside the dispersal consensus argue that, given the high costs involved, counseling programs can divert scarce resources away from the core of the voucher program. This can result in fewer eligible families being served—families who already often endure long waiting lists to receive assistance.[13] Thus, housing assistance for many urban poor families is readily sacrificed on the altar of dispersal. Even more of a concern would be if such counseling efforts were fueled by federal administrative rules giving local bureaucrats a strong incentive to promote dispersal, something advocated by prominent dispersalists such as the Urban Institute's Margery Turner (also see Katz and Turner 2001). While Turner (1998, 388) argues that "this kind of incentive structure does not mean that every family receiving Section 8 assistance must be pressured into moving to a low-poverty neighborhood," such pressure could indeed be substantial if bureaucrats needed to meet strict dispersal quotas in order to receive rewards or avoid sanctions. Moreover, it is important to remember that Turner's advocated "pressure" presumably would be applied to many extremely vulnerable urban families, often poor mothers and their young children (albeit not "every" one).

Beyond the mere didacticism of "mobility education," with its emphasis on convincing perhaps unconvinced voucher recipients of the joys of low-poverty suburban life (and perhaps, to paraphrase Marx and Engels, the idiocy of inner-city urban life as well), the DC normally supports more intensive interventions into the lives of the urban poor. The Katrina Move to Opportunity petition itself, for example, advocates that dispersal efforts include "counseling to assist in relocation" and, in order to be "most successful," further "transitional support in the form of support services for each family." Specifying the DC's frequently expressed perspective on this issue, housing researcher Kirk McClure (2005, 347) argues that what is needed in dispersal programs is "intensive housing placement assistance" to "guide households out of their impoverished neighborhoods." Although, he notes, "this may mean some reduction in the freedom of choice participating households enjoy, it could greatly improve the capacity of the program to serve...national goals." McClure (2005, 356) explains that

> program administrators should be expected to provide households with guidance that should include much more than explaining program rules.

> It should involve finding a rental unit in a neighborhood that serves the goals of income and racial integration .... This guidance should move to the level of case management serving not only the housing needs of the participating household, but also its employment, educational, and other needs. This guidance could coordinate housing placement with other services such as job training and placement, as well as help households find schools, shopping, and transportation.

All of the emphasis on "guidance" in this "intensive" placement assistance begins to conjure images of the repressive "therapeutic state" (see Thompson 1998).[14] The therapeutic state, explains political historian Andrew Polsky (1991, 3), "begins with the premise that some people are unable to adjust to the demands of everyday life" and therefore these "marginal citizens" are in "need [of] expert help" or therapy in order to do so. Since marginal citizens "cannot govern their own lives" the state "seeks to 'normalize' them" through their integration "into the social mainstream" (Polsky 1991, 4). Such an integration of the urban poor into the "social mainstream" is of course also the ultimate goal of dispersalists (see, for example, Lemann 1991; Orfield 2002), except that beyond the usual bourgeois conventions the *normal* is also understood spatially to include—at least for families with children—a suburban existence.

Overselling Evidence

Perhaps most disheartening from a scholarly vantage point is that, in their drive to promote their dispersal agenda, the DC consistently oversells the real but thin accumulated evidence supporting it. Take the Gang of 200's Katrina petition itself. Given its direct political intent—being a clarion call to shape public policy—it rather unsurprisingly exemplifies this tendency. It touts the "growing body of scientific research" coming from "careful studies" that demonstrate the "significant positive effects" of dispersal programs. While conceding that "not all families benefit equally" and "some need more support than others," the benefits accruing to the urban poor from such programs are characterized as "sizable."

The primary source of the research showing these "significant positive effects" comes from studies of the Gautreaux program in Chicago and the federal MTO demonstration. Yet, in the case of the former at least—where observed effects were the most positive—characterizing these findings as coming from "careful studies" that are part of "a growing body scientific research" is disingenuous at best. Such a characterization woefully ignores the multitude of limitations in the Gautreaux research—limitations that make it difficult to generalize the touted findings to the broader population of public housing residents.[15] As housing expert Susan Popkin and her colleagues (2000, 929–30) point out, Gautreaux participants were self-selected, heavily screened, and "many participants were not [even] current public housing residents" but instead were on the waiting list or were merely "related to people who had lived in public housing during the...[relevant] period." Moreover, 80 percent of families coming through the program did not even relocate, meaning that those who did "were likely the most determined and motivated." And the research design itself had limitations as well. It was not a random experiment and people were not tracked from before to after their move but surveyed after their move only. Given this retrospective research design and the problems involved with locating past Gautreaux families, "only a handful of participants who had either moved back to the city or lost their Section 8 assistance were included in these samples," making it probable that "many unsuccessful movers were excluded." The exclusion of these unsuccessful movers thus likely inflated the observed positive effects of the program (Popkin 2000, 929–30), effects commonly trumpeted by the DC in their determination to promote dispersal.

Although the MTO research avoided some of these limitations, it is wild overstatement to interpret its results as showing that the program—to return to the language of the Katrina petition—had "significant positive effects" that produced "sizable benefits" for its participants (see Clark 2008). As housing scholar David Varady (2005, xvii) summarizes, the interim MTO evaluation offers "mixed evidence regarding effectiveness," including "virtually no influence on any measure of educational attainment, and virtually no impact on employment, earnings, or receipt of public assistance."[16] Most interestingly, along some indicators of participant well-being, such as health, child behavior problems, and juvenile crime, the MTO research showed that *both* the experimental group (who were assisted with a "move to opportunity," usually to the suburbs) and the comparison group (who received a regular Section 8 voucher and moved a lesser distance) "did better than the control group" who stayed in pubic housing (Varady and Walker 2003, 353). Thus, the MTO research, rather than being clear and convincing evidence for the wisdom of dispersal policy, seems primarily to confirm the rather nonstartling notion that, because the quality of life in many public housing projects is abysmal, almost any move improves family well-being.

Even the evidence purporting to demonstrate the strong *neighborhood effects* in impoverished inner cities—the stone foundation upon which the DC was erected—turns out to be less than conclusive. The existence of such neighborhood effects, where living in a deprived neighborhood negatively and substantially affects social and economic outcomes for their residents, especially children, has been seen as not "warrant[ing] any strong generalizations," being "thin and contradictory," and "at best equivocal."[17] In fact, a major recent study of the issue (Elliott et al. 2006, 276) concludes that, while it is certainly the case that better neighborhoods have overall higher *rates* of children who have developed successfully, "the vast majority (typically 90 percent or more) of *individual* variation in success outcomes occurs *within,* not between neighborhoods." Thus, for a given child, the "practical advantage" of living in a better neighborhood is "quite modest." In contrast to the "conventional wisdom about the inner-city poor," disadvantaged neighborhoods exhibit "much more variation in the quality of families, schools, peer groups, and community agencies" than is commonly recognized. The successful development of children thus "depends on the *combined* influences" of many factors, including their neighborhood but also their "family, school, and peer group...[as well as] their own personal attributes, characteristics, and personal choices."

Slighting Alternatives

The flip side of the overselling of the evidence for dispersal is the slighting of evidence suggesting the viability of alternatives to it. Nothing illustrates this point more than the DC's dismissive perspective regarding the work of the thousands of urban-based community development corporations (CDCs). As pointed out in previous chapters, despite their mixed record of success, by any measure CDCs have garnered stunning achievements in the production of affordable housing for low-income families (see Bratt 2006a), especially when examined vis-à-vis the paltry scale of assisted mobility programs such as Gautreaux. Yet, such accomplishments are routinely either ignored (Briggs 2005a) or explained away (Lemann 1994) by dispersalists. When they are recognized, such recognition often comes with a "yes, but" qualification. "These organizations have helped revitalize inner city neighborhoods," Alan Berube and Bruce Katz (2005, 9) of Brookings, for example, affirm. "But"—they continue in the same sentence—"their inner-city focus has sometimes neglected the increasing decentralization of good employment and educational opportunities." The "outside game" advocate David Rusk strikes a similar chord. While acknowledging the prodigious accomplishments of CDCs, Rusk (1999, 18) nevertheless argues that their potential for ameliorating urban problems should be largely discounted because they have failed to win "the war against poverty itself."

One of the fundamental starting premises of the DC, like liberal expansionism more generally, is that helping the poor where they live—through place-based economic (or community) development—is destined to be of limited success.[18] Yet, as noted in chapter 3, a key piece of the evidence supporting this premise—that past attempts of the federal government to revitalize poor neighborhoods in cities over the last half century have failed—is highly suspect. Because many of these place-based programs were themselves flawed in design, it is not clear whether past failures should be attributed to those flaws or, as the DC presumes, the inherent near-impossibility of community development. In addition, even more important is the broader context surrounding these past efforts. Such programs have had to, in historian Alice O'Connor's (1999, 79) words, "swim…against the tide" of a plethora of other federal policies that have "encouraged the trends that impoverish communities in the first place."

When it does endorse efforts to redevelop poor communities in cities, such as with its embrace of the Housing Opportunities for People Everywhere VI program, the dispersal consensus's near obsession with dispersing the urban poor overwhelms any clear-headed analysis of such efforts. HOPE VI sought to remake public housing projects by usually demolishing existing buildings and replacing them with low-density mixed-income developments. A large number of researchers analyzing the HOPE VI program have been acutely troubled by the massive human costs it has imposed on the urban poor.[19] Finding significant involuntary displacement, the loss of affordable housing options for the most vulnerable, and land grabs and gentrification, among other problems, many have strongly condemned the program. It has been variously (and reproachfully) relabeled "HOPE Sick" or "HOPE (House Our Poor Elsewhere) VI," and cast as the "new face of urban renewal" or the "new slum clearance."[20] Contrast the sanguinity for HOPE VI expressed in the joint report produced by the Urban Institute and the Brookings Institution—the two, borrowing an apropos term from the legendary sociologist C. Wright Mills, *command posts* of the DC. "In our view," the multiple authors (who include Bruce Katz and Margery Turner) summarize, the

> evidence *strongly* supports continuation of the HOPE VI approach as a way to improve outcomes for distressed developments, residents, and neighborhoods. The program has achieved *substantial* success.... Therefore, HUD *should continue* to operate a targeted redevelopment program that provides funds for both physical revitalization and supportive services. (Popkin et al. 2004, 5; emphases added)

This assessment, while glowing, is, however, qualified. "The evidence also points," they next write, "to the urgent need for reforms in the HOPE VI program if it is to realize its full potential to improve the circumstances of very low-income families and communities" (Popkin et al. 2004, 5). Yet, the urgently needed reforms they call for in large part are simply ways to further their goal of dispersing the urban poor to the suburbs. What is needed "in particular," they argue, is stronger "assistance with relocation and supportive services," as well as giving "new attention ... to innovations such as 'enhanced vouchers'" (Popkin et al. 2004, 5). These so-called enhanced vouchers "provide counseling to encourage *moves to opportunity rich areas,* as well as long-term support to ensure a successful transition and progress toward self-sufficiency" (Popkin et al. 2004, 54; emphasis added).

The idea of ameliorating social problems where they exist is given so little consideration empirically by the DC that it can pervert its normative vision. For example, Berube (2006, 22) of Brookings describes a study showing how girls whose families were offered a voucher to move out of "deprived inner-city neighborhoods" were safer from sexual predation compared to those girls whose families didn't move. The data portrayed "a stark portrait" of the lives of teenage girls living in such deprived neighborhoods; these girls were "likely to face pressure from older men in the neighborhood for early, risky sex; to report being sexually harassed when they walk down the street; and to have experienced sexual violence or coerced sex." Therefore, he concludes, evidence of this sort "reminds us that policies to help low-income families in highly deprived neighborhoods to access better local environments can be defended on *social justice* grounds" (emphasis added). Yet, when confronted with this appalling reality, a more vigorous (and defensible) normative commitment to social justice would seem to compel us to be concerned not simply with whether those girls accessing better environments were safer; rather, our real concern should be with the deeper question of why American society cannot protect young, vulnerable girls from such egregious behavior wherever in America they happen to live. A strong commitment to "social justice" would seem to demand nothing less.[21]

Finding Another Path

Hurricane Katrina laid bare the tragedy and desperation that is American urban poverty and America's deep urban social problems. The television pictures from New Orleans during those days following the storm should be our generation's *How the Other Half Lives,* our *The Other America.* They should spawn a renewed and reenergized "war" on that poverty and its associated urban ills. The aim of my analysis in this chapter has been to challenge the dispersal consensus's near-hegemonic influence over the discourse that will shape that war's justification as well as its tactics.

This challenge has revealed some fundamental weaknesses in the dispersal consensus and, by extension, liberal expansionism more generally. These weaknesses suggest that liberal expansionism's normative desirability and policy efficacy is very much open to question. Such a conclusion in turn demands that another path for fighting the next antipoverty war be found.

Part III

ALTERNATIVES

5

THE LOCAL PUBLIC BALANCE SHEET

The local economic alternative development strategies (LEADS) have emerged as central to both reconstructing urban regimes in more progressive directions and developing a means to solve urban problems in ways superior to liberal expansionism. The next two chapters explore these strategies in more depth by returning to the elements of the alternative economic paradigm set out in chapter 2. Among these elements, two stand out as especially important because they cut across and buttress the entire LEADS project: the local public balance sheet, explored in this chapter, and the idea of community economic stability, explored in the next.

Background and Overview

The public balance sheet (PBS) concept, also known as social cost-benefit analysis, was developed almost three decades ago, and since then has made several appearances in the alternative economic development literature.[1] Scholars attribute its origin to a 1979 report, *Towards a Public Balance Sheet: Calculating the Costs and Benefits of Community Stabilization,* written by researcher David Smith for the National Center for Economic Alternatives (codirected at the time by two pioneers of alternative economic thought, political economists Gar Alperovitz and Jeff Faux).[2]

The concept's earliest applications addressed the development problems wrought by the wave of deindustrialization striking places such as Youngstown and Detroit during the late 1970s. Later analysts applied the concept to understand phenomena such as the real costs of economic growth on communities, the critique of the corporate-center approach to central-city revitalization, the economic viability of municipally owned economic enterprises, the proper use of government-provided development subsidies, and the recasting of the concept of economic efficiency.[3]

The term itself—*public* balance sheet—places the conceptual focus of policymaking squarely on the issue of the extent to which public or community benefits actually result from local development expenditures. So, at the most basic level, the PBS concept frames the policy question sharply in terms of the public versus the private: while local economic development efforts may aid corporations and other businesses—enhancing *private* balance sheets—the call to employ a PBS suggests a possible disjunction between such private benefits and those accruing to the public or to the community at-large.

For example, as progressive economic development expert Robert Giloth (1988, 344) has pointed out, examining "public and private balances sheets" raises serious questions about the level of public benefits generated by "mainstream development" efforts. Such "concerns about conventional development," he added, "have given rise to [alternative] community economic development strategies" that produce more concrete and direct public or community-wide benefits. In a similar vein, urban political economist and historian Marc Levine concludes his comprehensive critique of Baltimore's mainstream corporate-center development strategy by calling for cities to "deploy public resources consistent with the logic of . . . the public balance sheet—an approach that calculates the *social* costs and benefits of local policies, rather than simply underwriting developers' profits in the hope that 'trickle down' will occur" (1987, 119).

From the public balance sheet's general framework of casting economic development policymaking in private versus public terms derive two additional, and more specific, conceptual uses of the technique.

First, the public balance sheet can be employed as an "analytical tool for scrutinizing and measuring the social costs of private-sector development" (Feagin and Parker 1990, 289). The PBS is "a way of tallying up...the tangible, measurable, quantifiable, costs being imposed on citizens individually and collectively by the actions of the private sector" (Feagin and Parker 1990, 290). These social and community costs, imposed through both the operation of private-sector enterprises and, especially, through private investment decisions, "don't show up on any firm's ledger; no accountant writes them down. They're not charged against the income the firm makes from selling its products and services" (also see Greider 2009). While conventional economic theory conceives of such costs as examples of *externalities,* causing the market to *fail,* the PBS adopts a much more expansive notion of market failure in general and externalities in particular.

Second, the PBS can be utilized as a tool to guide activist and positive public intervention in the market economy; that is, as a guide for formulating public policies designed to generate local economic development. As a tool to formulate policy, Alperovitz and Faux (1979, iii) explain that the public balance sheet "compares the total taxpayer and public benefits from direct intervention to maintain local employment against the total costs." They therefore argue that "it provides *a more comprehensive and rational guide* than the narrow considerations of private profit and loss that are typically used to evaluate public action" (emphasis added).

Tallying Social Costs of Development

The public balance sheet demonstrates how the actions of the private sector impose significant costs on the public and the larger community. Conventional, that is, neoclassical, economic theory treats these social costs as *externalities*—costs that stem from market processes but are not experienced by market actors. Instead, these costs are externalized—that is, transferred to others, usually to the community at-large. The presence of externalities creates an instance where the competitive market will fail to maximize social welfare: "Because of the divergence between private and social [i.e., total community] returns," Harvard economists Edith Stokey and Richard Zeckhauser (1978, 304) wrote in their widely read statement of neoclassical theory, "uncoordinated individual actions lead to less than optimal results." Together with public goods/bads (essentially a variation of the externality problem), the need to correct for market failure provides the basic justification in conventional economic theory for government intervention into the market economy. As such, this reasoning underlies neoclassical economics' "normative theory of the state" (Bobrow and Dryzek 1987, 33).

Conventional economic theorists generally view the instances and scope of the externalities to be modest (Kuttner 1997).[4] Hence, in normative terms, most advocate a limited role for the public sector in society (see Stokey and Zeckhauser 1978; Friedman 1962). In contrast, PBS practitioners view externalities as profound and extensive—to the point that their existence serves as a challenge to the entire underlying logic of conventional economic theory. In his original work developing the concept, Smith (1979, 5), for example, writes that "the economic rationality of the 'profit-maximizing' private corporation does not necessarily lead to 'welfare maximization' for individuals and communities, since the market does not adequately measure, and in fact explicitly ignores, the public costs and benefits of private investment decisions." The noted urban sociologist Joe Feagin and a colleague's rationale for employing the PBS builds from an even more systemic critique of conventional economic theory, as well as the capitalist economic system it justifies (Feagin and Parker 1990, 290). That system "of necessity must transfer many internal costs to outsiders. In reality, the social costs of privately controlled industrial and real estate development are *not* 'external' to modern capitalism, but are as a rule an integral part of its everyday routine operation."[5]

The PBS conceives of the pervasive and substantial costs imposed on the public or community as resulting from both the decisions of private actors to invest and their decisions to disinvest.

Costs of Private *Dis*investment

The original conception of the PBS grew from an analysis of a case of massive capital disinvestment—the shutdown of the Lykes Campbell Works steel mill (part of its Youngstown Sheet and Tube subsidiary). "With little more warning than precedes a tornado," wrote Alperovitz and Faux (1979, i), "more than 4,000 jobs in the Ohio steel town were suddenly gone," to be followed by an estimated thirty-six hundred additional jobs lost in grocery stores, shops, banks, and other businesses suffering the ripple effects of the shutdown. This decision, made by the private corporation,[6] imposed massive costs on public taxpayers, who had to "bear costs of $60–70 million in adjustment assistance, unemployment compensation, revenue reduction, and increased government expenditures" (approximately $225 million in today's dollars).[7] From the point of view of Lykes, however, these costs had no bearing from an economic standpoint because such costs did not "show up on [its private] balance sheet" (Alperovitz and Faux 1979, iii). These expenses simply could be transferred (externalized) to public taxpayers (also see Jakle and Wilson 1992; Lustig 1985).

The public balance sheet holds that private actions to disinvest capital burden the public and the larger community with a plethora of liabilities—externalities usually not even acknowledged to exist in conventional economic analysis. Physical, social, human, fiscal, and political costs are all traced to these private decisions.

Regarding the first of these costs, one of the most exorbitant expenses foisted on the public at-large by private disinvestment results from the *physical* "throwing away" of established communities (Williamson, Imbroscio, and Alperovitz 2002, 13; Ricker 1998). Trillions of dollars of sunk investments in infrastructure—including roads and other transportation systems, housing, schools, hospitals, public utilities, as well as a host of industrial facilities (plants and equipment)—are left abandoned or vastly underutilized when disinvestment occurs and people and businesses, left with greatly diminished economic prospects, are forced to leave town.

The public balance sheet similarly can provide an accounting of the costly destruction of the *social* infrastructure (or social capital) that occurs when disinvestment causes widespread unemployment and transiency, disrupting established patterns of human interaction.[8] This social capital—"features of social organization, such as networks, norms and trust, traditions of civic involvement and social solidarity"—is increasingly seen as crucial for facilitating the widespread cooperation necessary for overcoming collective action problems. Because it appears to help facilitate collective action, a high level of social capital in a community "seems to be a precondition for economic development, as well as for effective government" (Putnam 1993, 36–37; also see Putnam 2000). The general public hence incurs significant costs when private decisions cause a level of community disinvestment that greatly depletes its stock of social capital.

Widespread disinvestment also imposes *human* costs on individuals and families. The unemployment and forced mobility caused by such disinvestment increases levels of anxiety and stress among individuals and leads to a decline in feelings of self-worth. These conditions, in turn, often cause deterioration in physical and psychological health. Heightened incidences of substance abuse, child and spousal abuse and neglect, and increased stress on family structures result as well.[9]

The Youngstown case described above points to the massive public *fiscal* costs that can stem from private disinvestment decisions. Most notably, such decisions can directly result in the need for increased government transfer payments (e.g., unemployment compensation and public assistance), the increased demand for other government services, and a decrease in public tax revenue. More systemically, the current political-economic context—marked as it is by the widespread disinvestment (actual or prospective) brought about by the heightened mobility of capital—imposes generalized fiscal costs on the broader public. Such a system allows mobile corporations to extract overly generous locational subsidies by pitting competing places against one another, creating a situation not unlike an arms race with its prisoners' dilemma game logic. In their pursuit of capital investment, players in the game of competing local jurisdictions, such as states and cities, irrationally oversupply inducements to attract mobile businesses, worsening the fiscal condition of all jurisdictions (Williamson, Imbroscio, and Alperovitz 2002). Moreover, there is an additional public fiscal burden incurred under these conditions: the "corporate surplus." The source of this burden is the asymmetry of information in the bargaining process that exists between the private and public sectors, where "the businessman knows just what incentives will be necessary in order to affect a decision in regard to location, but the city official does not." This asymmetry allows mobile corporations to extract "an amount over what would be strictly necessary to affect the decision about location"—that is, a "corporate surplus"—at the general public's expense (Jones and Bachelor 1986, 203).

Finally, there are *political* costs. Standing on the shoulders of venerable political thinkers such as John Stuart Mill and Alexis de Tocqueville, the political theorist Stephen Elkin (1999) shows why local government is the only forum where large numbers of people can learn the art of effective, public-spirited citizenship. Such a learning process occurs when citizens are able to consider (and deliberate over) what is truly in the public (as opposed to individual) interest (also see Elkin 2006; Frug and Barron 2008). Yet, the politics in localities plagued by substantial private disinvestment are "much more likely to teach futility than what is at stake in giving concrete meaning to the public interest" (Elkin 1999, 57). In these cases, he adds, "the citizens of such communities will simply be left out of local politics as a school of citizenship—or they will be assigned, as it were, to the wrong school." And since there are "a nontrivial number of citizens [who] live in such localities...the loss to a public-spirited citizenry is significant." Without a public-spirited citizenry, Elkin (1999, 56) warns, a republican regime built on popular sovereignty is imperiled by an excessive degree of "narrowness of concern on the part of citizens."

Costs of Private *In*vestment

Public balance sheet advocates point out that, just as costs are imposed on the public (or community) from private decisions to withdraw capital, the decisions of private actors to invest capital also can prove burdensome to the public or the wider community. Smith recognized this phenomenon in his original analysis of plant closings and corporate mobility:

> There are [also] very real costs imposed on communities at the receiving end of corporate relocations....Physical infrastructure, schools and social services must all be financed out of local operating and capital budgets. In addition, there can be serious impacts on local real estate markets as newcomers bid up the prices of available housing. Once again, corporate investment decisions impose a range of costs on the public that do not show up on the corporate balance sheet. (Smith 1979, 4)

In short, those established communities *thrown away* because of disinvestment need to be rebuilt somewhere—specifically, in places where private investors choose to move their capital. This replication (and duplication) comes at a substantial cost to communities receiving the investment and, by extension, the society as a whole.

Likewise, in their analysis of urban land development using the PBS, Feagin and Parker (1990, 289) also point to the costs imposed on the public and the wider community from private investment. The social costs of "modern real estate capitalism take a variety of forms," including "the shortage of affordable rental housing, large numbers of people displaced by developments,...enhanced traffic congestion, air and water pollution, constrained choices for consumers, ... and taxpayer burdens from tax subsidies for developers." So, once again, costs are imposed on, in Feagin and Parkers' (1990, 289) words, "the citizenry and their communities" by the private decisions of "developers, bankers, and other investors," who have no need to factor these additional expenses into their consideration of profit and loss. And, for those cities that of late have been experiencing massive gentrification, such costs of investment are even more significant than those from disinvestment (see Lees, Slater, and Wyly 2008).

Scholarship in the urban political economy field also has extensively documented this dynamic. This body of research finds its clearest manifestation in the many powerful critiques of the Petersonian perspective, which sees urban development policies as unambiguously promoting the well-being of cities (see chapters 2 and 3). The thrust of these critiques emphasize that, while economic growth brings benefits to local places such as increased employment and tax revenue, it also often comes at a steep price. Increases in tax revenue may be overwhelmed by larger increases in the demand for public services and the costs of additional infrastructure, while expanded job opportunities may largely go to residents of surrounding jurisdictions or new migrants to the area. Summing up this point in their now-classic book, *Urban Fortunes,* urbanists John Logan and Harvey Molotch (1987, 85) write that "for many places and times, growth is at best a mixed blessing." The public balance sheet makes a useful contribution to this research by providing an analytic framework to calculate and accentuate these public and community costs. In this way, the technique allows for a more balanced assessment of the pro-growth policies favored by the corporate interests that currently exercise hegemony over American urban governance.

Another lively body of research examining the social costs of development has been provoked by the ubiquitous phenomenon of urban sprawl. Once again, consistent with the PBS perspective, researchers find that the private decisions of investors, and the development patterns that result, impose burdensome costs on the public and the larger community. Such costs are not factored into investors' private economic calculations (Persky and Wiewel 1999).

In a comprehensive review of the effects of sprawl, urbanist Todd Swanstrom (2000) identifies and explicates these myriad costs. This pattern of urban development lessens the employment opportunities for poor residents of central cities, harms the overall economic vibrancy of the metropolitan region, drives up the cost of government services, increases the central-city tax burden, negatively affects the physical and psychological health of city dwellers and suburbanites alike, burdens the poor in central cities with additional consumer costs while fueling overconsumption and the assumption of burdensome debt in the suburbs, and exacerbates both central city and suburban crime rates. To this list we can add environmental costs such as additional air and water pollution, the loss of green space and agricultural output, and the damage to ecosystems (Benfield, Raimi, and Chen 1999; also see Williamson, Imbroscio, and Alperovitz 2002).

Surveying sprawl's extensive public costs leads Swanstrom (2000, 78–79) to reflect on the misguided way such costs are conceptualized by conventional economic analysis. Consistent with the public balance sheet critique, he expresses a similar dissatisfaction: "To speak of these spatial effects as 'externalities' [in the limited way that conventional economists conceive of that term] wrongly implies that they are marginal.... In fact, they are ubiquitous, complexly intertwined, and difficult to change."

Holding Private Actors Accountable

The public balance sheet focuses the attention of local development policy on the significant costs that private decisions impose, or externalize, on the public sector and the community as a whole. For practitioners of this approach, the policy implication logically derived from this insight is that, since it is the decisions of private actors that engender these costs, private actors should be held accountable for them.

At the broadest level, PBS advocates suggest that the present system, which allows private actors largely to evade responsibility, is normatively undesirable from a political perspective and empirically unsustainable from an economic perspective. Smith (1979, 4), for example, quotes the insight of economic theorist Peter Bearse, who proclaims—with poignancy—that "a philosophy of government which says that the function of government is simply to pick up the dirty linen of private enterprise without affecting incentives to dirty the linen would bankrupt government and corrupt the political process." In more specific terms, PBS practitioners prescribe policies designed to hold private actors accountable by either preventing behaviors that externalize significant costs in the first place or by requiring compensatory payments to be made.

On first glance, these general policy prescriptions seem roughly congruous with those of conventional economic analysis, which espouses the use of government to correct for negative externalities by proscribing the offending conduct or levying a tax or fee on it (Browning and Browning 1983; Stokey and Zeckhauser 1978). But once again, where the PBS diverges from conventional economics is in its expansive conceptualization of what is considered to be an externality problem warranting corrective action in the first place.

Some externality problems fit the conventional model well. For example, when production facilities pollute the air or water, this model prescribes environmental policies that either prevent the firm from polluting or charge the firm a fee for doing so. Likewise, to take an example from economic development policy, the externalities generated by excessive investment (and the intensification of land use it causes) commonly leads rapidly growing communities to either employ zoning power to constrain new development or to levy impact fees (exactions) on developers. The latter are fees based on the idea that land development imposes additional physical costs for roads, sewers, schools, and so forth, costs that should be borne by the private developers rather than by public taxpayers.

In contrast, conceptualizing externalities more expansively—as the PBS concept does—inspires a range of LEADS-type innovative and socially transformative policy prescriptions.

Take, for example, the case of impact fees (exactions). Traditional exactions simply require developers to provide *themselves* with the infrastructure needed to serve their new projects, "with amenities...accru[ing] to the property supplying them" and "local governments...merely [acting] as conduits for payments" rather than "fulfilling broader public policy goals with the funds" (Garber 1989, 16). Later, however, the understanding of the range and scope of the development costs externalized onto the community was broadened, leading to the implementation of more innovative and redistributive exactions. Urban theorist Judith Garber (1989, 16) recounted this evolution: "By the 1960s," she writes, "the *effects* of the ultimate use of land began to be treated as fair game by local governments, although those effects were often physically [i.e., spatially] removed from the development site." In short, she added, "exactions were redefined to include the obligation incurred when property transactions create social, economic, or environmental costs to the larger community." Such an understanding of the external costs of property development, Garber (1990, 9–10) observed, opened the door for "a greatly expanded repertoire of methods for collecting social debts inherent in land use."

Notable among this repertoire are *linkage* or *linkage development* policies. Such policies usually impose a fee (or exaction) on private investors in exchange for granting them the right to develop a city's prime real estate. The rationale for this fee is the *link* drawn between that development and the exacerbation of the city's social, economic, and environmental problems. To compensate the larger community, cities obligate developers to contribute to a special fund targeted to address pressing community needs for child care, job training, public transportation, and, most important, affordable housing (Euchner and McGovern 2003).[10] It is unsurprising that several analyses of urban problems invoke the public balance sheet as the rationale for the adoption of linkage policies.

A Vermont law requiring that an economic impact statement be prepared to evaluate large development projects provides another example. Once again, we see a case where a more expansive understanding of the external costs imposed by private investment leads to innovative policy. Based on the impact statement required by this law, a citizen review commission rejected Wal-Mart's attempt to open a large store in the state. When the commission examined the full range of economic effects applying the "type of full-cost accounting" used by these impact statements (an accounting method not unlike the PBS), it concluded that this prospective investment "would cost the community $3 for every $1 in benefits it created, as a result of its adverse [external] impact on local businesses and infrastructure" (Morris 1998, 15; also see Mitchell 2006).

Cases involving private capital *dis*investment provide further examples. Here, we also see how the PBS's expansive conceptualization of externalities inspires LEADS-type innovative and socially transformative policy ideas.

Conventional economic analysis rarely conceives of disinvestment as an externality problem for which private investors should be held accountable. It instead sees disinvestment as part of the normal operation of well-functioning, rather than failing, market processes, as private actors reallocate capital to secure the highest possible (risk-adjusted) returns (see Berliner 1999). In contrast, the public balance sheet traces *extensive* external costs to disinvestment, such as the physical, social, human, fiscal, and political costs described above. And the process of actually coming to terms with the extent of these costs wholly transforms the parameters and dimensions of appropriate policy prescriptions.

Such a transformed understanding crystallized in the mind of a federal judge presiding over legal action to prevent the shutdown at Youngstown. The catastrophic social consequences of this disinvestment drew the judge to a radically new and innovative understanding of property law, one that suggested the possible existence of what progressive historian, lawyer, and activist Staughton Lynd (1987a, 927) calls a "community property right." The judge stated that

> it seems to me that a property right has risen from this lengthy, long estab-lished relationship between United States Steel, the steel industry as an in-stitution, the community in Youngstown, the people in Mahoning County and the Mahoning Valley in having given and devoted their lives to this in-dustry....I think the law can recognize the property right to the extent that U.S. Steel cannot leave the Mahoning Valley and the Youngstown area in a state of waste, that it cannot completely abandon its obligation to the com-munity, because certain vested rights have arisen out of this long relation-ship and institution. (Quoted in Lynd 1987a, 940)

In the end, however, the judge could not find the legal basis for this new community property right, and ruled in favor of the company. Vesting com-munities with rights over private property to hold private actors account-able for the external costs they impose thus remained, as Lynd (1987a, 941) notes, "visionary, without apparent lodgment in existing law." Neverthe-less, the public balance sheet's expansive conceptualization of these exter-nalities can catalyze a transformation in both legal doctrine and the policy prescriptions enabled by doctrinal standards.

The same phenomenon provoked a metamorphosis in thinking about the proper uses of local government's power of eminent domain. Emi-nent domain is the power to take private property without the owner's consent upon paying just compensation if a "public purpose" is served. Tra-ditionally, it has been employed to facilitate the process of land assembly to encourage private development or enhance public infrastructure. But by the 1980s, local communities began to see this power in a more transformative light, understanding its potential to be used innovatively as protection against the worst pangs of corporate flight (Portz 1990). Many communities (including Oakland, California, New Bedford, Massachusetts, and Pittsburgh, Pennsylvania) attempted (or considered) using this power to condemn, that is, to acquire, the business facilities of enterprises seeking to relocate or close operations. Most interesting is that the basis for this action lay in the understanding that disinvestment imposed far-ranging externalities on communities. It therefore was argued that the effort to mitigate these costs (by preserving otherwise lost jobs) constituted a clear *public purpose,* hence opening the door for the legitimate use of eminent domain (see Elkin 2006). Even though these efforts ultimately proved unsuccessful—because they either were disallowed by the courts or were not fully followed through by communities themselves—we nonetheless again see how the expansive conceptualization of externalities spawns innovation in the formulation of local development policy.

Guiding Public Intervention

The public balance sheet has been used to draw attention to the social costs of private development—an essentially passive and negative exercise that merely tallies costs and exacts accountability. Yet, it also can play a more activist and explicit role in policymaking by promoting the use of positive government to accomplish desirable ends. Specifically, it can serve as a tool to guide public intervention into the market economy to regenerate local economies, often via the LEADS-type efforts sketched in previous chapters.

Questioning Market Judgments

The key postulate underlying the public balance sheet policy prescriptions is that policymakers err when they assume economic behavior is desirable or undesirable solely based on the actions of traditional market investors. In specific terms, policymakers should not deem economic activities to be inefficient simply because investors have shunned them due to ostensible limited profit potential. Alternatively, when private actors do invest, this action should not automatically and unquestionably indicate an efficient use of societal resources.

PBS practitioners adduce many reasons for not blindly accepting this so-called *judgment of the market* as their guide for prescribing economic development policies.

Market Failure   First and foremost, the market may be failing in any number of ways, especially by not taking into consideration the full range of positive and negative externalities that affect the public (or the larger community). Insofar as the market is failing, its judgments will not reflect the maximization of social welfare; therefore, it logically follows that such judgments should not be the sole basis for policy prescriptions (Smith 1979).

Plural Values   In the case of disinvestment by private actors, the economic activities in question still might be judged profitable by market criteria, just not profitable *enough* for large corporations demanding annual returns topping 20 percent (see Williamson, Imbroscio, and Alperovitz 2002; Osborne and Gaebler 1992). In contrast, as Alperovitz and Faux (1984, 149) noted, "when the public sector—either a government or a collection of people connected by their geographic community—is seen as an investor in its own right, perception of profits can change dramatically." Relatively low profit levels might be acceptable to a local polity or community in order to enhance other values it deems desirable—for example, economic stability, equality, or community—that is, other values beyond simply maximum economic efficiency. Recognizing this plurality of values, the PBS allows for the design of economic development policies that better reflect the normative ideals of democratic decision making.

Socially Constructed Markets   The workings of market processes are not driven exclusively by neutral, impersonal forces. Markets are, instead, socially constructed, and therefore infected with myriad other values and biases apart from strict economic rationality. Nowhere is this phenomenon more evident than in America's inner cities, where racial prejudices warp and distort economic decision making (see Dymski 1997). As political scientist Adolph Reed (1988, 170) points out, "parcels of [urban] land occupied by minorities are underutilized...because the presence of minority populations lowers market values." Race, filtered through the conceptual lens of largely white investors, *in and of itself* determines investment risks and land values.

Miscalculations   Finally, market actors may simply make miscalculations about the economic viability of certain investments, causing an overinvestment in unprofitable ventures and an underinvestment in profitable ones. The former is clearly illustrated by the multibillion-dollar losses racked up by the savings-and-loan industry in 1980s or the more recent subprime lending fiasco (Kuttner 1997, 2007). A glimpse of the latter can be found in the results of an Ohio program that conducted feasibility studies of several industrial plants slated for shut down. Most such studies showed that, on close scrutiny, many of these firms turned out to be economically viable after all—an indication of how many plants regularly closed by their corporate owners might instead be saved or retooled (Williamson, Imbroscio, and Alperovitz, 2002).

Intervening More Rationally

Having rejected the *judgment of the market* as a flawed guide for economic development policy, the public balance sheet approach instead examines the full range of taxpayer and public benefits generated by a policy in comparison to total societal costs. As noted above, Alperovitz and Faux (1979, iii) stress that the technique therefore "provides a more comprehensive and rational guide" for public intervention because it does not simply focus on "the narrow considerations of private profit and loss." Although the private profit criterion remains an important factor in this guide—without which gross inefficiencies might arise—the PBS situates this criterion within a broader analytic framework.

Policy prescriptions again vary in a general sense according to whether the economic development issue at hand involves disinvestment or investment. In the case of private *dis*investment, the PBS becomes a tool to evaluate whether public resources should be committed to sustain some economic activity eschewed by the private sector. In cases where the private sector desires to *in*vest, this tool evaluates whether such investment should be encouraged or discouraged based on, for example, whether it tends to strengthen or weaken the local economy.

Most of the early PBS work focused on the appropriate public policy response to private *dis*investment, especially in the form of plant closures. Alperovitz and Faux (1984), for example, explain how an (ultimately unsuccessful) effort to reopen and modernize the Campbell Works steel mill in Youngstown (under the ownership of a locally based corporation) justifiably could have been granted a subsidy of several hundred million dollars. When evaluated according to the accounting framework of the PBS, a tally of the massive level of government revenue losses averted, added together with the expectation of moderate private returns, combined to make the planned reopening effort a potentially worthy public investment.

Activist-scholars Dan Luria and Jack Russell (1981) used the PBS framework in a similar way to justify public subsidy for their plan to "rationally reindustrialize" Detroit. The following excerpt from their analysis expresses the logic of their policy prescriptions (remembering of course that the dollar figures are from 1980):

> Imagine a Detroit enterprise that employs 250 workers earning $15,000 each year, of whom two-thirds own homes and half live in Detroit. The enterprise, let us say, is losing $500,000 per year. Assuming that closing the facility makes private accounting sense to its owners, let us ask whether closing the facility is also rational for the total society. On the negative side, operating the plant costs society $500,000, the private loss. On the positive side, keeping the enterprise open garners the society about $172,000 in property taxes, $57,000 in worker-paid city income taxes, $138,000 in state income taxes, and $487,000 in federal income taxes. It also saves $920,000 in unemployment insurance (a one-time cost), welfare, and food stamps transfer payments. Adding these social benefits, one gets about $1,770,000 in year one and $850,000 each year thereafter. Netting out the annual $500,000 loss, over a decade society is better off to the tune of $4.4 million by keeping the plant open. (Luria and Russell 1981, 31)

Thus when the balance sheet employed is a public one, what is economically irrational can potentially be transformed into what is, instead, actually quite rational.

The PBS also can be utilized to formulate appropriate economic development policy in cases in which private actors seek to *in*vest in a local economy. In these cases the technique examines the full range of public and community benefits compared to total social costs in order to determine whether this investment should be encouraged or discouraged. Rather than simply letting the market judge the issue, the PBS evaluates private investment according to a broader set of criteria, especially its tendency to strengthen or weaken the local economy.

This type of evaluation was a central objective of an economic development initiative launched in the city of St. Paul, Minnesota, in the 1980s. The St. Paul initiative, which sought to create a more "self-reliant city" by building a "homegrown economy," evaluated new business development "not only for the services or products...[these businesses] offer but for the way they affect the local economy" (Office of Mayor, St. Paul 1983, 12). Of particular importance was the understanding of the crucial role played by import substitution in strengthening local economies, an understanding gleaned from the seminal and highly influential work of the heterodox economic thinker Jane Jacobs (1969, 1984). A key economic development official explained the approach this way: to the "extent we had businesses in St. Paul that would essentially be importing things into the city and exporting capital out, this was a net loss to St. Paul." The goal of the city's development policy under this initiative, he added, "was to reverse this situation...by understanding that certain kinds of businesses were good [on this score] and others were not" and encouraging the development of the former, while discouraging the latter (as quoted in Imbroscio 1997, 79).

Hence, in cases involving both *dis*investment and *in*vestment, the public balance sheet can potentially guide more rational interventions by considering whether they generate greater public/community benefits compared to total societal costs (rather than relying solely on market-based criteria and judgments).

Yet, at first glance, it is not altogether clear what the PBS would add here to the current practice of mainstream local development policy. Consider cases in which public resources need to be committed to sustain economic activities otherwise shunned by the private sector. Public subsidization, of one form or another, almost always finds its justification in the claim that these subsidies generate greater benefits for the broader community in relation to overall costs (e.g., tax incentives for business attraction and infrastructure expenditures for items such as sport stadiums and convention centers). Therefore, the utilization of the PBS to guide policy formulation seems simply to buttress what these officials claim they already do.

Nevertheless, the widespread use of the PBS as a policymaking tool would bring about two significant modifications to current practice.

First, local development policy might more intensely accentuate the benefits accruing to the public and the community at-large. Reviewing various approaches to development policy, economic development experts Peter Fisher and Alan Peters (1998, 217) explain how policy guided by the PBS would reflect this emphasis. For those who "take a public balance sheet approach," they write, a cost-benefit analysis would be conducted of development policy that weighs "the public benefits against the public costs." Advocates of the approach call for the use of public funds only for those "projects or firms that satisfy public-interest performance standards regarding labor practices, workplace safety, environmental record, wage levels, or the provisions of health insurance."

For many critics of local economic policy, this change would inject a much-needed corrective into current practice, mitigating its considerable biases. As urbanists Timothy Barnekov and Daniel Rich (1989, 216) demonstrated, in actuality the use of public subsidies often fails to provide substantial public/community benefits compared to the benefits garnered by private actors, despite the claims of local development officials to the contrary. They point out, for example, that "local economic development programs designed to use public funds to leverage private investment frequently result in reverse leverage—that is, private enterprise often leverages public funds to accomplish its own development objectives."

Second, local development policymaking might be less constrained by the ideological blinders currently delimiting appropriate modes of public intervention. For example, though the current practice of development policy clearly views massive public subsidy as a legitimate role for public policy—witness the billions spent by states and cities on tax incentives and infrastructure expenditures—the expenditure of public funds goes almost exclusively to support privatistic forms of local development, where "priority...[is] given to the needs of the private sector, and public resources must be focused on the creation and enhancement of private investment opportunities" (Barnekov and Rich 1989, 213). By placing the accent on the *public,* the PBS potentially moves local policymaking away from this strict orthodoxy of privatism and toward more imaginative and innovative development policies, conceivably of a LEADS-type nature.

In fact, if the public benefits outweighed total societal costs, the PBS might even warrant the most radical of LEADS-type public interventions: local public ownership of productive economic assets. Rather than justifying so-called lemon socialism, where the public costs exceed public benefits, the PBS would only prescribe the creation of public enterprises producing the opposite result. As noted in chapter 1, many cities have pursued public ownership in various forms as a local development strategy. As such, they have owned or operated enterprises in realms of commerce such as telecommunications, venture capital provision, real estate, commercial and retail services, professional sports, recreation, and a variety of ecological areas (also see Williamson, Imbroscio, and Alperovitz 2002). Significantly in this regard, even mainstream thinkers such as David Osborne and Ted Gaebler understand the value of casting off the shackles of privatism in order to fashion innovative development solutions involving local public ownership. As part of their *reinventing government* agenda, Osborne and Gaebler (1992, 216) point out that "in reality, there are several good reasons why government [by engaging in public enterprise] *should* sometimes compete with the private sector." The wider use of the PBS as a policymaking tool for local economic development would likely facilitate the conditions supporting enhanced creative policy formulation along these lines.

Challenges and Responses

The public balance sheet hence can be employed both as a tool for tallying the social costs of private development decisions and as a guide for public intervention. Nonetheless, the technique faces serious challenges—challenges that PBS partisans need to confront head on.

A key objection of conventional economists to the widespread use of the PBS would be that the technique encourages the propping up of firms unable to attract sufficient productive economic resources (land, labor, and capital) through the private market. Such actions are seen as creating barriers to the dynamic movement of these resources out of declining industries and technologies to those on the rise. Under these conditions economic processes supposedly would be too static, resulting in large losses in economic efficiency.

This issue raises a legitimate concern, one that even ardent supporters of the PBS recognized (Alperovitz and Faux 1984). However, it can be addressed on two levels.

First, recall that the technique still factors investment returns (e.g., privately profitably) into its accounting framework (albeit as one of many ledger entries). Hence, if investment returns were extremely poor in a given enterprise due to anemic demand for its product, the PBS most likely would *not* prescribe that public resources be committed to it. Take for example the scenario described by Luria and Russell (1981) excerpted above. If their hypothetical enterprise were likely to lose $1 million annually rather than $500,000, public intervention into market processes would not be deemed rational, as total societal returns from this intervention would be negative.

Nonetheless, conventional economists no doubt would continue to question the PBS logic of subsidizing firms not sanctioned by the market (after all, Luria and Russell's hypothetical enterprise *is* losing $500,000 a year). This action will hence still be inhibiting market dynamism by obstructing the flow of productive resources (especially capital) into more efficient uses. Therefore, this objection must be addressed on a second, more profound level.

Addressing this objection entails evoking another key element of the alternative economic paradigm set out in chapter 2—community economic stability. While the economic *dynamism* of the marketplace clearly yields efficiency gains for society, such gains also result from the economic *stability* of communities—something likely to be enhanced if the PBS were in widespread use. For example, we saw above how the community economic *instability* engendered by capital mobility and disinvestment results in the inefficient throwing away of physical infrastructure and the erosion of social capital, among other significant costs. We also saw how this same economic instability wrought by urban sprawl leads to myriad inefficiencies for both cities and suburbs alike. So, if market dynamism and community stability *both* produce efficiencies for society, it remains an open question *which* force is more powerful and, more precisely, what the appropriate trade-off should be between them.

Unfortunately, there currently exists a lacuna in the knowledge base needed to answer this question. This lacuna is due in large part to the methodological biases built into the conventional neoclassical approach that imperiously reigns over the modern study of economics. Rather than approaching research questions in a value-free manner, as conventional economists usually claim, neoclassical economics intensely focuses on documenting the virtues of market dynamism, while practically ignoring the virtues of community stability (see Markusen 2001).

Pointing to our lack of useable knowledge regarding the relative efficiencies of dynamism and stability raises another more general challenge facing the public balance sheet. Like all attempts to make decision making more comprehensive and rational, the technique demands a considerable amount of information. In the case of the PBS, it is necessary to understand with accuracy and empirical rigor the effects of private-sector economic activities on communities (see Wyly, forthcoming). Much of this information is not currently available, however. Once again, the deficiency of required knowledge stems in part from the biases built in to the discipline of economics. In addition, much of the required data is highly intangible in nature, such as the human, social, or political costs imposed on communities by private disinvestment decisions. This intangibility poses obvious operationalization and measurement problems for the PBS.

The most befitting response to this challenge to the development of a workable local PBS is simply to accept it. It should be treated as a call to frame and execute a reconstituted agenda for methodologically sophisticated and empirically rigorous economic development research (as one part of the alternative economic paradigm set forth in chapter 2). Unlike much of the work currently conducted in the field, this agenda affords researchers an opportunity to produce socially useful studies that can have a positive, progressive impact on the quality of public decision making and local community life (see Wyly, forthcoming).

The local public balance sheet thus clearly is a potentially valuable tool to facilitate improved local economic development efforts. It is useful for tallying the social costs of economic activities, giving policymakers a rationale for holding private investors to account (often via LEADS-type policy prescriptions). It also is useful as a guide for LEADS-type public interventions into market processes, providing a means to make such actions potentially more rational and more progressive.

Yet, much more than employing the local PBS technique is needed if the two central constructive goals of this book—progressive urban regime reconstruction and the amelioration of urban problems—are to be realized. Additional ways to move toward these goals need to be identified, clearly understood, and, ultimately, put into practice.

6

A Triad for Community
Economic Stability

Community economic stability refers to a condition where places "possess job opportunities and a general level of economic activity…adequate to provide a decent standard of living for their populations over a sustained period of time" (Williamson, Imbroscio, and Alperovitz 2002, xiv).[1] This is an important element of the new alternative economic paradigm because conventional economics, with its obsessive focus on market dynamism, fails to grasp the economic benefits arising from such stability. To realize such benefits, however, this community economic stability must first somehow be enhanced in a more basic sense. The local public balance sheet can contribute to enhancing community economic stability in the myriad ways explicated in the previous chapter. Yet, if the nature of urban governance and the severity of urban problems are to be, respectively, transformed and ameliorated, additional means must be found to promote this stability.

The orthodox means to achieve the necessary community economic stability advocated by scores of urbanists is liberal expansionist in nature (see, for example, Dreier, Mollenkopf, and Swanstrom 2004; Kantor 1995).

Most basically, such an approach involves a greatly augmented role for the federal government to shore up the economic and fiscal bases of America's cities and facilitate greater metropolitan regionalism in urban governance and policymaking. Given that liberal expansionism is flawed on both normative and programmatic grounds (something to be further fleshed out in part 4), it is clear that another path toward enhanced community economic stability must be found. One such path, explored below, is inspired by, and largely draws upon, the local economic alternative development strategies (LEADS).

Irrespective of the particular means followed to achieve community economic stability, the basic economic development problematic that must be overcome is threefold: first, the conditions must be right to capture capital investment initially; second, such captured investment must be augmented by ensuring that it yields the maximum advantage to the local economy; and, third, mechanisms must be in place to root this investment securely in place. Solving this problematic is largely a matter of successfully tackling the challenges posed by what I identity as the *inducing, multiplying, and anchoring triad.*

Overview of the Triad

There are several ways the division of labor between state and market can be innovatively restructured in the current political economy of cities. Nonetheless, as the perceptive work of political economist Charles Lindblom taught us, as long as the political-economic system remains fundamentally market-oriented, the options available to public officials for capturing business investment in their communities are circumscribed. Specifically, Lindblom (1977, 173) observed that "constitutional rules—especially the laws of private property—specify that, although governments can forbid certain kinds of activity, they cannot *command* business to perform. They must *induce* rather than command" (emphases added; also see Elkin 2006). For, as Lindblom and a colleague further explained, "a business manager creates new jobs and otherwise performs only if he or she *voluntarily* decides to do so in the pursuit of profit" (Lindblom and Woodhouse 1993, 91, emphasis added). Since business managers are currently *not* voluntarily investing enough job-creating capital in the many cities now lacking community economic stability, they must be *induced or enticed* to do so if such stability is to be enhanced. Inducements—in essence government-provided benefits to businesses that enhance the profitability of capital investments—are the first leg of the triad for enhancing community economic stability.

The second leg consists of efforts to ensure that the capital that is invested in cities has the maximum economic impact on local economies. For what becomes crucial for local economic development and job generation is not simply how much investment and income flows into a local economy; it is also important how much investment and income circulates within it (Power 1996). When injected economic resources circulate extensively, they produce a *high multiplier effect.* Some initial level of economic activity ripples or spins off through the local economy, augmenting (or multiplying) its economic impact. Consider, for example, if new business investment created jobs for fifty employed workers earning $45,000 annually. Each worker

> obviously will have money to spend on food, clothing, entertainment, and the like—hence creating additional jobs for persons providing those goods and services. If a town or city has a multiplier of 1.5, then for every two new jobs created, a third will naturally spin-off the other two. If, however, this multiplier can be raised from 1.5 to, say, 2.5, then for each two new jobs created *three more* new jobs also will be added, for a total of five. (Williamson, Imbroscio, and Alperovitz 2002, 166)

Thus, the greater the local multiplier effect, the greater number of jobs created in a community to help meet local employment needs and hence enhance community economic stability.

Third, since investment capital induced to locate in particular areas tends to be flighty, the creation of jobs via inducements is not enough; such jobs must also remain rooted in place if economically stable communities are to be maintained. Capital mobility is clearly far from absolute, of course, as many factors act as a brake on such mobility, including the high costs of the sunk investments of businesses in particular places (Savitch and Kantor 1993; Stone 1989). Moreover, successful efforts to increase local multipliers—the second leg of the community economic stability triad— also tend to wed capital to specific locations. Nonetheless, despite these counterweights, under current conditions *enough* capital investment clearly remains mobile *enough* to threaten the stability of many local economies (Elkin 2006). Therefore, the community economic stability effort requires a third leg—job *anchoring*. Anchoring efforts help root capital investment more securely in local economies, and have the added benefit of helping to reduce (to a more manageable level) the aggregate amount of new capital investment that must be initially induced in the first place (from the triad's first leg).

In sum, communities with a vigorous and effective inducement process, high internal multipliers, and sufficient capital-investment anchors also are likely to enjoy a stable local economic base.

Inducing

The first challenge facing efforts to promote community economic stability involves the need to induce or entice business managers to invest capital where they otherwise would not. Such inducements—that is, government-provided benefits to businesses that enhance profitability—come in many forms. Unfortunately, many of the most well-worn or often-advocated forms are of limited value or are otherwise troublingly problematic.

One of these often-advocated forms is based around efforts of the central government to achieve the desired spatial flows of investment via federal taxing and spending mechanisms (see Peterson 1981; Sundquist 1975). As the economic fortunes of local communities waned, they would receive additional federal fiscal resources (revenues and development assistance) via a compensatory formula (Kantor 1995). This approach is, of course, solidly of a liberal expansionist nature. Therefore, in light of the difficulties such liberal expansionist-type efforts have with garnering the necessary political feasibility (see chapter 3 and part 4), it is unlikely to be a promising path toward greater community economic stability (also see Imbroscio 1993).

When considering inducements less expansionist in nature, we again see problems with the most common forms. These forms involve tax breaks and other incentives to cut business capital costs to attract or retain mobile businesses. Such state and local *job chasing* efforts are ineffective at best and often deleterious to the stability of local economies (Williamson, Imbroscio, and Alperovitz 2002; also see Oden and Mueller 1999; Wolman 1996).

The competition for investment resulting from these efforts becomes zero-(or even negative-) sum. Most places need to supply increasingly generous incentives to be able to continue to attract investment or keep competitors from luring it away (Levy 1992; Peretz 1986). And, moreover, evidence suggests this tax and incentive competition to induce business investment generally fails to accomplish the goal of bringing jobs to where they are needed to enhance community stability. As economic development experts Peter Fisher and Alan Peters (1998, 219) conclude in their comprehensive study of the issue, insofar as this competition does result in a spatial redistribution of employment, it generally fails to "shift...jobs from places with low unemployment to places with high unemployment" (also see Fisher and Peters 2004).

Thus the essence of the challenge of the triad's first leg is to find more *positive* locally oriented inducement strategies. Along these lines, it is important to note that for the purposes of facilitating community stability, the most effective inducements are those that help create the kind of local business climate able to spawn significant business development indigenously, from *within* the local economy itself. In this way inducements do not simply lure businesses from other locales (many of which also may have highly precarious economies) in a kind of zero-sum game of interjurisdictional competition.

So, in order to realize the objective of the first leg of the triad, a central issue becomes how this indigenous development process can be engendered. The key here is to promote the kind of local economic environment supportive of locally generated *enterprise development,* that is, the creation and expansion of (often) small-scale, entrepreneurial businesses springing from existing local resources (Schweke 1985; Friedman 1986; also see Eisinger 1988). Since many such businesses will inevitably have short life-spans, and still others may leave the locale that spawned them, what becomes important is the overall development *process* that generates and regenerates such new enterprises with great rapidity and dynamism (see Jacobs 1969; Imbroscio 1997).

Perhaps the most important element in this process of continual indigenous enterprise development and regeneration is the availability of finance, especially in the form of seed capital to such businesses (see Schweke 1985). These inducements are crucial because of the difficulties young businesses face in securing financing for start-ups or expansions—a problem greatly exacerbated in times of generally tight credit. Such seed capital could come in a number of forms, ranging from small micro-loans (of $35,000 or less) for entrepreneurs starting home-based micro-businesses (see McCulloch and Woo 2008; Servon 1999) to venture capital (for both equity and debt finance) for enterprises with significant growth potential. Further inducements to spawn indigenous enterprise development include the provision of a range of technical assistance to enterprises and—even more direct and stimulative—the creation of a number of small business incubators. These small business incubators work to cultivate new and growing firms by providing fledgling business start-ups with low-cost commercial or industrial rental spaces, as well as a range of shared business services and management training (see Knopp 2008). Additional important inducements include help with locating and exploiting new markets for their goods and services, including those markets created by the expenditures of the local public and nonprofit sectors (see Schweke 1985; Imbroscio 1997).

Beyond these efforts at stimulating indigenous enterprise development, other more general inducement options also positive in nature can be identified. Perhaps the most important is the most fundamental: the provision of strong basic public services in a community. To thrive, businesses "need to know that they can rely on high-quality, well-administrated public services to facilitate the conduct of their enterprises" (Lynch 1996, 6). For instance, flood control and snow removal "must be reliable and timely"; highways, local roads, and bridges "must be in good repair"; police and fire protection "must be there when needed"; the court system "must be professional, impartial, and quick to resolve contract disputes"; and public schools and institutions of higher learning "must help to generate a skilled and well-trained workforce." Such a strong level of quality service provision facilitates cities' ability to spur economic growth and generate jobs because businesses will be induced to invest capital in such places at higher rates (Lynch 1996). As a result, local community economic stability is likely to be significantly enhanced.

Multiplying

The augmentation of local multipliers, the second leg in the triad for achieving community economic stability, occurs when income circulates extensively within the local economy. The key to augmenting multipliers is to enhance the degree of *interdependence* among local economic agents. Enhancing these interdependencies in a local economy is, in turn, largely a matter of facilitating the development of rich weblike networks of interaction between local producers, suppliers, wholesalers, retailers, and consumers (Meehan 1987).

The most basic strategy to create and nurture such networks is to replace goods and services currently imported from elsewhere with those locally produced. Such an economic process, known as *import replacement* or *import substitution* (Jacobs 1984; Watkins 1980), enhances local economic interdependencies as local buyers and sellers become tightly linked to one another via frequent business transactions (see Shuman 2006). Toward this end, there are two general ways to substitute for imports in a local economy: local purchasers (businesses, households, or governments) can begin to *buy locally* those goods and services they currently import; or local producers can begin to meet local needs now satisfied by external sources, that is, *producing locally* what was previously imported.

Buy local strategies come in three basic forms. Each targets a distinct economic sector. The first strategy is to promote local buyer-supplier networks, encouraging local businesses to purchase goods and services from one another. These networks strengthen the economic linkages among a community's business sector in three steps: (1) identifying products that local businesses currently import, (2) communicating the existence of this potential new market to appropriate local businesses, and (3) brokering matches between the local buyers and suppliers (Persky, Ranney, and Wiewel 1993). The second strategy focuses on household consumers. It encourages local consumers through advertising and marketing efforts to buy from local rather than nonlocal businesses (Meyer 1991). Finally, the local public sector can use its own procurement efforts to enhance local purchasing, especially by giving local firms advantages over nonlocal firms when bidding for government contracts (Williamson, Imbroscio, and Alperovitz 2002). The localist writer and activist Michael Shuman (2006, 170) points out that these advantages can be justified by the higher multipliers such firms yield for a local economy: "If a city can foresee that a local bidder will deliver two to three times the local jobs and tax revenue as a nonlocal bidder," Shuman asks, "why shouldn't it take this into account in its contracts?"[2]

Produce local strategies offer a second route to import substitution. Here the idea is to increase local productive capacity to meet local needs, rather than simply getting purchasers to buy locally. For example, in the promotion of local buyer-supplier networks discussed above, produce local strategies would go a step further than simply linking businesses together. These strategies would attempt to stimulate the local production of goods and services that are currently imported because no local supplier exists, either by aiding local firms' new product development or by facilitating business start-ups to meet this demand. Economic development initiatives might include specialized job training, the provision of technical assistance (for business administration or product development), or general financial assistance to develop new product lines or to help meet the start-up costs for the development of new enterprises (see Black 1991).

Beyond the effort to substitute for imports, local economic interdependencies, and hence local economic multipliers, can be augmented by facilitating the development and flourishing of certain *types* of businesses. Most helpful in this regard are businesses that are small and, regardless of size, those that are locally (i.e., independently) owned (Shuman 2006). Small businesses tend to require a variety of business support services and factor inputs, as less of these services and goods are provided internal to the firm.

This dynamic weds small businesses to numerous other businesses via their spin-off purchases, many of which are likely to be local, hence enhancing local economic interdependencies (Fisher 1988). Business that are locally owned, regardless of size, also tend to enhance local economic interdependencies because they, too, tend to purchase business services and factor inputs locally (especially compared with large, absentee-owned businesses that often purchase centrally). Moreover, local, independent ownership tends to keep profits circulating (i.e., multiplying) locally because these monies are not siphoned off to corporate headquarters and absentee owners in far-flung locations (Mitchell 2000; Shuman 2006).

Supporting the development and flourishing of small businesses in the local economy could be greatly advanced by the *enterprise development* efforts discussed above, such as the provision of seed capital, the creation of incubators, and assistance with new market development. More general support of such businesses could come via the creation of effective and well-funded small business assistance centers (see Blakely 1989). Because many of these indigenous small businesses will be owned by local residents, enterprise development efforts also advance the goal of increasing the degree of local ownership in the local economy. In addition, the efforts to enhance import substitution—the buy local and produce local strategies—also advance this goal.

However, because these import substitution strategies emphasize the spatial character of businesses rather than their ownership status, some of the locally sited businesses promoted may not themselves be locally *owned*. Thus, additional efforts to promote local ownership are warranted. Along these lines, especially salient are the efforts of local communities to assist their locally owned retail enterprises in their struggle against corporate chains, such as Wal-Mart (Frug and Barron 2008). Local land-use and zoning policies can be structured to favor local retailers, local taxes on chain stores can be increased, and efforts to expand retailer-owned purchasing cooperatives can be supported to give small merchants purchasing advantages similar to those enjoyed by chain stores (see Mitchell 2006, 2000).

Another means by which local multipliers can be enhanced in a community is through the creation of local currencies or local exchange systems. Perhaps surprisingly, there were more than three hundred such currencies or systems operating in the United States by the early 2000s (Williamson, Imbroscio, and Alperovitz 2002). Since local currencies must, by definition, be spent locally, wealth translated into them recirculates within a community rather than quickly flowing outward, greatly enhancing local multipliers (Meeker-Lowry 1996). For example, in the Ithaca HOURS program, perhaps the best-known and best-developed U.S. local currency, the local multiplier has been estimated to be at an impressive 6.0, meaning that with $85,000 in circulation over $500,000 in trade is generated each year (Hargraves 1998).

Although there are a variety of ways to establish such currencies and exchange systems,[3] the simplest method is to print local scrip, which then serves as an alternative to regular paper money (as in the case of the Ithaca program). Such systems are, also perhaps surprisingly, perfectly legal (Williamson, Imbroscio, and Alperovitz 2002; Grover 2006). To get the system started, small quantities are given to commercial entities (such as local businesses) who agree, in turn, to accept it for goods and services. Once a number of businesses have agreed to accept it, other methods of currency distribution can be employed. For example, grants to nonprofit organizations from local philanthropies can be awarded in the local scrip, or the local scrip can be used by participating businesses to pay the wages of willing employees, who perhaps receive a slight bonus in pay when it is received in this form. In addition, on the public sector side, Shuman (2006, 187) suggests that "bonuses or raises to public employees" could be paid in local scrip and such scrip could be accepted "for partial payment of taxes, both of which Philadelphia did during the Great Depression." Additionally, given the "strong public benefits to spending the [local] currency," another analyst (Grover 2006) suggests that "local governments could give businesses and individuals "a small reward, in dollars, for making transactions" in local scrip, perhaps in the range of 5 percent. This reward could help incentivize its use, since as of now—in the Ithaca HOURS case at least—circulation is lower than it might otherwise be because "not enough individual benefit exists for the majority of people to overcome the inconvenience of using the [local as opposed to national] currency" (Grover 2006, 734–35).

Undergirding all of these efforts to increase economic multipliers in local communities are attempts to better understand the ways economic resources (especially income and expenditures) flow across community boundaries (see Gunn and Gunn 1991). By tracking income and expenditure flows, local officials can better understand how and why some resources remain in local economies while others *leak* out (Huber 2000). With this information, a focus can be given to the ways that such leaks can be plugged, for example, by substituting local products for imports. Studies tracking these resource flows have been undertaken in several cities over the past few decades and over time have become more methodologically sophisticated and empirically grounded (see Yin 2004; Cole 1994; Gunn and Gunn 1991).

Anchoring

The third leg of the triad aims to root investment more securely in communities, helping to keep jobs from fleeing the places where they are needed to promote community economic stability. We already have seen one powerful means to achieve this goal, in efforts to increase local multipliers by augmenting the degree of interdependency among a community's economic agents. When businesses have established relationships with other nearby suppliers, wholesalers, retailers, and consumers, they are more likely to remain rooted in place in order to maintain and nurture these relationships (Berk and Swanstrom 1995). As pointed out in chapter 2's discussion of *asset specificities,* the social capital (especially trust) stemming from this frequent, place-specific interaction is not easily reproduced in new settings, limiting the degree of capital mobility. Moreover, interdependent enterprises, especially those in related areas of commerce, may form spatially rooted business networks, or clusters. Such networks allow similar enterprises to join together to carry out certain business activities (such as marketing, worker training, or technology development) that individual firms could not pursue effectively acting alone (Rast 1999).

Another powerful way to more securely anchor business enterprise in communities is by changing the nature in which such enterprises are owned and controlled. Commonly, either an individual or a traditional business corporation owns an economic enterprise. In contrast, various alternative models of business ownership exist, where ownership and control are held in a more collective or community-oriented fashion. Such models can help anchor jobs and businesses in communities, as these various collectivities (or community-oriented entities) tend to be more wedded to particular places (Shuman 1998; Gunn and Gunn 1991).

The most well-known and well-developed of these alternative models is employee ownership. In the United States today, there are approximately ten thousand employee stock ownership plans (or ESOPs), with some $600 billion in assets (McCulloch and Woo 2008). Unfortunately, only a minority of existing ESOPs, about 30 percent of those in privately held companies, are majority worker-owned firms, and only 40 to 50 percent of those companies grant full voting rights to worker-shareholders. Nonetheless, the trends are for more and more ESOPs to evolve toward greater employee stock holdings and greater democratic governance, and even partial employee ownership can yield workers significant leverage over capital investment decisions (Alperovitz 2005; Olson 1987). Unlike more traditional business structures, when employees are the owners and controllers of businesses they often have a strong incentive to ensure that their enterprises continue to operate in or near the communities where they reside (see Dahl 1985).

Another well-known and well-developed alternative ownership model is the community development corporation. CDCs are nonprofit, community-based organizations designed to spur economic regeneration in a particular area, usually an inner-city neighborhood (or group of neighborhoods) that is suffering disinvestment (see Vidal 1992). Like worker-owned firms, CDCs number in the several thousands, and are dispersed throughout the United States (but concentrated heavily in cities). However, despite their substantial numbers, the contributions CDCs have made hitherto to the cause of anchoring capital in place have been somewhat modest (see Giloth 2007b; DeFilippis 2004). Rather than owning and operating (and thus anchoring) business enterprises, most CDCs have concentrated on the more limited goal of developing housing in their communities. In part, this focus has been due to some earlier business failures during the era when CDCs were newly emerging in the late 1960s and early 1970s. Nonetheless, despite the housing-oriented focus of most CDCs, some larger and more sophisticated ones do in fact successfully own and operate small and medium-sized enterprises that generate revenue and create substantial employment for local residents (Alperovitz 2005). As CDCs have grown more sophisticated over the past two decades, their potential for developing, owning, and operating community-rooted businesses has increased markedly (Williamson, Imbroscio, and Alperovitz 2002).

A third alternative ownership model is the consumer cooperative. Consumer cooperatives are designed to provide quality consumer goods and services to their members at a reasonable price. They, too, are found throughout the United States and number in the thousands, existing mostly in the areas of health care, housing, retail grocery, and rural electricity (Williamson, Imbroscio, and Alperovitz 2002). The members of the cooperative normally democratically govern it, based on the one-person, one-vote principle. This democratic ownership and control by cooperative members tends to root businesses in the particular communities served by the cooperative, as most members have significant ties to such communities (see Hammond 1987). The key to the further development of this alternative model (as an anchoring strategy) is to extend the cooperative form of ownership beyond the areas where it currently has been most present, especially the retail grocery industry (Imbroscio, Williamson, and Alperovitz 2003).

The development of *publicly* owned businesses of various sorts, on a decentralized (especially municipal) level, offers a way government power can be used directly to anchor jobs in communities. Municipal enterprise has a venerable history in the United States, especially in the areas of public utilities such as water, sewer, and electricity, as well as nonutility enterprises such as hospitals, recreational facilities, parking structures, and airports and seaports. What is surprising is that, even after a strong wave of privatization, local-scaled public ownership of economic enterprises remains remarkably robust in twenty-first-century America (Alperovitz 2005). Growing beyond more traditional forms that tend to have a public-goods character, many relatively recently created municipal enterprises have moved into areas of commerce historically dominated by the private sector. Local governments have run business operations in an eclectic array of fields, including training and consulting, fertilizer and soil enhancer production, equity investment in commercial development, bottling tap water for sale, auto towing, real estate, retailing and retail merchandising, and professional sports (Imbroscio, Williamson, and Alperovitz 2003). Existing local public enterprises have been shown to operate efficiently, and are largely nonideological in nature, being commonly associated with good government notions of *public entrepreneurialism* or *reinventing government* (see, for example, Osborne and Gaebler 1992). In general, these enterprises offer a rooted source of employment for local residents and a potential healthy revenue stream that local governments can tap to fund needed public services.

A final alternative ownership model to anchor jobs locally involves *community* (rather than direct public) ownership. Community-owned corporations are not unlike traditional corporations save one crucial factor: they are owned exclusively or primarily by citizens living in or strongly connected to a local community. Community members have banded together and pooled their resources to buy a number of small businesses in many parts of America, including coffee shops, restaurants, theaters, retail outlets, and several department stores (Mitchell 2006; Williamson, Imbroscio, and Alperovitz 2002). Wisconsin's National Football League franchise, the Green Bay Packers, stands as perhaps the most celebrated example of a community-owned corporation. The world of professional sports includes many other examples, especially in minor league baseball, where in several cases shareholding local fans own their minor league teams (see Kraker 2000). Citing the precedent of Ben and Jerry's ice cream, which restricted its first stock issue to buyers residing in Vermont, Shuman (1999, 52) suggests the creation of "a new kind of business structure" to facilitate the development of this model, where members of the local community would

be the only ones able to own voting shares of stock. "With all voting shareholders residing in the community," Shuman (1998, 101) points out, "it's
unlikely that the firm would move operations elsewhere."

A last anchoring strategy involves the innovative use of the power of
eminent domain. By the 1980s many local governments (including Oakland, California, New Bedford, Massachusetts, and Pittsburgh, Pennsylvania) began to see this power as a means to keep productive capital from
fleeing their communities (Lynd 1987a). Eminent domain affords localities
the power to acquire property held privately, as long as a public purpose is
served and just compensation paid. The idea here is for cities to condemn
(acquire) the operations and capital facilities of a business seeking to relocate or shut down, and then sell or lease the enterprise to another entrepreneur willing to run it locally (see Elkin 2006; Portz 1990). Although such
efforts in the 1980s were unsuccessful in part because of an inhospitable
legal environment, their legality was never fully and conclusively tested in
the courts (Eisinger 1988). The U.S. Supreme Court continues to hold, as
affirmed the 2005 case of *Kelo v. New London* (Connecticut), an expansive
view of what actions constitute a public purpose—virtually anything that
creates jobs and enhances tax revenue. Thus, the door remains potentially
open for using eminent domain power in such an innovative manner to
anchor capital in communities.

Yet, this same *Kelo* decision also spawned a wave of hostility to eminent
domain across the country, as many states enacted or considered enacting
legislation to restrict its use (see Frug and Barron 2008). This hostility was
in large part rooted in the regressive nature of eminent domain use in the
New London case, where property was taken from ordinary citizens and
transferred to well-heeled private interests (Jost 2008). The current climate
is likely, however, to also imperil its more progressive and innovative uses
to promote community economic stability. As one observer recently commented, the "post-*Kelo* backlash" has left city officials "hyper-cautious on
approaching eminent domain issues" (as quoted in Jost 2008, 278). The
nub of the legal vulnerability of eminent domain is that, when the ownership of the condemned property is given over to private interests, the
public purpose requirement may no longer be satisfied because there is not
a *public use* of such property as called for by the U.S. Constitution. One
way the innovative use of eminent domain set out above might be more
legally acceptable, then, is if the acquired operations and capital facilities of

businesses seeking to relocate are retained by local government rather than being transferred to private parties. Yet, such an expansive role for public ownership in America's property rights-oriented cultural context would no doubt need to be part of a broader urban social movement built around the pursuit of a LEADS-type policy agenda.[4]

Returning to the general goal of community economic stability, it is important to keep in mind that many of the anchoring strategies detailed above also serve as *value recapture* mechanisms (see Carr 1999), especially those involving alternative ownership models.[5] Value recapture mechanisms allow for the increasing market values of property to be directed in ways that benefit community residents. As such, the increase in the level of economic activity brought about by successful community stabilization will be realized to a greater degree by the population for which it is intended (rather than being appropriated by those already economically advantaged or by outside investors).

Employee-owned firms, the business activities of CDCs, cooperatives, community-owned corporations, and, to some extent, decentralized public enterprise all allow for the enhanced market value of property to be better *captured* by lower-income community residents (Blackwell and McCulloch 2002). Another crucial value recapture mechanism not yet discussed but playing a key role in community economic stabilization efforts is the community land trust (CLT). CLTs allow for a community-based institution to retain title to land, holding it in permanent stewardship through the trust, while making it available via long-term leases to individuals or businesses for housing or commercial development (see Bourassa 2006; Davis and Demetrowitz 2003). In this arrangement, individuals may own the homes or enterprises occupying the land, but since this land is owned by the community trust, any increase in its value will accrue back to the broader community. CLTs thus can be an extremely valuable tool to ensure that urban revitalization efforts actually advance community stability rather than bringing about community destabilization. The latter, of course, often occurs in the process of gentrification (see Lees, Slater, and Wyly 2008; Carr 1999). And, on a further positive note, CLTs have been rapidly proliferating in the United States, from around sixty in the 1980s to around two hundred by 2006 (Davis 2006). Moreover, and most salutary for fostering community economic stability, recently a diverse array of local governments have taken leading roles in establishing, funding, and supporting

CLTs including Las Vegas, Nevada; Irvine, California; Chicago, Illinois; Sarasota County, Florida; Austin, Texas; Chaska, Minnesota; Delray Beach, Florida; and Highland Park, Illinois (Jacobus and Brown 2007).

Challenges and Responses

Like the local public balance sheet highlighted in the last chapter, some serious challenges confront this path to community economic stability, challenges that must be confronted head-on with forceful responses.

The first challenge concerns the heightened degree of capital mobility documented by Paul Peterson (1981), among others. Technological advances in communication, transportation, and production have left capital largely detached from specific places. While the capital-anchoring strategies discussed above can help mitigate this mobility, conventional economists would still question the wisdom of doing so due to the potentially high macroeconomic efficiency costs involved.[6] What such economists misunderstand, however, is that these same technological advances unfettering capital can, almost ironically, be put in service of the goal of enhancing community economic stability. For such advances actually make the dispersal of business operations *more* feasible, as production facilities, distribution centers, administrative offices, and market outlets can be located almost anywhere (Power 1996; also see Kotkin and Zimmerman 2006; Shuman 2006). In short, the kinds of technical determinants of business firm location—such as physical geography, the proximity to natural resources or markets, or the logistical need for administrative coordination at a central location—become less important given the new technological environment of production (Williamson, Imbroscio, and Alperovitz 2002). Therefore, capital investment can occur in a variety of places without imposing substantial efficiency losses on the economy as a whole.

A second challenge concerns the issue of capital mobility directly. In light of the powerful forces of economic globalization impelling capital investment away from the United States altogether, will the mitigation of this mobility supplied via the strategies discussed above be enough to enhance the economic stability of specific communities? Although it is not possible to answer this question definitively until such strategies are pursued on a large enough scale, there are some favorable trends pointing to the idea that a significant increase in broad-based community economic stability is, even in this era of economic globalization, not hopelessly beyond reach.

For example, while globalization has ushered a decline in the percentage of the American workforce involved in manufacturing and the rise of service jobs, this sectoral change actually—and, again, almost ironically—has led to a significant *localization* of the economy. Whereas manufacturing markets tend to be worldwide, service activities—in areas such as retail, government, medical, educational, repair, personal and professional services, utilities, and real estate—all tend to be highly localized. As these service activities have increased in importance, the percentage of U.S. economic activity that is local has actually *grown,* from about 40 percent in the 1940s to about 60 percent by the 1990s (Alperovitz 2005). In addition, the predicted long-term increase in energy costs, especially the decline of cheap oil—"the lubricant of quick, inexpensive transportation links around the world"—has the potential to slow the ongoing march of economic globalization considerably (Rohter 2008, A1). Should this long-term trend materialize, as many believe it will, and in light of larger concerns about global climate change, there could be a significant and sustained turn toward the local, especially given the major inefficiencies in global-scale production and distribution systems (Shuman 2006). Therefore, the task of enhancing the stability of local economies in the globalized economy, while daunting, seems at a minimum to be conceivable and, possibly, even achievable (see Elkin 2006).

The third, and in many ways deepest, challenge involves funding. Although some of the initiatives discussed above will be more or less self-financing, most will require external (most likely public) funding in varying degrees, especially in the initial phase of start-up. The key dilemma is that the absence of community economic stability also brings with it a dearth of local fiscal capacity to fund the efforts necessary to enhance it. Liberal expansionism of course has a ready-made solution to this dilemma: use the superior resources of the federal government to fund a compensatory revenue sharing scheme administrated nationally to funnel monies (and perhaps direct economic development grants) to localities suffering fiscal stress (see Kantor 1995). In such a scheme, intergovernmental transfers would be adjusted upward to ensure that declining places unable to fund development efforts would have the fiscal means to do so. Yet, as noted above, given that the liberal expansionist approach has great difficulties achieving the necessary degree of political feasibility (also see part 4 below), it is highly likely that other sources of funding would need to be found.

So, from where might such funding come? Consider first that cities now routinely spend massive amounts of revenue on corporate-center local economic development strategies, most of which fail to add much to community economic stability and often detract from it. Thus, a first source of funding for the triad could come from a significant redirection of resources away from such failed strategies. As more and more critical scrutiny focuses on exposing the folly of such strategies (following the perceptive work of Marc Levine, 1987, 2000), the necessary redirection in revenues can garner significant momentum.

Second, there exist a number of largely untapped innovative local finance sources to help meet this goal. One such source is to administer linked deposit programs, as many cities, such as Chicago, Pittsburgh, and Santa Monica, have done. Linked deposit programs allow cities to place temporarily idle monies (which accumulate just after revenue collections or bond offers) only in financial institutions that invest in the local economy (Rosen 1988; Clarke and Gaile 1998). Along these same lines, cities seeking to fund initiatives in the triad could specify that such local investments be earmarked for this purpose. Another source of innovative local finance is the issue of tax-free "mini-bonds" or "mini-munis"—smaller-denominated securities (in amounts as small as $250) that allow local citizens to invest their savings in their municipalities while, at the same, diverting income from centralized taxation. Over the years, several local governments and authorities have issued such securities, including the cities of New Orleans, Philadelphia, East Brunswick, New Jersey, and Rochester, New York (Imbroscio 1997).

Most cities have a number of institutions that, by their nature, are already largely rooted or "anchored" in place, hence their designation as "anchor institutions." Prominent examples include universities and hospitals—so-called eds and meds—as well as churches, museums and other cultural facilities, public utilities, and community foundations (Cleveland Foundation 2008). These anchor institutions are huge economic engines in urban economies (see Bartik and Erickcek 2008; Harkavy and Zuckerman 1999), spending billions each year on business activities such as real estate development and procurement. Targeting these expenditures to the development of the triad initiatives could serve as a third source of funding. One such effort is under way in Cleveland, where the procurement dollars of its anchor institutions are being targeted to build a network of employee-owned cooperatives. The first, a commercial laundry, has lined up major contracts with large clinics and hospitals in Cleveland's "University Circle" area (Miller 2009; Bernstein 2009).

By far the largest and potentially most efficacious untapped pool of innovative finance to fund the triad initiatives is found in the trillions of dollars in state and local public employee pension funds. Discussing this option, the progressive economic journalist William Greider (2005) refers to this massive pool of investment capital as the "New Colossus." Several such pension funds already devote some small portion of their monies to so-called Economically Targeted Investments designed to stabilize the local economies where fund participants live and work. If this amount were increased from the current level of about 2 percent to 10 percent, and explicitly made available for community economic stabilization, an estimated $200 billion (or more) of additional investment revenue could flow to such efforts (Williamson, Imbroscio, and Alperovitz 2002). Although most pension funds are controlled on the state, rather than local, level, funds do operate on the local level in many larger cities and counties, such as New York, Los Angeles, San Francisco, and Chicago. Even funds operating on the state level, such as those in New York and California, have begun to target investments to urban revitalization, while over two dozen more states were found in a recent survey to be "potential" or "possible" investors in such urban revitalization efforts (Strauss et al. 2004; also see Greider 2005).

Looking to the Political

This chapter has highlighted how community economic stability can be enhanced in significant ways. Achieving this stability is necessary if the two central constructive goals of this book—the progressive reconstruction of urban regimes and the amelioration of urban problems—are to be realized. The particular means explored here to stabilize communities drew heavily upon the local economic alternative development strategies (or LEADS) discussed throughout the book. Although this chapter has demonstrated that such strategies have the *potential* to enhance community economic stability, that potential is heavily bound up with the crucial question of whether the LEADS approach itself can garner the necessary political support to be feasible. And, indeed, an even more basic political question is whether the LEADS are also normatively desirable (in the sense that they *should* be pursued).

Part IV

On Politics

The Desirable and the Feasible

7

THE FOLLY OF LIBERAL POLITICS

Any comprehensive analysis of the particular practices constituting a given politics revolves around the exploration of two overarching evaluative questions: Is such a politics normatively desirable? If so, can it be feasibly practiced? (cf. Elkin 1987; Banfield and Grodzins 1958).

Following this framework, a critique of the liberal politics underlying both conventional urban regime theory and liberal expansionism can be advanced. A key remaining question from this overall critique of liberal politics is whether the new politics underlying the local economic alternative development strategies (or LEADS) offers a politically superior alternative to both conventional urban regime theory and liberal expansionism.

The Politics of Liberal Expansionism

Liberal expansionist politics is neither feasible nor, perhaps surprisingly given its many fervent advocates and proselytizers, terribly desirable.

Some of the barriers hampering its political feasibility have already been identified in earlier chapters, and I shall return to these later in the analysis below. But the prior question for political analysis always involves the question of normative desirability—would we desire to practice such a politics in the first place (or live in society where it is practiced)? It is my contention that we would (or at least should) not.

Normative Undesirability of Liberal Expansionism

The defining feature of liberal expansionist politics is its deep contempt both for the established spatial pattern of human settlement in contemporary American metropolitan areas and the related established jurisdictional boundaries constitutive of such areas. In essence, liberal expansionism affords these established spatial patterns of settlement and jurisdictional boundaries very little political legitimacy and cultural authenticity. For liberal expansionism, such patterns of settlement and jurisdictional boundaries fundamentally lack such legitimacy because they are seen as the legacy of a plethora of historic and ongoing injustices, usually perpetrated by the state. Similarly, such patterns and boundaries also fundamentally lack authenticity because liberal expansionism holds that forces external to the individual—whether it be the wrongful or neglectful actions of state or private institutions, the prejudicial behavior of other individuals, or the cumulative psychological imprint of the historic injustices—largely drive decisions regarding residential choice. Seeing such patterns and boundaries as fundamentally politically illegitimate and culturally inauthentic, there is little reason to respect and conserve either them or the place-based communities to which they give rise. In fact, the moral imperative for liberal expansionists runs very much in the opposite direction: social justice demands their disruption, *with extreme prejudice* (see, especially, Fiss 2003).

This prescriptive stance came into view vividly in earlier chapters (see part 2). For liberal expansionism, established political boundaries, especially the legal separation between central cities and their affluent suburbs, enable the continuance of the dysfunctional *inside game,* in which central cities and community developers remain isolated from the resources necessary to ameliorate urban problems. Therefore, as we saw in chapter 3, liberal expansionists ardently advocate that such boundaries be supplanted via the creation of metropolitan-wide institutions that expand the scope of governance as much as possible to the regional level (see Dreier, Mollenkopf, and Swanstrom 2004; Orfield 2002; Rusk 1999). Likewise, established spatial patterns of human settlement perpetuate what is deemed by liberal expansionists to be the central evil of American society: racial segregation (see, especially, Massey and Denton 1993) and, more of late, segregation by economic status (see, especially, Dreier, Mollenkopf, and Swanstrom 2004). As we saw in chapter 4, liberal expansionists thus believe public policy must be "deliberate about greater spatial inclusion." This is to say, policy must mitigate this segregation by dispersing most of the urban poor away from their minority-dominated inner-city communities to white-dominated suburbs, while facilitating the resettlement of higher-income "in-movers" into central cities (Briggs 2008, 134; 2005c, 251).

In this light, many have seen the politics of liberal expansionism as normatively compelling, even heroic, as it evokes the courageous mid-twentieth century struggles against state-enforced Jim Crow segregation in the American South and the federal War on Poverty of the 1960s. And, indeed, the ongoing struggle to eradicate vestiges of racial discrimination and the fight against poverty and inequality remain central goals in the effort to solve urban problems. Yet, on closer scrutiny, the normative desirability of liberal expansionist politics appears highly dubious. In fact, irrespective of the historic origins of established patterns of settlement and political boundaries, there are nevertheless—*pace* liberal expansionism—good normative reasons to respect and conserve such patterns and boundaries and the place-based communities they engender (cf. Glaser, Parker, and Li 2003).

How could this possibly be, a skeptic might justifiably ask? Does not justice demand we right historic wrongs? The answer is that it very much does—and this book is dedicated to that cause via its two central constructive goals: progressively reconstructing urban regimes and effectively combating entrenched urban problems. Thus, the key normative problem with liberal expansionism involves not its ends but rather its means. Such means would create or perpetuate a variety of undesirable political practices that, taken together, paint a picture of a future political life that is normatively unappealing.

These undesirable political practices include (1) the disempowerment of the historically disenfranchised; (2) the vitiation of local control; (3) the demand for excessive spatial mobility; (4) a faulty conceptualization of the self; (5) an accommodation to corporate power; (6) a limited basis on which to create a strong, politically independent citizenry; (7) a tendency toward elitism; and (8) an overreliance on the centralized, bureaucratic state. Each is elaborated on below.

Empowerment   Consider first the established political boundaries in the typical American metropolis. From the perspective of liberal expansionism, such boundaries result from unjust laws established by state governments that are historically designed to facilitate racial and economic exclusion by making the annexation efforts of central cities more difficult and easing the incorporation of new suburban jurisdictions. These state-level laws, as well as actions and inactions of the federal government supporting them, fueled the creation of a multitude of separate political jurisdictions within the same metropolitan area, arbitrarily fragmenting regional governmental authority (Dreier, Mollenkopf, and Swanstrom 2004; Rusk 1993). Yet, while this view of history may indeed be correct, there have been unintended normative benefits from this political fragmentation. These benefits are largely unappreciated and undervalued by liberal expansionists.

One such normative benefit is the political empowerment of the historically disempowered. As discussed in chapter 3, the well-known case of the Louisville city-county consolidation (or merger, as it was known locally) demonstrated clearly how established political boundaries, especially the separation of central cities from suburbs, facilitated minority, especially African American, political empowerment (see Savitch and Vogel 2004). Liberal expansionism of course dismisses this idea, claiming that this separation actually awards minorities a *hollow prize,* given the difficult economic and fiscal conditions challenging many central cities (Kraus and Swanstrom 2001). But what this assessment misses is how an even deeper disempowerment of minorities results from expansionist political designs. As the progressive political scientist J. Phillip Thompson (2002, 447) points out, expansionist proposals are quite troubling because

> they have uniformly minimized the danger of political marginalization of minorities in broader political collectives. How is it possible to begin a multiracial coalition-building process when, from the outset, the terms of the

discussion exclude issues of urgent concern to racial minorities…If democratic, broad, and participatory coalitions are the goal, what gives policy intellectuals or, for that matter, the white middle class the democratic right to decide what issues should be left off the table?[1]

If the answer to these questions, Thompson concludes, "is that 'the white middle class is, after all, the majority,' then perhaps there is some wisdom in blacks wanting to hold onto their limited political autonomy in black-run cities, even if they are being financially starved" (Thompson 2002, 447–48).

Returning to the Louisville case, two prominent urbanists based in that city, Hank Savitch and Ronald Vogel (2004), demonstrate that the issue extends beyond minority disempowerment. It also involves a disempowerment of the central city as a whole acting as a separate political entity engaged in regional-level political struggles. Established political boundaries in Louisville before the merger allowed the central city to advocate effectively on behalf of its citizens for its interests in regional politics, involving matters such as fiscal equity and sprawl-promoting transportation policies. But once the central city's interests were neutralized by, to use Thompson's (2002, 448) apt phrase, the "broader political collective" created by the merger, Savitch and Vogel report that the "absolute necessity to defend the urban core" was greatly reduced as such changes "eviscerate[d]…[this core's] major advocates." This evisceration, in turn, took away the "institutional expression" of pro-city positions regarding transportation measures and other regional issues (Savitch and Vogel 2004, 776).[2]

More generally, by pursuing expansionism—whether it involves merging established political boundaries into a unified whole or dispersing poor minorities from the inner cities to largely white suburbs—what is lost politically is a genuine diversity of voices. In particular, distinctive perspectives in a broader regional-level political discourse, whether rooted in class, race, ethnic, or spatial concerns, are muted by the amalgamation or assimilation resulting from expansionist efforts. As a consequence, this discourse is impoverished, and the vibrancy and health of democratic politics is correspondingly enervated.

Similarly, the poor, inner-city *ghettos* (or, less pejoratively, *enclaves*) that are the scourge of liberal expansionism—and rightly so given the often abysmal social conditions plaguing such areas—nonetheless also can serve as the site for effective political mobilization and empowerment of the economically and socially disadvantaged (see Clawson 2003; Betancur and Gills 1993). The possibility of such mobilization is enhanced given the spatial proximity of many persons living under such conditions. It is relatedly enhanced because social problems—most notably poverty—are highly visible when more concentrated spatially rather than diffused over a wide area (Goldsmith and Blakely 1992).

Moreover, central cities often provide a strong political voice for the poor as compared with suburbs. As the political scientist Margaret Weir reminds us, central cities unlike suburbs have a "legacy of organizations dedicated to serving the poor," resulting from previous waves of European immigration and later innovations such as the War on Poverty efforts of the 1960s (2009, 7–8). The poor's "greater advantage in cities stems from the presence of…[these] organizations," as well as from those "public bureaucracies [such as public hospitals] for which service to the poor is a central mission." Central cities are also more likely to be home for organizing networks empowering the poor, such as the Association of Community Organizations for Reform Now (ACORN) and the Industrial Areas Foundation (IAF).

Liberal expansionism is, however, largely blind to these realities.[3] This is most likely because such realities suggest something anathema to liberal expansionists: that these established patterns of settlement have positive effects in a political sense that must be balanced against the social harms caused by concentrated poverty and metropolitan fragmentation. In a broader sense, this possibility for enhanced political mobilization also suggests the normative superiority of addressing urban problems where they currently exist rather than using expansionist measures to foster a spatially oriented solution.

Local Control   A related issue involves the principle of local control. Through the lens of liberal expansionism, local control holds little normative value[4] since, as noted above, this perspective affords the jurisdictions exercising such control little political legitimacy in the first place. Local control is especially noxious to liberal expansionists because, as exercised in the contemporary American metropolis, it is seen as greatly exacerbating racial and class segregation. Most notably, localized political power enables affluent jurisdictions to engage in a variety of exclusionary practices (mostly involving zoning and other land-use regulations) that limit the entry of the less affluent into these jurisdictions. This practice, in turn, supposedly condemns the less affluent to be segregated in poorer places elsewhere in the metropolitan region.

Once again, in the face of the widespread use of local regulatory power to promote exclusion, the politics of liberal expansionism—with its impulse to vitiate local control—appears normatively compelling. But, also once again, this perspective remains largely blind to the many positive normative attributes flowing from local control, upon which the negative impacts of exclusionary actions must be balanced. Such attributes, articulated through the ages by the likes of Aristotle, Alexis de Tocqueville, and Robert Dahl, are well known (see, for example, Elkin 1987; Shuman 2006).

Nonetheless, liberal expansionists do indeed have a point, and a good deal of evidence, regarding the exclusionary effects of local regulations, especially zoning. So, to see why a politics where such local control has been vitiated would not be normatively desirable, we need to envision a polity where the capacity for localities to control land use is extremely curtailed.

Such a vision has been most forcefully advocated by Brookings Institution economist Anthony Downs over many years (see especially 1993, 1994; also see 1973, 1981). Downs's "three decades of concern with this issue" (1993, 260–61) left him convinced that "the restrictive behavior of local governments, expressed through their regulations, is by far the most important single cause of high housing costs." According to Downs, the result is a dearth of affordable housing in many suburbs, blocking avenues of entry into them by the less well-off. To unblock these avenues, he advocates a strategy of comprehensive deregulation, where most—if not all—of these "restrictive behaviors" practiced by local governments would be relaxed or eliminated via the commands of higher-level governments.

Yet, as the venerable progressive scholar and activist Chester Hartman (1991, 1165) points out, where this perspective is normatively defective is in "its failure to assess regulations against the quite obvious benefits they also can and do bring." Many local regulations are "specifically designed to benefit lower-income housing consumers," Hartman explains, citing "condominium conversions controls, just-cause eviction statutes, rent controls, and inclusionary zoning laws" as examples. Other regulations, he adds, serve "important environmental, historic, health, and safety functions," noting that "even those land-use regulations that indisputably add to [housing] costs for the most part have a tangible social benefit."

A number of sophisticated urban political theorists go a step further.[5] Urban problems result not from cities having too much power but rather from having too little. This phenomenon is what Harvard law professor Gerald Frug (1999) calls *city powerlessness,* the inability to exercise the full range of powers over land use and other economic matters due to the historical erosion of cities' status in legal doctrine. Such powerlessness leaves cities hamstrung in their struggles against the demands of growth-machine-type interests and the controllers of capital more generally (see, especially, Garber 1990). Thus, what is required is an enhancement, rather than a curtailment, of local powers in order to achieve more normatively desirable political outcomes. These include distributive justice (Garber 1990); participatory democracy (Frug 1999); less corporate-dominated urban regimes (Elkin 2006); and a more egalitarian middle-class-oriented city (Frug and Barron 2008). Along these same lines, many of the local economic alternative development strategies (LEADS) developed in earlier chapters—such as the public ownership of land, the transformative potential of eminent domain, and an array of uses of the local public balance sheet—require a legal environment where city power to regulate land use is expansive and extensive.

Moreover, there is a strong case to be made that regulatory powers over land use ought to be even further extended to other locally controlled entities, such as community-based development organizations. Evidence for the normative attractiveness of this idea comes from the widely heralded experience of inner-city community revitalization carried out by the Dudley Street Neighborhood Initiative (DSNI) in Boston. Empowered two decades ago with eminent domain authority over vacant properties in the neighborhood, the DSNI was able to gain "effective control over local land uses" allowing the community-controlled organization to direct neighborhood development "in accordance with a development plan determined by the DSNI itself" (King 2004, 114). From these efforts, more than five hundred parcels of vacant land have been transformed into affordable housing (including the creation of a community land trust, which helps limit displacement from more recent gentrification), as well as community gardens, playgrounds, and other community facilities (Toups 2000; also see Medoff and Sklar 1994).

Thus, even in the difficult case of the regulation of land use, the vitiation of local control can be seen as far from an unadulterated good. Although most liberal expansionists ideally would hope to retain local land-use regulations with redistributive impacts (or that provide social benefits) and repeal exclusionary ones, the impulse to vitiate local control—which is so strong in liberal expansionism—would likely sound the death knell for both. This, in turn, closes off important avenues for the empowerment of cities against growth-machine interests and, conceivably, also weakens the ability of community-based organizations to fight abandonment or gentrification.

Spatial Mobility   The case of exclusionary local land-use regulations and their ostensible role in *blocking* the entry of some persons into certain jurisdictions raises yet another normatively troubling aspect of liberal expansionist politics: it demands an excessive degree of individual spatial mobility.

For liberal expansionism, the notion of spatial mobility being blocked (or at least impeded) extends well beyond the exclusionary impact of land-use regulations. In fact, such a notion is a central premise behind much of the liberal expansionist view of the contemporary American metropolis. This perspective sees a myriad of instances of blocked or impeded individual mobility resulting primarily from deleterious actions or neglectful inactions of the state. Many minorities are thus seen as *trapped* in segregated neighborhoods, unable to move to white-dominated ones because of, for example, the state's failure to adopt and/or enforce strict fair housing and lending laws (see Squires and Kubrin 2005; Massey and Denton 1993).[6] The urban poor are seen as similarly trapped in inner cities for a plethora of reasons, including the availability of publicly assisted housing and social services there rather than in suburbs (Orfield 2002; Kasarda 1992). And, more blue-collar, working-class people are seen as trapped in declining older suburbs because exclusionary zoning practices prevent them from moving into more affluent areas, even though they may be employed there (Dreier, Mollenkopf, and Swanstrom 2004).

Even elements of the middle class are seen by liberal expansionism as suffering impeded mobility under current conditions. Middle-class families with children, for example, are seen as trapped in suburban jurisdictions because concerns about public schools and safety prevent them from moving to central cities (see Dreier, Mollenkopf, and Swanstrom 2004). Others of middle-class status seeking a racially or ethnically diverse residential setting are seen as trapped instead in exclusively white (or black) areas because of the lack of public support for integrated neighborhoods (see Smith 1993; Ellen 2000). And those relatively affluent homebuyers with preferences for higher residential density are seen as trapped in low-density areas because building restrictions and other policies overly encourage sprawled development (see Levine 2006).

This list could continue, but the point is clear: in the liberal expansionist view of the world, the chief normative deficiency of the contemporary American metropolis, and the reason urban problems such as economic and racial segregation are so acute, is that the actions or inactions of the state limit individual spatial mobility. Such mobility would, in this view, otherwise be widespread if it were not, *unnaturally,* blocked. And, for liberal expansionists, as with all philosophical liberals, such blockage is a supreme iniquity. For liberalism, as the eminent political theorist Michael Walzer (1990, 12) makes clear, is most basically the "theoretical endorsement" of movement, with individual mobility representing the very "enactment of liberty" and "pursuit of... happiness" itself.

The problem with this aspect of liberal expansionist politics is not so much that it empirically misdiagnoses the situation. It clearly does that—at least to a degree. For example, it was pointed out in chapter 4 that, to quote the astute work of housing policy expert Edward Goetz (2003, 241), the widely held assumption that most poor families "*want* to move to outlying areas" is "questionable." Moreover, while housing discrimination based on race or ethnicity is still prevalent, many blacks are reluctant to move to largely white neighborhoods even if they could (Charles 2005; Clark 2009). Likewise, in contrast to liberal expansionism's strong emphasis on residential diversity, University of Chicago political theorist Iris Young (2000, 216) compellingly argued that "people often want to cluster in affinity groups defined by ethnicity, religion, language, sexual orientation, or lifestyle." And, moreover, sprawl and suburban living have proven to be quite popular among its denizens, as political scientist Thad Williamson's (forthcoming, 167 MS) rigorous empirical analysis emphatically demonstrates. "Americans, taken collectively," Williamson notes, "have a *strong* preference for suburban communities in which...the key constituents of sprawl are present" (emphasis added).

Yet, from the perspective of normative desirability, the real problem for liberal expansionism is that this politics, if practiced, spawns an unattractive version of political and social life. This unattractiveness results because the instrument utilized to solve urban problems is massive residential upheaval, as many people would need to be shuffled about through regional space until the desired racial and economic mix in each metropolitan jurisdiction, or neighborhood, was achieved. Clearly, any politics, if it is to be normatively desirable, must allow free movement for those wishing to change residences (Imbroscio 2004a). But liberal expansionism is predicated on something much more—it demands an excessive degree of geographic mobility, creating in turn a degree of residential instability in the metropolitan population base that is incompatible with the flourishing of a vibrant and healthy democratic polity.

There is a plethora of work in democratic theory documenting the link between the hypermobility of citizens and the corrosion of political life. In a notable example, political theorist Richard Dagger (1997, 162) points out that the "unsettling effects" of "widespread mobility" on the nature of citizenship are readily manifest. What is most important, he notes,

> is the tendency of residential mobility to loosen the ties that bind individuals into a community. Citizenship grows out of attachment to place and its people—out of a sense of community—that only forms over time. Those who move about frequently are not likely to acquire this attachment. Even those who seem rooted to a place are affected, for they are likely to feel abandoned as the faces about them become less familiar and their neighborhoods less neighborly.

Along similar lines, the political theorist Stephen Elkin (1987, 148–49) explains how the key to a healthy democratic polity is a certain level of public-spiritedness, where political choices among citizens and leaders become an exercise in deliberative "reason-giving." Reason-giving involves *justification,* rather than simply an aggregation of "wants and interests," which in turn involves "elicit[ing] arguments about what is beneficial to us as a political community." But "to give reasons requires that there be *memory,*" as citizens and leaders "cannot be disembodied reasoners coming from nowhere and without history" because "not everything can be debated in the present" and the citizenry must have a sense of "what has been tried and has failed and what is likely to be deeply disagreeable." And such memory requires, not surprisingly, a substantial *"continuity* among citizens," something that Elkin believes is already deficient given the "present rates of movement both into and out of the city." (Elkin 1987, 183; emphasis added). This problem is thus likely to be especially acute if liberal expansionism were put into actual practice.[7]

Conception of the Self   To understand another undesirable feature of liberal expansionism's politics, recall that this perspective embraces hypermobility because it sees the state's arbitrary or unnatural impeding of such mobility as the chief normative deficiency of the contemporary American metropolis. Yet, by embracing this understanding of urban problems, liberal expansionists are, most likely unwittingly, also embracing the same faulty conception of the self that vexes philosophical liberalism more generally.

To see the state as arbitrarily or unnaturally blocking (or impeding) individual mobility that would otherwise occur is to claim that the state is in essence not remaining *neutral* with respect to the *good* (or the *good life*); or otherwise put, it is to see the state as arbitrarily imposing a set of values on its citizens rather than letting them freely choose their own ends. But as numerous communitarian and civic republican theorists have pointed out, the possibility of this ideal of liberal neutrality requires that each person's self be conceived as *unencumbered* by any social roles involving obligations or relationships not freely chosen (see, for example, Sandel 1982, 1996). This requirement arises because state neutrality finds its justification in the idea that people are potentially choosing freely, something impossible unless individuals are devoid of such social roles—that is, unless the self exists in an unencumbered form. Social selves are of course not unencumbered, but rather always *situated,* meaning that they are constituted by obligations or relationships existing prior to choice.

Thus, the aspiration for neutrality in liberal politics is misguided. Likewise, liberal expansionism's aspiration to apply this neutrality principle to the contemporary American metropolis is also misguided. Such an aspiration assumes, as noted above, that we see selves as unencumbered, essentially untethered by their social roles and, if not for the pernicious actions of the state, able to exercise free choice with respect to the *good life* as expressed by their spatial mobility. Although it is clearly the case that spatial choice in the contemporary American metropolis is indeed to a degree impeded, liberal expansionism's mistake is to conceive of such a condition as the American metropolis's *chief* normative deficiency. For, to do so, is to build a politics around a conception of self that is ontologically flawed.

Corporate Power   Another undesirable feature of liberal expansionism's politics involves its tepid reaction to the immense political power wielded by large business corporations. In this regard, what political theorists and progressive activists Joshua Cohen and Joel Rogers (1996, 21) attribute to liberal politics in general applies to liberal expansionist politics in particular: "it is deeply accommodating to corporate power—preferring to mop up after its damage is done to controlling it in the first place" (also see Noble 2004). The problematic nature of this aspect of liberal expansionist politics is revealed in an insight quoted in relation to the public balance sheet: "A philosophy of government which says that the function of government is simply to pick up the dirty linen of private enterprise without affecting incentives to dirty the linen would bankrupt government and corrupt the political process."[8] And, for liberal expansionists, the mopping up or picking up of the dirty linen takes shape most prominently in the form of the expansion of the national-level welfare and regulatory state—something that does little to challenge corporate power save to extract some social surplus for public coffers and curb corporations' more egregious excesses.

While, as Cohen and Rogers (1996, 21) point out, there was a period in America where "reasonable progress on egalitarian ideals could be reached without directly contesting corporate power"—roughly during American capitalism's so-called *golden age* from the late 1940s to the late 1970s— "that world is now gone" (*long* gone, we might now add; cf. Greider 2009). Henceforth the United States has witnessed an explosion in economic inequality to levels that political economist and social theorist Gar Alperovitz (2004) characterizes—with only slight hyperbole—as *medieval,*[9] with all of the concomitant dark implications for democracy. While sophisticated liberal expansionists such as Dreier, Mollenkopf, and Swanstrom (2004) do see the need to countervail corporate power via enhanced labor power, the means to this end is the expansion of conventional unionization by reforming labor law rather than altering the existing division of labor between market and state (as set out in part 1).[10] This conventional path greatly limits the political potential for progressive systemic change because such

change, as Alperovitz (2005, 5) points out, "involves, above all, questions
of how property is owned and controlled—the locus of real power in most
systems." And this locus remains untouched by the political demands of
the mainstream American labor movement.

Citizenship   The key role played by an expanded national welfare and
regulatory state for liberal expansionist politics reminds us of the kinship
between that politics and European-style social democracy (see Dreier,
Mollenkopf, and Swanstrom 2004; Bratt 2006b). Liberal expansionism
is, in fact, simply a spatially oriented (urban-focused) application of what
Elkin (2006, 266) appropriately calls social democracy's "close [American]
first cousin"—New Deal/Great Society liberalism. Although there are serious questions about its ongoing fiscal sustainability in the face of economic
globalization (see Pierson 2001), in the European context this politics has
historically produced reduced levels of inequality and poverty, something
clearly normatively attractive. On the other hand, as Elkin (2006, 266)
notes, social democracy, like its American first cousin, "is deeply centralist
in its orientation," weakening the local control that, as pointed out above,
is crucial for a healthy democracy (also see Greider 2009). Even in light of
this (and other related) defects, Elkin (2006, 278) concedes that "social democracies may be very attractive...regimes." Their chief problem from a
normative perspective, then, is a general incongruence with American political aspirations inherited from its founders to be a *commercial republic,*
built around limited centralized government, individual liberty, and republican ideals (also see Elkin 1987). Such "foreign imports," he concludes,
"have little hold on our affections," and, despite normative attractiveness
in the abstract, "may not increase the well-being" of the American polity
(Elkin 2006, 267 and 278).

In fact, the normative attractiveness of social democratic-type politics,
even in the abstract, can be questioned. Consider that at the very heart of
republican ideals lies a concern for popularly controlled government animated by the considerations and deeds of a free and independent citizenry
(Pettit 1997). The key to this independence historically was widespread
property ownership, as best represented by the Jeffersonian notion of the
yeoman farmer or small business owner of nineteenth-century America
(see Dahl 1985). Only under such conditions, Thomas Jefferson himself
wrote, could citizens "safely and advantageously reserve to themselves

a wholesome control over their public affairs." In contrast, "dependence," according to Jefferson, "begets subservience and venality, suffocates the germ of virtue."[11] In this regard, such property ownership and self-employment facilitated that necessary citizen independence because it served as a bulwark against the state and other large, powerful institutions. In the now-familiar story, the industrialization of the late nineteenth and early twentieth centuries wiped away these conditions, to the point where nine out of ten people in America today are employees, creating what historian and social theorist Michael Lind (2007, 149) calls, fittingly, the "proletarianization" of American society. In essence, Lind adds, the "American ideal of the largely self-sufficient citizen-producer has been replaced by the citizen-consumer."

The politics of liberal expansionism, with its social-democratic orientations, embraces this proletarianization. Social democrats, Lind (2007, 150) explains, "are willing to jettison the older republican ideal of self-reliant citizens in favor of the ideal of the middle class worker-consumer who relies on generous government welfare programs." In the latter view, what is most important is societal affluence (so that wages will be higher) and a large and extensive welfare state (so that collective social security can be guaranteed). Although such a system does come with some normative appeal, from the perspective of republican politics, wage earners and social welfare-receivers remain dependent on their (often large corporate) employers and the (often overly bureaucratic and centralized) state. And this remains the case no matter how middle class their income and consumption levels might be. Hence, liberal expansionism, by focusing on income and consumption rather than assets and ownership, offers no mechanism to restore the institutional basis necessary for an independent citizenry. The politics it breeds thus fails to satisfy America's venerable republican aspirations.[12]

Elitism   Broadening out this critique yields another normatively undesirable feature of liberal expansionist politics: its strong tendencies toward elitism. As Cohen and Rogers (1996, 20–1) explain:

> While liberals often have reasonable views about political outcomes (some equality, some decent living standards, some personal freedom), they are elitists as to means. They don't believe that people of ordinary ability

and intelligence are capable of running the society themselves. And so to achieve their ends they typically favor the kinder and gentler administration of people—usually through the state—to popular organization. (also see Greider 2009)

Along these lines, practically nothing in the vast panoply of liberal expansionist institutional and policy prescriptions involves direct democratic or community control of decision making in an *empowered participatory* (Fung and Wright 2003) or *strong democratic* (Barber 1984) fashion. Most notable for our purposes is that liberal expansionists' focus on state, especially welfare state, programs to solve urban problems leaves them "barely [able to] contemplate what a more popular administration of the economy might look like" (Cohen and Rogers 1996, 21).[13] And elitism flows from liberal expansionism's expansionist impulse as well as its liberalism. Its incredulousness about the normative value of local control leaves it favoring larger political jurisdictions that, as we saw in the case of the Louisville merger, tend to facilitate the augmentation of elite political power.

State-Centrism   Finally, liberal expansionism's heavy reliance on the state, especially the centralized state apparatus, creates its own set of normative problems. Many such problems have been astutely identified by Thompson (1998) in his critique of what he calls *liberal universalism,* a broader conception than liberal expansionism but closely related to it. For example, as Thompson (1998, 202) points out, "entrusting"—as both liberal expansionism and liberal universalism do—the "moral or physical integration [of persons] to...large bureaucracies seriously threatens the viability of local democracy and social stability—especially with respect to African-Americans, the targets of moral and physical integration." We saw this phenomenon most vividly in chapter 4. Liberal expansionists advocate using the federal housing bureaucracy to integrate the urban poor via dispersal efforts into physical areas (often white-dominated suburbs) where middle-class moral norms predominate.

Moreover, reflecting on the historical experience in the 1950s, 1960s, and 1970s with urban renewal "slum clearance" and "intrusive welfare agencies," Thompson (1998, 202) additionally warns that "an overly empowered state can wreak havoc on the social networks and self-esteem of poor African-Americans." He adds that "many argue that the state continues to play such a role," and indeed we again saw ample evidence for this argument in chapter 4. Such evidence included, for example, liberal expansionists' strong advocacy and defense of the dispersal-oriented HOPE VI program (aptly labeled by a leading housing expert as the "new slum clearance"[14]), and their advocacy of a variety of repressive measures suggestive of a *therapeutic state* (Polsky 1991) designed primarily to fuel the dispersal of poor African Americans from inner cities. "It is difficult to imagine," Thompson (1998, 202–3) says in summary, "state-centered strategies producing democratic outcomes; they are likely to further weaken local democracy and undermine personal autonomy for the very people they are supposed to help" (cf. Greider 2009).

Political Infeasibility of Liberal Expansionism

Turning to the question of political feasibility, recall that much analysis of liberal expansionism's difficulties on this criterion was offered in chapter 3. To recapitulate, the basic, nagging problem for liberal expansionist politics is the formidable character of what was identified as Type II constraints on that feasibility. In essence, expansionist designs, while potentially capturing more resources for state-directed redistributive efforts, also enlarge the political landscape in more politically conservative directions. This change, in turn, undermines the political will to engage in such redistribution.

Many other scholars have produced related analyses with consistent findings. For example, returning to Thompson's critique of state-centered strategies (of which liberal expansionism is one), we find that such strategies are burdened with feasibility problems as well as normative ones: "The political support for...[them] must come from the [largely suburban] white middle class, who," as Thompson (1998, 201) effectively argues, "are not interested in the special problems of poor African-Americans." Likewise, political theorist Jeff Spinner-Halev (forthcoming), with equal effectiveness, argues that, although liberal expansionists blame—rightly to a degree—state actions in the postwar period (especially those of the federal government) for creating many of the worst urban problems in the first place, these state actions were to a large degree done in response to the popular will exercised by the majority of the nation. Therefore, there is little reason to expect that these same democratic processes will now yield political support for the substantial reorientation in federal priorities required by liberal expansionism.

Alperovitz adds a broader but also wholly consistent analysis of the political infeasibility of liberal expansionist-type approaches. Specifically, he points out—bluntly but perceptively—that "there is very little doubt about what has happened to undermine liberal redistributive strategies." Such strategies, Alperovitz (2005, 14–15) explains, are contingent on strong labor unions, but in the United States unions have been in "radical decline" for decades. This "downward trend...[is] all but certain to continue" as "responsible estimates suggest union membership...in the private sector may sink below 5 percent by 2020."[15] He notes in addition that economic globalization also plays a role, increasing "the already enormous power of the large corporation economically and politically," while fueling world-wide competition for investment that pressures national governments to reduce business tax rates "thereby...implicitly reduc[ing]...[their] capacity...to spend on redistributive social programs." Finally, echoing Thompson and drawing on another insightful analysis (Edsall and Edsall 1991), Alperovitz (2005, 16) points to the strong role played by racial conflict in the United States. Such conflict broke the New Deal coalition in the 1970s and 1980s, and left the "the largely white suburban middle class...no longer willing to pay for a progressive political agenda it believes will mainly benefit the black and Hispanic poor."

The Politics of Urban Regime Theory

Because conventional urban regime theory hitherto has been largely an explanatory rather than a prescriptive theory, the politics underlying it are less well developed than the politics of liberal expansionism. Therefore, there is less of a basis upon which to build a political critique of it, something reflected in the more limited nature of the discussion below. Nonetheless, within some of the empirical analyses proffered by key regime theorists, we do find attempts at political prescription, and even the more purely explanatory aspects of urban regime theory are strongly suggestive of how its associated politics might be practiced.

Normative Undesirability of Regime Theory

The politics of urban regime theory avoids many of the shortcomings of liberal expansionist politics. Regime theory has focused almost exclusively on governance within the political bounds of central cities, while devoting little prescriptive attention to disrupting established patterns of urban settlement. In essence, then, urban regime theory does not advance a politics of expansionism, and thus avoids many of its attendant normative difficulties.

Nonetheless, conventional urban regime theory is still steeped in the same deep philosophical liberalism as liberal expansionism. As a result, its politics shares many of the normatively problematic features of liberal expansionism. Among these features three stand out.

First, and most crucial, urban regime theory clearly remains accommodating to corporate power. As chapter 1 made clear, the liberalism at its theoretic core leads regime theory to endorse and embrace a strict distinction between matters deemed public and those deemed private. Holding to this distinction, regime theory conceptualizes the division of labor between the state and the market as largely static, taking "as a given" an urban economy dominated by private corporations (Stone 1991, 294). The political possibilities for contesting and moderating corporate power by reconstructing this division are left unconsidered.

Second, like liberal expansionist politics, the politics of urban regime theory exhibits strong elitist tendencies. Nearly all of the analytic focus of conventional versions of the theory is on elites and their relations to one another, especially in the coalition building process (see Stoker 1995; Horan 2002). As political scientist Cynthia Horan (2002, 27) correctly notes, the "inequalities generated by broader relations—of the economy, state, and race—[that] structure elite interactions" are only weakly theorized. This phenomenon is especially the case in regard to economic relations, which is severely neglected by conventional urban regime theory (see chapter 2). While the leading regime theorist, Clarence Stone (1993), holds out the possibility of building *lower-class opportunity expansion regimes* animated by mass mobilization (his chief normative aspiration), in the final analysis he affords such nonelite oriented regimes little hope of coming into being (Davies 2002; Mossberger 2009). Subsequently, they have been given only scant systematic attention in urban regime analysis. In the end, then, with the construction of mass-based, progressive regimes off the table, the prescriptive politics of conventional urban regime theory simply seeks, in the best case scenario, to convince business-sector elites and elites running large nonprofits to devote an increasing share of resources to support improvements to urban education systems and related social services (see Imbroscio 2004c and chapter 1).

A third normatively problematic feature of this politics goes directly to these prescriptive elements. As pointed out in chapters 1 and 2, urban regime theory focuses its attention regarding political reform on collective consumption rather than on economic production, seeking to recast policies within the social welfare arena rather than within the realm of economic development (also see Imbroscio 1998 and 2004c). Like liberal expansionism, then, the politics of conventional urban regime theory with its collective consumption focus does little to create the conditions likely to advance the republican ideal of an engaged and self-reliant citizenship.

Within the social welfare arena a chief focus of some key regime theorists, notably Clarence Stone and his several collaborators, has been public education systems (see, for example, Stone et al. 2001; Stone, Orr, and Worgs 2006). Although an improvement in the general level of formal education undoubtedly can contribute to a degree to the advancement of republican ideals, this feature of urban regime theory's politics raises a larger concern for the overall health and vibrancy of a democratic polity. Namely, a politics that sees formal education as the chief means to redress economic and social ills is a politics almost certainly rooted in inegalitarianism and hierarchy. This is because it is exceedingly unlikely that any more than a relatively few can advance economically by becoming more educated (see, for example, Lafer 2002; Davies 2004; Fitzgerald 1993), a trend that is accelerating in the present era.[16] In this regard, what urban regime theory's focus on formal education reveals more precisely is philosophical liberalism's instrumental privileging of individual *mobility*—in this case *social* rather than geographic or spatial (Lasch 1991).[17] Inspired by the writings of Kentucky-based philosopher and poet Wendell Berry, the late social theorist Christopher Lasch (1995, 77) cogently and eloquently noted that

> high rates of [social] mobility are by no means inconsistent with a system of stratification that concentrates power and privilege in a ruling elite. Indeed, the circulation of elites strengthens the principle of hierarchy, furnishing elites with fresh talent and legitimating their ascendancy as a function of merit rather than birth.

What is more important for a healthy democracy than high rates of social mobility, Lasch (1995) pointed out, is the broad-based instillation of citizen competency, a goal to which formal education of course can partially help realize. But when formal education is seen as the primary means for improving the poor social and economic conditions of a community (rather than the more systemic development efforts discussed in previous chapters), the primary result is to allow select individuals to escape such conditions rather than to enable a more generalized uplift of the broader community.[18]

Political Infeasibility of Regime Theory

The politics of conventional urban regime theory, at least considered pre-scriptively, is also politically infeasible. The heart of that politics revolves around the reform of urban education systems (see Stone et al. 2001). But since conventional urban regime theory eschews any effort to reconstitute urban governance in progressive directions (see chapter 1 and Imbroscio 2004c), these reform efforts take place within the context of traditional urban regime forms. In such regimes, the corporate business sector holds the key to "get[ting] things done" (Stone 1989, 227) because it maintains control over the necessary resources. Therefore, the process of instituting significant education reform requires garnering strong corporate business support for the pro-education liberal agenda (i.e., corporate liberalism).

Yet, such support is likely to be marginal, at best, given the growth-oriented political priorities of corporate business elites (Logan and Molotch 1987). Although urban regime theory hopes to overcome this political roadblock by appealing to the corporate business sector's clear need for well-trained workers, such a hope is likely to flounder as the number of skilled workers actually required is relatively small vis-à-vis the large pool of workers within most metropolitan labor markets (Imbroscio 1998; also see Lafer 2002; Fitzgerald 1993). Thus it would appear that the corporate liberalism of urban regime theory is, like liberal expansionism, liable to be politically infeasible.

8

The Possibilities of an
Alternative Politics

Taken together, the preceding chapters have exposed the misguided nature of the two orthodoxies that have taken hold within the academic study of urban America—conventional urban regime theory's understanding of the nature of urban governance and liberal expansionism's understanding of the policies to address urban problems. But I began by stating that the ultimate goal of advancing this argument is eminently practical: The key failings of these orthodoxies lie not only with their deleterious impact on academic study. Instead, it is that they are detrimental to real world political practice. In particular, while the state of urban governance in America is dismal and the human suffering from its urban problems severe, neither conventional urban regime theory nor liberal expansionism offer a compelling prescriptive guide for bringing about a significant transformation in these conditions.

Along similar lines, the progressive political theorists and activists Joshua Cohen and Joel Rogers (1996, 20)—reflecting on the condition of America as a whole—perceptively and inspirationally write that

people sharing a commitment to democratic values need to get more serious about a *constructive* political project, not just about protesting or correcting the exercise of power at the margins. Left to its own devices, this
society is headed toward truly ruinous division, inequality, and squalor
for much of the population. To prevent that, an alternative future needs to
be described, its values declared, sides taken in arguments for its advance.
(emphasis added)

And, most crucially, they add: "All this will require a sharp break with
conventional liberal politics."

In my reconsideration of urban America, I, too, see the need for such a
sharp break with conventional liberal politics—specifically its manifestation in the forms of urban regime theory and liberal expansionism. The
particular substance of the break I call for is embodied by the array of local
economic alternative development strategies (LEADS) discussed throughout much of the book. These LEADS, I have claimed, offer the potential to bring about a transformation in the state of the urban condition in
America by facilitating the progressive reconstruction of urban regimes
and providing a superior means for addressing urban problems.

To fully comprehend the nature of this potential, as well as its concomitant implications, we need to evaluate the particular practices constituting
the politics of the LEADS. Using the two overarching questions introduced in the last chapter, we must first ask: Are these political practices
normatively *desirable*—which is to say, would we wish to practice such politics if we could? Otherwise put, would we wish to live in a society where
it is practiced? And, if so, then secondly, can such a politics be *feasibly* practiced in ways that bring about the necessary transformations in the state of
the urban condition? More directly framed, the second question we must
ask is, Could the LEADS be the vehicle through which the two central
constructive goals of this project—progressive urban regime reconstruction and the amelioration of urban problems—actually can be realized in
contemporary American cities?

Engaging and wrestling with these questions requires recognizing the
difficulties involved with answering them fully and definitively. Given
their inherent complexity, and in many cases the lack of well-developed
experiences with the (now only nascent) LEADS approach, such answers
must perforce be partial and tentative.

The Essence of the Local Economic Alternative Development Strategies

As a prelude to this exercise, it is first useful to distill the essence of the LEADS approach. Such a distillation is especially salutary given that the approach's various elements have thus far been presented in multiple forms.

Significant Features

The LEADS can best be understood through an identification and explication of their five most significant features: a focus on restructuring the state-market division, an attentiveness to place-community, decentralization in scale, the orientation toward commercialist (or productionist) values, and the promotion of social and economic equity.

Restructuring Focus   The first significant feature of the LEADS is that they often involve a restructuring of the division of labor between the state and the market. Rather than accept philosophical liberalism's strict *public-private distinction*—where wealth creation and economic development functions are overwhelmingly dominated by the traditional, for-profit private sector—many of the key elements of the LEADS are built upon the notion that such functions can be carried out by entities of a different sort. In this sense, they transcend both the market and the state.[1] These entities are collectivist in orientation and often nonprofit or publicly owned in institutional form; prominent examples include community-based or municipal enterprises, as well as enterprises that are employee or cooperatively owned.

Place-Community Attentiveness   Another significant feature of the LEADS is their strong attentiveness to established place-based communities—that is, groupings of persons organized around, and rooted in, spatial relations—manifest on either the neighborhood or municipal-wide scale. What is valued most heavily is the health and vibrancy of these *places*—that is, their community development. Of particular concern is whether or not their local economies possess the necessary stability. This stabilization of places thus becomes the vehicle to enhance individual well-being, which contrasts with the liberal perspective that gives direct individual utility priority without regard to where people happen to live. And, with the strong emphasis on place, the established boundaries among communities (whether explicitly political or more of a cultural nature) and the related patterns of settlement (especially the human relationships growing from these patterns) are accorded great respect and deemed worthy of conservation.

Decentralized Scale   The LEADS also are strongly localist in spirit and form. None are built upon a weighty intervention of centralized state structures or the garnering of substantial resources from larger-order institutions. Many, in fact, grow from the grassroots efforts of urban residents to redevelop their communities on a neighborhood level. More generally, the LEADS look mostly inward, to the local economy and its untapped resources and possible hidden economic opportunities. Although the power of the state to facilitate economic development plays a substantial role—employing local public balance sheets, for example—this state power is largely exercised on a decentralized level by the *local* state. At this highly localized scale, the character of such power can morph from the modern liberal state's traditional bureaucratic form into something more akin to the institutions of civil society.[2]

Commercial Orientation   The orientation of the LEADS is decidedly commercial. They are, above all, efforts to facilitate local economic development—job and wealth creation and a general level of commercial vibrancy within the local economy. This commercialism is, however, tempered: the community-oriented and collectivist nature of many of the LEADS builds in recognition that, in contrast to philosophical liberalism, only part of human well-being (or utility) can be satisfied via material means.[3] In addition, the focus of LEADS development efforts is on promoting *entrepreneurial* enterprise, organized on a small or medium scale, rather than enterprise in its large and bureaucratic corporate form.

Equity Emphasis   Finally, the LEADS place a strong emphasis on promoting economic and social equity, specifically the amelioration of entrenched urban poverty and inequality and the myriad social problems arising from such conditions. Such equity promotion revolves around three key axes. First, much of the equity promoted is of a spatial nature. In an effort to mitigate uneven development, many of the LEADS—especially those rooted in the community economics movement—focus on the revitalization of the city's more disinvested neighborhoods. A second key axis is the concern—highlighted by the local public balance sheet—for a more equitable sharing of costs and benefits in the development process among the public and private sectors. The goal here is to better balance these costs and benefits, so as to ensure the broader public or community interest is well served by development efforts, rather than simply a narrow set of private interests. A third axis is the effort to broaden ownership via collectivist economic institutions, so that asset building and wealth accumulation becomes possible for the economically disadvantaged.

Is It Desirable?

The politics of the LEADS, as we shall see, is not beset by the many normative deficiencies afflicting the liberal politics of conventional urban regime theory and liberal expansionism. LEADS politics keeps an emphasis on promoting equity but does not also carry with it the normatively problematic political characteristics of urban regime theory and liberal expansionism. But, as we shall also see, the politics of the LEADS comes with its *own* set of potential normative deficiencies—deficiencies that must be taken into account when evaluating its overall desirability.

Transcending Liberalism's Normative Deficiencies

Examining more closely the five significant features of the LEADS reveals an understanding of how their politics transcends the normative deficiencies of the liberal politics of conventional urban regime theory and liberal expansionism. Once again, these five significant features are: a restructuring focus, place-community attentiveness, decentralized scale, commercial orientation, and an equity emphasis.

Restructuring Focus   Whereas both liberal expansionism and urban regime theory are deeply accommodating to corporate power, the focus of the LEADS on restructuring the division of labor between state and market presents a significant challenge to such power. Most notably, such restructurings make possible the building of alternative urban regimes—such as community-based regimes, petty-bourgeois regimes, and local-statist regimes. These regime types would be free of excessive corporate domination, as their governing coalitions are not built upon an alliance between those interests and local public officials.

Place-Community Attentiveness   By being attentive to place communities, the politics of the LEADS does not fuel the hyperspatial mobility of individuals so central to liberalism, with its attendant conception of the self as unencumbered. Instead of shuffling significant numbers of people through regional space, the strong emphasis of the efforts of the LEADS to ameliorate urban problems is on the development of communities as presently constituted by established patterns of settlement. Moreover, this place-community attentiveness deemphasizes the hyper social mobility of individuals; the key goal, instead, is the uplift of the broader place community rather than a few select individuals within it. Additionally, the impulse to conserve *places* leaves established political boundaries and related patterns of settlement intact, thus avoiding the disempowerment of minority (and other traditionally disadvantaged) interests that stems from expansionist political designs or expansionist assimilation efforts.

Decentralized Scale   The decentralized scale most straightforwardly allows the LEADS to avoid the strong propensity in liberal expansionist politics to vitiate local control. Politically, the LEADS look inward rather than outward in their quest to solve urban problems. In addition, their small-scale orientation militates against the elite political control that bigness can foster, such as in the case of liberal expansionism's larger-order political designs. Indeed, many elements of the LEADS involve grassroots, community-based efforts undertaken on a neighborhood level. Thus, a key impulse in LEADS politics is to enhance the direct community control over decision making, often animated by significant citizen participation. Finally, the decentralized scale of the LEADS mitigates the worst aspects of state-driven actions. Because such actions are pursued largely by the state operating on a localized level, they tend to be less bureaucratic in nature and subject to a greater degree of democratic control by the local citizenry.

Commercial Orientation   The commercial orientation of the LEADS most clearly facilitates the citizen independence so important to the classic republican ideal of popular government controlled by a free and self-reliant people. Both liberal expansionism and urban regime theory, in contrast, tend to breed citizen dependence. They rely heavily on enhanced citizen consumption via an expanded welfare state and an increase in wage levels within the corporate-controlled economy. The politics of the LEADS mitigates such dependence, however, because it is strongly *productionist* in nature, with a key focus on direct citizen ownership and control of productive assets. Whether as independent producers operating small, locally rooted entrepreneurial businesses, or as partial owners of a collectively controlled enterprise (as a worker, community member, citizen of a municipality, or a cooperative shareholder), such ownership and control of productive assets affords the citizenry a higher degree of independence from large bureaucratic institutions in both the public and private sectors. This independence, in turn, breeds a politics where republican ideals and virtues can flourish, allowing citizens to—in the words of Thomas Jefferson—"safely and advantageously reserve to themselves a wholesome control over public affairs."[4]

Equity Emphasis   Although the politics of both liberal expansionism and urban regime theory are undoubtedly committed to the normative goal of economic and social equity, there are clear limits to this commitment. The root of these limits lies partly in the elitism infiltrating both of these approaches, such as the hierarchy and inegalitarianism bred by urban regime theory's focus on formal education as the principal means to redress economic and social ills. More broadly, the economic equality desired in all liberal politics is the equality of economic *opportunity*—essentially the equal right to become unequal.[5] Such limits also result from the failure of this politics to mount any serious challenge to corporate power, as such a challenge is both means and end to any serious effort to enhance social and economic equity. In contrast, the politics of the LEADS attack inequities more forthrightly and profoundly. This politics seeks a restructuring of the state-market division to reduce the current corporate domination of urban politics, while avoiding elitism by employing strategies that seek the collective betterment of *whole* communities.

Normative Challenges to the Local Economic Alternative Development Strategies

Although the politics of the LEADS appears to provide many useful correctives to the normative deficiencies in the politics of liberal expansionism and urban regime theory, it faces its *own* normative challenges. Because these challenges involve deep and complex issues, both within the realm of political philosophy and empirical social science, they cannot be fully assessed here. Nonetheless, it is possible to get a general flavor for the kinds of normative challenges confronting the LEADS, as well as whether such challenges might be overcome.

Restructuring Focus   The central normative challenge confronting the restructuring of the state-market division concerns the degree to which the economic institutions involved in these efforts can generate and sustain a sufficient level of economic activity and jobs for a local community. This challenge looms large in political terms because a generalized penury saps the health of any democratic polity. Persons struggling mightily with multiple and deep economic woes are less likely to be public-spirited citizens (see Elkin 1999) and governing regimes are more likely to be corrupted by the powerful (see Dahl 1985).

Recall that the restructuring of the state-market division moves away from the strict *public-private distinction,* and as such aims to alter the form of the local economic base. Specifically, the idea is to reorient that base away from its current domination by the traditional, for-profit, and largely corporate private sector, toward one where many economic institutions are owned and controlled in a more collectivist fashion and often operate as nonprofits or publicly owned enterprises. But the key question is whether these collectivist institutions can be the basis upon which to construct an efficient and prosperous local economy.

When considered in a general sense, the historical record of economic collectivism suggests the prospects for such a felicitous outcome are rather gloomy. The twentieth century is full of failed experiments with collectivist ownership structures, suggesting that the traditional, for-profit corporate-dominated economy represents the only viable option path. Corporate capitalism perhaps then represents a sort of end of history.[6] On the other hand, when one looks at the experiences of particular collectivist institutional forms, especially those operating on decentralized levels, the prospects somewhat brighten (DeFilippis 2004).

Take, for example, the two most potentially efficacious ownership forms that result from state-market restructuring: employee-owned firms (via employee stock ownership plans, or ESOPs) and the commercial and business activities of community organizations (especially community development corporations, or CDCs). Regarding ESOPs, a plethora of studies have documented that such firms are "as productive or more productive than comparable non-ESOP firms," and that ESOPs register, on average, greater annual sales growth than non-ESOPs. Moreover, as such firms become more controlled by their workers, they generally become more rather than less productive (Alperovitz 2005, 87). Regarding CDCs, the conventional wisdom is that, while they are well-suited for the more limited goal of affordable housing production, their ability to operate productive economic ventures is limited (see Vidal 1992). Nonetheless, substantial evidence suggests such a view to be outdated, being rooted largely in the experiences of then newly emerging CDCs from the late 1960s and early 1970s. Since that time, numerous CDCs—especially large and sophisticated ones—have successfully owned and operated a number of economic ventures, ranging from retail stores, restaurants, manufacturers, real estate development firms, and construction companies (see Alperovitz 2005).

Place-Community Attentiveness   The strong attentiveness to place-communities raises another normative challenge to the politics of the LEADS. Specifically, in light of technological advances in communication and transportation, and the social and economic trends toward an ever more cosmopolitan and globalized world, is not the focus on place-based community now quaint? Are not other kinds of communities—nongeographic "communities of interest," for example—more significant to urbanites than their particular cities, or even their neighborhoods? (See Lowndes 1995, 163). If so, is not the strong attentiveness to established place-communities normatively misguided, when people these days care little about where they happen to live and would nonchalantly abandon such places if circumstances warranted?

It turns out that, in reality, people still care a great deal about where they live, and are similarly very much attached to place-based communities. Even people with a high degree of freedom to choose their place communities will tend to, as the political theorist Loren King (2004, 216) notes: "develop loyalties to particular places as sites of formative associations and practices." Along similar lines, and drawing on a wide range of empirical literature in geography, planning, urban studies, and social psychology, community psychologists Lynne Manzo and Douglas Perkins

(2001, 20) find that, despite the many countervailing trends, "it is evident that...emotional bonds to places [experienced by human beings] are a real and important phenomenon" (also see Manzo and Perkins 2006).

One key essence of this phenomenon is the experienced condition of "place dependence" (Cox 2001, 14). People engage in certain place-specific sociospatial practices that "tend to get routinized, and for very good reasons...[as] they not only facilitate realization of individual ends," but also "create a world of predictability and confidence" (Cox and Mair 1988, 312). There is then, they note, "a resistance to change." While contingency may reign for a time, once settled, "the workplace, the living place and the particular spatial system of everyday life which they jointly constitute tend to acquire for people a certain necessity." Children get used to particular schools, mutual aid relationships are formed with particular neighbors, babysitters, parks, doctors, and dentists are all located, homes may be purchased, and social networks are "laboriously constructed," all as an "identification with a particular place" becomes more powerful (Cox 2001, 14; Cox and Mair 1988, 313).

Decentralized Scale   The obvious (and age-old) normatively problematic issue with decentralization concerns the issue of equity. In light of the economic spatial segregation in the American metropolis that so concerns liberal expansionists (Dreier, Mollenkopf, and Swanstrom 2004), focusing on smaller units (or boxes; see Rusk 1993)—whether neighborhoods or municipalities—can reinforce and even exacerbate inequities across space. Under such conditions, it is feared that poor jurisdictions and areas will thus remain poor, while affluent ones will be able to maintain their privileged status.

The dilemma here, however, is that the *means* liberals advocate to address this inequity—state-directed redistribution via expansionist designs—is itself politically infeasible. As explained in the last chapter, such efforts require that Type II constraints on feasibility be overcome—that is, the necessary political will for redistribution must be generated. Yet the enlarged political landscape concomitant with expansionism works to undermine this political will. Thus the liberal solution is really no solution at all, so the only path left to promote equity is the decentralized one. It, too, is problematic, of course, given Type I constraints, that is, the limited internal resources available in poorer jurisdictions to address urban problems.

Whether such difficulties can be overcome is an issue returned to in the discussion of political feasibility below.

A related classic normative concern of American liberals, from James Madison on, is that decentralized political scales of decision making and action provide inadequate protection for individual, and especially minority, rights (see Henig 1985; Elkin 2006). Liberals draw heavily upon the ugly history of state-enforced racial segregation in the American South during much of the twentieth century to confirm such fears. And they see the federal-level actions of the 1950s and 1960s spurred by the civil rights movement as strong evidence that the centralized state is the best, and perhaps only, effective guarantor of a minority's rights, whether a racial/ethnic group or the poor and vulnerable. Thus, liberal expansionists ultimately place great credence in the willingness and capacity of the federal government to right historic injustices by preventing localized polities from mistreating their vulnerable citizens.

Although it is certainly the case that many localized polities have a history of such behavior, the overall historical record of the federal government is not much better. U.S. history is replete with cases in which the federal government took a lead role in repressing the individual rights of minorities. In particular, its record of violating the rights of political minorities (who were often also ethnic minorities) considered a threat to national security—such as communists, labor and peace activists, or "enemy aliens"—has been especially abysmal. Such acts of repression date as early as the 1798 passage of the Alien and Sedition Acts and continued throughout the twentieth century. Prominent examples include the Red Scare following World War I, the internment of Japanese Americans during World War II, McCarthyism, and, most recently, the twenty-first century infringements of civil liberties associated with the so-called War on Terror.[7] Moreover, throughout the twentieth century and into the twenty-first, the federal government has more often than not also been the leader of the so-called War on Drugs, perhaps the most salient contemporary force behind the curtailment of the liberties of poor, urban African Americans (see Thompson 2003).[8] And, as we saw in chapter 4, many of the more repressive aspects of dispersal-type housing measures are (or would be, if adopted) federal-level policies. In a more general sense, it is highly ironic that liberal expansionists turn to the same entity—the federal government—to be the savior of cities and the urban citizenry whom they, rightly to a degree, also vociferously blame for creating or exacerbating urban problems in first place (see Dreier, Mollenkopf, and Swanstrom 2004; Fiss 2003).

Commercial Orientation   The central normative challenge raised by the commercial orientation of the LEADS is whether such an orientation breeds a local politics too focused on wealth generation and economic development—or, put more bluntly, on the crass pursuit of money. Specifically, would such a politics be devoid of compassion, especially toward those unable or unwilling to contribute much if anything to economic production? Similarly, would such persons not be considered full-fledged citizens and, as a consequence, denied mutual respect, given their limited economic contribution? Thus, would not the practice of this politics undermine the two key aspirations for cities advanced in this book: to ameliorate the human suffering resulting from entrenched urban problems and to create vibrant democratic and egalitarian urban regimes?

This is exactly the thrust of much of the hostile critical reaction of liberal egalitarians to Paul Peterson's idea of *City Limits*.[9] Peterson (1981) famously argued that cities must—and thus should—pursue economic development policy and eschew efforts to help the urban poor via redistribution, though Peterson did favor redistributive efforts undertaken by the central government. Is not the politics of the LEADS subject to the same charge?

Perhaps. Yet, unlike Peterson's conception of the local economy, the LEADS approach envisions that many of the economic institutions engaging in commercial endeavors will be community-based and collectivist in form. Such forms tend to temper the impulse to see material means as the sole path to promote human well-being. Moreover, since the LEADS seek the collective betterment of *whole* communities, as opposed to individual-level social mobility, there is a greater likelihood that a communitarian ethic of caring would take hold where the strong assume obligations to help care for the weak (see Etzioni 1993). Similarly, to promote mutual respect and equal citizenship, this communitarian ethic might help facilitate the development of a broader conception of what counts as "production," to include unpaid caregiving and a variety of volunteer activities (cf. Goodin 2000). Finally, as the work of political theorist Stephen Elkin (1987, 2006) on the nature of a *commercial republic* makes clear, even when an economy is structured in a more traditional, individualist form, a commercial orientation is not incompatible with, and can even buttress, a strong degree of both economic and political equality.

Equity Emphasis   The strong emphasis on equity in the politics of the LEADS raises another venerable normative concern frequently raised by liberals. This concern, expressed by liberal political theorists such as James Madison, Alexis de Tocqueville, and John Stuart Mill, is that equality will somehow destroy or weaken liberty (see Dahl 1985). Along these lines, the fear is that the mass of citizens will use democratic equality to repress the rights of minorities, especially propertied minorities (i.e., the wealthy) or those holding nonconformist or dissenting opinions or practicing unorthodox lifestyles. A related and, for this discussion, more apropos concern is that the particular actions necessary to enforce and reproduce equity themselves require continuous and significant violations of liberty (see, for example, Nozick 1974). In general, then, at a minimum equality and liberty are seen to be in a somewhat strict trade-off. Hence a politics with too strong an egalitarian impulse can threaten the foundations and practices of a free society.

That said, the degree to which the politics of the LEADS poses a threat to liberty is very much an open question. The answer to that question will most likely turn on the crucial issue of how liberty is defined, specifically what counts as a violation of, or reduction in, liberty. To bring this issue more into focus, consider one stark example from earlier chapters—the use of eminent domain power by cities to condemn (acquire) the operations and capital facilities of businesses seeking to relocate or shut down. From the libertarian vantage point of the so-called property-rights movement, the use of eminent domain in almost any form, let alone in this proactive and aggressive way, represents an egregious violation of liberty (Berliner 2006). On the other hand, many economic progressives (see Lynd 1987a), and even some liberals (see Elkin 2006), see the use of eminent domain to condemn businesses threatening to depart or shut down as within the legitimate purview of democratically controlled, localized public power. Thus, whether or not the strong emphasis on promoting equity in the LEADS will pose significant normative problems by unduly restricting liberty is, ultimately, a political question—that is, one that can only be settled via the struggle over political ideas itself.

In sum, then, from this brief survey it is clear that the politics of the LEADS faces some deep normative challenges. Yet, it appears that such challenges can be adequately addressed, suggesting that LEADS politics may very well be normatively desirable (or at least not prima facie normatively undesirable).

Is It Feasible?

The politics of the LEADS may well be normatively desirable, but that matters little if it cannot be feasibly practiced. Perhaps like its liberal rivals, the LEADS are also politically infeasible. Hence, the status quo in urban America—marked as it is by poorly functioning, inegalitarian, and largely undemocratic governing regimes and an array of severe and entrenched social problems—is likely to endure for the foreseeable future. As we shall see below, however, there is at least some reason to be hopeful that the LEADS are indeed—potentially at least—politically feasible.

Recall that the political feasibility of liberal expansionism is stymied by the existence of Type II constraints: engaging in expansionism in order to provide access to the resources needed for liberal redistributive efforts requires a parallel expansion of the polity in conservative (e.g., suburban) directions. This expansion, in turn, undermines the political will to redistribute. Also recall that, because it does little to reconstitute traditional regime forms in progressive directions, the politics of the other reigning orthodoxy—conventional urban regime theory—requires the strong support of the central actor in those traditional regime forms, the corporate business sector. This support is necessary in order to promote its key prescriptive reforms, that is, the enhancement of urban education systems and related social services. Yet, given the growth-machine-type priorities of local corporate business elites, corporate support for these initiatives is unlikely to be more than token or marginal (see Logan and Molotch 1987).

Thus, any politics that is likely to be feasible cannot be based upon liberal expansionism or corporate liberalism. And, it is indeed the case that the LEADS eschew both of those paths. Yet, while steering clear of the impediments crippling the feasibly of liberal urban politics, the LEADS nonetheless confront their *own* set of political impediments: (1) Type I

constraints, where the resource base upon which to address urban problems is unavailable locally due to the fiscal stress of cities and their citizens,
and (2) the need to reconstitute urban regimes progressively, so as to create
the political environment supportive of the proliferation and scaling up
of the LEADS. Staring these formidable impediments directly in the face
evokes the realization that the political feasibility of the LEADS is quite
the hard swath to mow.[10]

Nonetheless, while formidable, they perhaps are not insurmountable.
It is at least conceivable that they could be overcome. Consider, first, the
Type I constraints. The key to lessening these constraints is found in what
might be called the *structure-altering* potential of the LEADS.[11] That is, once
the LEADS are operating at a sufficient scale, they possess the potential to
change the structural context that gives rise to Type I constraints in the first
place. By slowing capital mobility and stabilizing local fiscal and economic
bases, the LEADS thus can create the very structural conditions that allow
for their further development. With this further development comes a further lessening of Type I constraints, which in turn facilitates an even further
development of the LEADS. And with this change in the structural context
of city politics it now becomes more possible to reconstitute urban regimes
in politically progressive directions. This is because a more progressive set of
actors in local civil society or, alternatively, the local state itself is empowered
in ways allowing alternative regime forms to be viable (see chapters 1 and 2).
The subsequent institutionalization of such viable regimes in turn helps
counter the inevitable political resistance likely to be mounted by corporate
business interests against the proliferation and scaling up of the LEADS.

The key problem is how this salutary structural dynamic might be
unleashed in the first place, especially in light of the largely unfavorable
(corporate-dominated) political climate in cities. What would be necessary
to alter this climate, so that the LEADS could be brought up to a sufficient
scale where such a dynamic might kick in?

First, and most fundamental, what would be required is a new, urban-
based political (and social) movement built around the LEADS. In time,
this movement would need to give rise to new, localized political formations that would eventually grow into political parties, with platforms devoted to enhancing the scope and scale of the LEADS and animated by an
ideology supportive of these practices. Such new political formations and
political parties would likely be needed because it is highly improbable that

the established major political parties could accommodate the demands of this movement, given these parties' close political alliances with corporate America and their affinity for neoliberal globalization.[12]

Along these lines, the Kentucky-based agrarian philosopher Wendell Berry (1996, 412) suggests that such a "new political scheme of opposed parties...is beginning to take form" (though perhaps temporarily derailed by the events of September 11, 2001 and their aftermath). "This is essentially a two-party system, and it divides over the fundamental issue of community. One of these parties holds that community has no value; the other holds that it does. One is the party of the global economy; the other I would call simply the party of local community" (also see Faux 2006). This split—between the party of the global economy and the party of local community—brings with it an altogether new ideological (and dialogical) divide (cf. Hess 2009). Again, to quote Berry (1996, 412), in order to understand and respond effectively to America's deepest problems "the old political alignments have become virtually useless.... The dialogue of Democrats and Republicans or of liberals and conservatives is likewise useless to us."

What is needed, then, is a new oppositional ideology, built around the LEADS and standing against market-oriented conservatism *and* liberalism—whether in its 'neo' variety (see Hackworth 2007) or, given its normative and feasibility problems, its New Deal/Great Society variety as well (as expressed in liberal expansionism). Much of the basis of this new oppositional ideology to support and buttress the LEADS could lie from within the five significant features of the LEADS themselves: the restructuring of the state-market division, attentiveness to place-community, decentralization, the orientation to commercialist or productionist values, and the promotion of social and economic equity.

But would such an ideology gain the necessary level of support? Although this question is difficult to answer in the abstract, there are at least two reasons to believe it possibly could.

First, although both liberalism and conservatism, and the political parties they undergird, still command large and, in many instances, passionate partisans, it is clear that much of the American citizenry has for some time been only weakly attached to these ideologies (see Alperovitz 2005; Lasch 1995; Dionne 1991). As political economist and social theorist Gar Alperovitz (2005, 236) reminds us, millions have "expressed their discontent by breaking with the major political parties to vote for Ross Perot,

Pat Buchanan, and Ralph Nader," all of whom, in different ways, expressed a populist orientation (also see Greider 2009). Barack Obama's more recent message of "hope and change" resonated most effectively when it struck a similar populist chord. Many citizens seem to be unsatisfied with *both* the centralized statism promised by liberalism *and* the unmitigated free market promised by conservatism (see Isaac 2003; Noble 2004; Greider 2009). Big government is as disliked as corporate hegemony. But the absence of any coherent and attractive ideological *third way* leaves millions clinging to one or the other ideology, mostly out of fear that the worst aspects of the ideology with which they differ will come into being. A new ideology that cuts through the current dysfunctional ideological divide might appeal to this large political bloc (see Shuman 2006; Greider 2009).

Second, it is equally clear that all of the constitutive values of the new oppositional ideology have an enduringly popular appeal. Democracy is favored over corporate power and control, place-community over hyper-mobility and rootlessness, populism over elitism, self-help/self-reliant production over consumption and the welfare state, localism over globalism, basic equity and fairness over stark inequities (see Noble 2004). Moreover, these values transcend the traditional notions of the Left and the Right (cf. Shuman 2006; Alperovitz 2005). For instance, while many contemporary liberals would object to an ideology that (1) failed to emphasize social and geographic mobility, (2) limited the role of the centralized welfare state, and (3) tended toward a parochial focus on the local, many contemporary conservatives would register similar objections to (1) limits on the political power of corporations and elites, (2) efforts to counterbalance economic globalization, and (3) the fight for greater equity. Whether enough of those who feel no deep attachment to either liberalism or conservatism would embrace the new oppositional ideology is the central—but very much open—question.

The construction of the necessary urban political movement to support the proliferation and scaling up of the LEADS of course requires more than an appealing oppositional ideology. Such a movement must be able to grow out of the organizational makeup that currently exists in urban communities, since it would be next to impossible to build this movement from scratch. Where might this organizational basis lie?

One source might be those groups traditionally focused on fighting for social justice—community organizing groups, the community/social movement oriented elements of the (weakened but not completely dead) labor movement, left-leaning religious congregations, broad-minded civil rights organizations, and even some progressive elements within local Democratic Party structures. On the other side of the coin might be organizations dedicated to more "conservative" causes: fiscal watchdog groups (concerned about the waste of taxpayer subsidies on corporate center development), organizations dedicated to promoting small business (since such businesses play a prominent role in the LEADS approach), and those groups critical of excessive governmental spending on social services and welfare (which they see as ineffective). Such a forged coalition of Left and Right would represent not a convergence toward some amorphous center (as presently understood), but rather a political force with an ideological underpinning altogether different from anything easily categorized on present terms. This political force might be one possible manifestation of Wendell Berry's notion of the *party of local community*.[13]

Even more fundamental as an organizational basis for a LEADS-oriented political movement would be the people and institutions already on the ground in cities engaged in operating key elements of the LEADS themselves. This list would include a large subset of the ten thousand worker-owned firms, the forty-six hundred community development corporations, the three hundred community development finance institutions, the two hundred community land trusts, the numerous organizations dedicated to economic localism, as well as many of the tens of thousands of urban-based cooperatives and municipal enterprises.[14] These institutions most often operate independent of one another, without any serious recognition of their kinship in organizational form, guiding philosophy, and programmatic goals. If linked together and united in a common purpose via umbrella organizations and the new oppositional ideology, they could form the nucleus of an emergent (and potentially formidable) political movement dedicated to augmenting the scope and scale of the LEADS.

A Beginning, Not an End

Clearly, a case can be made for the proposition that the politics of the LEADS is both normatively desirable and, perhaps, politically feasible. There is of course much that is still unknown about the politics of the

LEADS, and my analysis in this last chapter only provides an initial assessment of this politics.

My objective in this book, taken as a whole, has been to initiate a conversation in which urbanists give due reconsideration to the orthodoxies of conventional urban regime theory and liberal expansionism, while also engaging the primer on the local economic alternative development strategies I have provided within these pages. As I have restated repeatedly, the ultimate goal of initiating this conversation is eminently practical. It is hoped that such discourse can be translated into tangible actions—actions that help relieve the human suffering from America's urban problems (laid so bare by the aftermath of Hurricane Katrina), while making urban governance (via progressive regime reconstruction) once again the pride of American democracy. With such practical considerations foremost in our minds: Let the conversation begin.

NOTES

Preface

1. See, for example, Jacobs 1961; Mollenkopf 1983; Jackson 1985; Thompson 1998; Reed and Steinberg 2006.

2. In a retort to Friedrich Hayek's dedication of his 1944 classic polemic *The Road to Serfdom* to "socialists of all parties," Hackworth (2007: xiv) tellingly dedicates his fine recent book, *The Neoliberal City,* to "liberals of *all* parties" (emphasis added). Thus, while his analysis emphasizes neoliberalism, the spirit of its critique is broader in focus (also see Purcell 2008).

3. While Purcell uses the term *radical* to describe this scholarship, I prefer the term *critical* because it is less burdened with a particular set of theoretic presuppositions and political commitments.

Introduction

1. See, for example, DeLeon 1992; DiGaetano and Klemanski 1993; Harding 1994; Imbroscio 1997; Stone 1993; Kantor, Savitch, and Haddock 1997; Bailey 1999; Brown 1999; Lauria 1997b; Orr and Stoker 1994; Ramsey 1996; Sites 1997; Stoker and Mossberger 1994; Ward 1996.

2. In a recent book reviewing the state of the art of *Theories of Urban Politics* (see Davies and Imbroscio 2009), regime theory was shown to pervade much of the field. It made an appearance in the coverage of over one half of the volume's subjects, including the chapters on poverty, community power, leadership, race, bureaucracy, new institutionalism, and social movements (in addition to being the main subject of one chapter itself, see Mossberger 2009). For other recent work

engaging urban regime theory, see also, for example, Collins 2008; McGovern 2009; Burns 2003; Davies 2002, 2003; Hamel and Jouve 2008; Gendron 2006; Mossberger and Stoker 2001; Horan 2002; Austin and McCaffrey 2002; Sapotichne, Jones, and Wolfe 2007; Gendron and Domhoff 2009; Stone 2005; De Socio 2007; Hackworth 2007; Bennett and Spirou 2006; Holman 2007.

3. See, most seminally, Dahl 1961 on pluralism and Hunter 1953 on elitism.

4. For a fuller treatment of these arguments, see Imbroscio forthcoming.

5. See, respectively, Haveman 1977; Clavel 1986; Vidal 1992; Stone et al. 1999.

6. In developing the term *liberal expansionism* I am influenced by J. Phillip Thompson's penetrating critique of what he labels *liberal universalism* (see Thompson 1998). Although there is a strong affinity between my term and Thompson's, one key difference is that my term evokes a greater emphasis on the explicitly spatial (i.e., expansionist) nature of the set of ideas I am critiquing.

7. The idea of expansionism in my term *liberal expansionism* comes directly from liberal expansionists themselves. For example, former Albuquerque, New Mexico, mayor-turned-scholar David Rusk—a leading advocate of this approach—opens his widely influential liberal expansionist tract, *Inside Game/Outside Game,* by employing this conceptualization. Albuquerque should be heralded as a model for others, Rusk (1999, 1) writes, because it "*expanded*" its boundaries" through aggressive annexation and "such *expansion* had big advantages" (emphases added).

8. Similarly, urban-issues newspaper columnist Neal Peirce (2008, 1) cites with approval the idea of the Urban Land Institute's John McIlwain "to rename HUD [the Department of Housing and Urban Development] the Department of Housing and *Metropolitan* Development...Why? To think more *expansively,* to make connections." (emphases added).

9. See Orfield 2002, 1998; Rusk 1999; Turner 1998; Goering and Feins 2003. The ideological affinity of Brookings and the Urban Institute has also spawned some high-profile collaborations to advocate liberal expansionist ideas (see, for example, Katz and Turner 2001).

10. See, for example, Florida 2002; Kanter 1995; Kantor 1995; Dreier, Mollenkopf, and Swanstrom 2004.

11. See Lasch 1991; cf. Swanstrom 1993.

12. My deep gratitude goes to Amanda LeDuke for help with developing the LEADS acronym. Broader inspiration came from the work of progressive writer and activist Michael Shuman. Shuman (2006) cleverly and effectively contrasts his idea of LOIS (local ownership and import substitution) with the contrasting idea of TINA (There Is No Alternative), an acronym closely associated with the declarations made by former British prime minister Margaret Thatcher to justify her neoliberal economic program.

13. See, for example, Okun 1975.

1. Reconceiving the State-Market Division

1. See, most seminally, Aglietta 1976; Lipietz 1986; for an application to urban politics, see Painter 1995.

2. Also see the review of the urban regime theory literature in Mossberger 2009.

3. For overview of Stone's enormous contribution to the field of U.S. urban politics over the last quarter century, see Orr and Johnson 2008.

4. See Stone 1997, 1989; also see Kantor, Savitch, and Haddock 1997.

5. Also see Bhaskar 1979; Giddens 1979; Sowell 1992.

6. Along these lines, progressive political scientist Adolph Reed has made a similar point. In his critique of sociologist William Julius Wilson's (1987) famous liberal analysis of urban poverty, *The Truly Disadvantaged,* Reed (1988, 170) perceptively noted that because "Wilson cannot see that history is made by human action...[his] argument does not juxtapose race and class but race and *economics,* which he treats as beyond the scope of social intervention." The apropos title of Reed's essay is "The Liberal Technocrat."

7. For a partial and inchoate exception, see Stone 1989, 215–16, 243–44.

8. See Alperovitz 2005; Imbroscio, Williamson, and Alperovitz 2003; Elkin 2006; Eisinger 1988; Hornack and Lynd 1987; Lynd 1987a; Portz 1990; Imbroscio 1997; Fisher 1987; Osborne and Gaebler 1992; Frug 1980.

9. See Williamson, Imbroscio, and Alperovitz 2002; Clavel 1986; Osborne and Gaebler 1992; Sagalyn 1990; Alperovitz 2005; Babcock 1990; Bowman 1987; Cummings, Koebel, and Whitt 1989; Fisher 1988; Kieschnick 1981.

10. Bruyn 1987; Imbroscio 1997; Brown 1993; Lane 1988; McArthur 1993.

11. See Williamson, Imbroscio, and Alperovitz 2002; Vidal 1992; Parzen and Kieschnick 1992; Purdy and Sexton 1995; DeFilippis 2004; Gunn and Gunn 1991; Imbroscio, Williamson, and Alperovitz 2003; Hammond 1987.

12. See Mitchell 2006; Imbroscio, Williamson, and Alperovitz 2003; Chalkley 1991; Greider 1993; Perlman 1997; Wiewel and Mier 1986.

13. Examples have included the Rochester Red Barons and the Syracuse SkyChiefs and, in a partial sense, the Wisconsin Timber Rattlers. See Imbroscio, Williamson, and Alperovitz 2003; Mahtesian 1996; Spirou and Jurie 1997; Williamson, Imbroscio, and Alperovitz 2002.

14. See Harvey 1991; Mayer 1988; Scott 1988; Eisinger 1988; Noyelle 1986; Piore and Sabel 1984.

15. For reviews of these typologies, see Mossberger 2009, Sites 1997, and Stoker 1995.

16. Cf. Berk and Swanstrom 1994; Unger 1987; Elkin 2006; Lasch 1991.

17. See Frug 1980; Garber 1990; Hartog 1983.

18. See O'Connor 1973; Offe 1984; Habermas 1975.

19. Some regime theorists, it should be noted, implicitly acknowledge this point. Most notable here is Elkin (1987). He suggests that various adjustments to the division of labor—adjustments that will enhance the vibrancy of urban democracy—need not come "at the expense of the city's economic vitality" (Elkin 1987, 179). But see Davies (2002) for a critique of Elkin's perspective on this issue.

20. As the eminent British social theorist R. H. Tawney argued decades ago: the "objection to public ownership, in so far as it is intelligent, is largely an objection to over-centralisation. But the remedy for over-centralisation is not the maintenance of functionless property in private hands, but the decentralized ownership of public property" (as quoted in Schumacher 1975, 252–53).

2. Reengaging Economics

1. See especially Poulantzas 1974; O'Connor 1973; Offe 1974; Block 1977; Habermas 1975.

2. The idea that only *enough* business investment need be contingent for the economic dependency dynamic to take hold was central to Lindblom's original conception of state-market relations that formed the foundation of regime theory (see Lindblom 1977; Elkin 1987, 1982).

3. See Clavel and Kleniewski 1990. Also see Imbroscio 1997.

4. See Collins 2008; Eisinger 2000; Staley 2001; Hackworth 2007; Barnekov and Rich 1989; Imbroscio 1997; Krumholz 1991; Reed 1988; Riposa and Andranovich 1988; Squires 1989; Burns and Gober 1998; Mier and Fitzgerald 1991; Sanders 2005; Zimbalist and Noll 1997.

5. See Williamson, Imbroscio, and Alperovitz 2002; Alperovitz and Faux 1984; Bluestone and Harrison 1987; Dudley 1994; Elkin 1999; Jakle and Wilson 1992; New York Times 1996; Moore 1996; Ricker 1998; Wilson 1987.

6. See Alperovitz and Faux 1984; Feagin and Parker 1990; Harte 1986; Wyly, forthcoming; Fisher and Peters 1998; Levine 1987, 1988; Luria and Russell 1981; Smith 1979; as well as chapter 5 below.

7. Giloth 1988; Morris 1998; Lynd 1987a; Eisinger 1988; Imbroscio 1997; Persky and Wiewel 1999.

8. For an excellent introduction and overview of Jacobs's economic thinking, see Polsky 1988.

3. Reassessing the Shaming of the Inside Game

1. This endorsement is repeated in Dreier, Mollenkopf, and Swanstrom (2004, 9).

2. See, for example, Stoecker 1997; Marquez 1993; Shipp 1996; Swinney 1998.

3. Swanstrom's earlier work (1993, 74) assessed liberal expansionism's compulsion to move poor urban residents to the suburbs this way:

> The economistic concept…implies that the best way to move people out of poverty is to encourage them to give up their particular cultural values, be willing to move out of the ghetto, and become Benthamite utility maximizers….The community development approach to urban poverty makes more sense. I am not suggesting that the racism that penetrates urban economic relations in the United States today is good or should be nurtured. I am suggesting, however, that the conventional approach of requiring African-Americans to give up their cultural commitments and ties to the black community in order to assimilate into white middle class society is both unrealistic, given the continued strength of racism in this country, and probably racist (suggesting that poor black communities have no social ties on which to build).

4. See, for example, Elkin 2006; Levine 2000; Eisinger 2000; Staley 2001; Barnekov and Rich 1989; Krumholz 1991; Reed 1988; Riposa and Andranovich 1988; Squires 1989; Mier and Fitzgerald 1991; Sanders 2005; Zimbalist and Noll 1997; Levine 1987.

5. See Elkin 1987; Krumholz 1991; Clavel and Wiewel 1991; Weiher 1989; Ganz 1986; Barnekov and Rich 1989; Fainstein et al. 1983.

6. Also see Dreier, Mollenkopf, and Swanstrom 2001, 207; 2004, 253.

7. See Swanstrom 1988, 1993; Frug and Barron 2008; Henig 1992; Stone 1987; Stone 1989; Goetz 1990; Elkin 1987; Logan and Molotch 1987; as well as chapter 2.

8. See chapter 4. Another measure on which Dreier, Mollenkopf, and Swanstrom (2004, 145, 258) pinned their liberal expansionist hopes was Bridges to Work, a federal demonstration program from the Clinton administration that ostensibly "helped poor residents of ghetto neighborhoods in five cities get access to suburban jobs through improved transportation." Bridges to Work is characterized as "potentially significant" and an example of the ways regional transportation planning agencies can use their funding in "innovative and flexible ways." However, another liberal expansionist, Margery Turner (2008, 173) of the Urban Institute, notes that rigorous evaluations of this program found, quite predictably perhaps, "no statistically significant effects on employment or income overall," a finding Turner laments as "disappointing."

9. See Rusk 1993; Orfield 2002; Dreier, Mollenkopf, and Swanstrom 2004.

10. And, moreover, more recent work strongly suggests that this hoped for salvation from merger has not occurred (see Savitch, Vogel, and Ye, forthcoming).

11. Also see Weir (2000, 133–34) on the elite oriented nature of the development of expansionist institutions in the Minneapolis case.

12. Also see, for example, Brookings Institution 2002; Katz and Muro 2005; Peirce 2004; Greenblatt 2002, 2003.

13. Continuing, Dreier, Mollenkopf, and Swanstrom (2001, 249; 2004, 299) approvingly add that "further investment in the housing, economic development, and infrastructure of the South Bronx would encourage middle-class people to move in." This migration is exactly what is happening, as by 2005 a front-page *New York Times* headline screams of classic gentrification and its concomitant displacement: "Goodbye South Bronx Blight, Hello Trendy SoBro" (Berger 2005; also see Lees, Slater, and Wyly 2008).

14. At this writing in the spring of 2009 it is too early to judge whether the same will be true of the urban policies of new Democratic presidential administration of Barack Obama. One hint,

however, comes from President Obama's address to the U.S. Conference of Mayors during the campaign. In that address, the *New York Times* reported, Obama sternly warned America's mayors that they "should not count on significant additional help from Washington" (Broder 2008).

15. This conclusion is a key reason why many progressive (as opposed to liberal) urbanists have called for the development of a third progressive political party in America, however difficult such an enterprise might be (see, for example, Cohen and Rogers 1996). Also see chapter 8 below.

4. Rethinking the Dispersal Consensus

1. On the Left, see Reed and Steinberg 2006, but also Greenbaum 2006; Thompson 2003; Bennett and Reed 1999; Goetz 2003; on the Right, see, for example, Husock 2003; Rockwell 1994; MacDonald 1997.

2. See Goetz 2003; Galster 2005; Bennett, Smith, and Wright 2006; Greenbaum et al. 2008; Imbroscio 2008.

3. See, for example, Rosenbaum 1991, 1995; Rosenbaum et al. 1991; Rosenbaum and Popkin 1991; Rubinowitz and Rosenbaum 2000; Kling et al. 2004; Kling, Liebman, and Katz 2007; Turney et al. 2006; as well as the reviews of several MTO studies offered by Goering, Feins, and Richardson 2003 and Goering 2003.

4. In fact, in an Orwellian "Freedom is Slavery"-type twist, some elements of the DC view improving poor neighborhoods as actually promoting unfreedom, as it anchors the poor to those areas rather than spurring them to make a so-called move to opportunity (for strong statements of this view, see Orfield 1998; Kasarda 1992; also see Rusk 1999).

5. See, for example, Polikoff 2006; Rubinowitz and Rosenbaum 2000; Fiss 2003.

6. Political theorist Don Herzog's (1989) critique of consent theory elucidates what is at issue here (see Imbroscio 2004b). In this critique, Herzog posits "the principle of alternatives," which states, "to say some action was voluntary requires that there were alternatives...[a principle] built into the syntax of consent and voluntary action" (Herzog 1989, 225). And, he adds that

> not any alternatives will do. They have to be not excessively costly, but reasonable. When the proverbial gunman issues his proverbial ultimatum and you hand over your wallet, your action isn't voluntary. True, you had an alternative: you could have permitted him to shoot you. When you renounce that alternative, though, and adopt the other, you aren't consenting or acting voluntarily. You're being coerced. (Herzog 1989, 226–27)

7. See Goetz 2003; Zaterman, Gross, and Kalenak 2001; Varady and Walker 2003; Basgal and Villarreal 2001; Varady 2005. Also see, especially, Glaser, Parker, and Li 2003 on this point.

8. Researchers Stefanie DeLuca and James Rosenbaum (2003), however, did not find this behavior among Gautreaux participants. But for several reasons this result may not be generalizable to a larger population of the urban poor (see Popkin et al. 2000 and discussion below).

9. See, for example, Briggs 1997a, 1997b; Goetz 2003; Hochschild 2003; Kleit and Manzo 2006; Weir 2009.

10. Interestingly, the book's cover even reflects this stance, as the title "Choosing a Better Life" is set off in a color scheme with the words "a" and "Life" in very light tones, causing them to fade into the background and leaving only the words "Choosing Better" to appear at a glance (anyone doubting this visual effect simply needs to examine the book's cover, an effect even more striking on its spine). Choosing to move to low-poverty suburbia, "The Better Life," thus becomes a case of making better life choices. It is of course most likely that the book's authors had little or no control over its cover design, and hence cannot be blamed for this particular piece of visual propaganda. Nonetheless, someone (or some group of persons) with creative control in one of the DC's house publishing outlets, the Urban Institute Press, did design and sign off on this biased color scheme,

promoting—whether consciously or not—the idea that people are currently making the wrong choices about where to live.

11. As the political theorist Stephen White (1987, 121) explains, many see a "latent authoritarianism" lurking behind efforts to attribute these *real* interests (also see Polsby 1980).

12. On the considerable social and cultural distance between those studying poor inner city neighborhoods and those living in them, see Wacquant (1997, 348). Reed and Steinberg (2006, 3) ask, pointedly, "How is it that this Gang of 200, from their ivory towers and gilded offices, presume to speak for the poor?"

13. See Basgal and Villarreal 2001; Zaterman, Gross, and Kalenak 2001; Varady 2005; Turnham and Khadduri 2001.

14. Similarly, Reed and Steinberg (2006, 5) link the Gang of 200's Katrina petition to the "stereotype of the 'urban underclass,'" arguing that such a stereotype is "insidious" because "it defines poor people's lives as only objects for 'our' administration." And they ask: "Just who makes up the circle of 'we' anyway?" (For a similar formulation, see Bennett, Smith, and Wright 2006).

15. See Popkin et al. 2000; Crump 2003; Goetz 2003; Varady and Walker 2003; Basgal and Villarreal 2001.

16. Also see Kling et al. 2004; Kling, Liebman, and Katz 2007; Turney et al. 2006; Geronimus and Thompson 2004.

17. Jencks and Mayer 1990, 176; Galster and Zobel 1998, 605; Jargowsky 2002, 443. See Dreier, Mollenkopf, and Swanstrom (2004, 328), who offer these citations and quotes. Also see Van Ham and Manley, forthcoming.

18. While "community development (area-based upgrading)" can be a "cure strategy" in the mind of some key members of the DC such as Xavier Briggs (2005a, 330; 2005c, 251), a crucial part of such upgrading must include the creation of "mixed-income and mixed-tenure housing development, to attract diverse in-movers" (also see Briggs 2005b). Therefore, many of the poor would not be helped where they live in this upgrading, because they will have to be relocated to make way for these higher income "in-movers" (also see the discussion of HOPE VI below).

19. See, for example, Bennett and Reed 1999; Goetz 2003; Williams 2003; Crump 2002; Bennett, Smith, and Wright 2006; Manzo, Kleit, and Crouch 2008.

20. See, respectively, Williams 2003; Vale 2006; Bennett and Reed 1999; Goetz 2000. Also see Greenbaum et al. 2008.

21. Fiss's (2003) normative vision is perverted in a similar way. The *only* way to achieve "racial justice" in America in his view is through dispersal; there can be no justice for most African Americans absent a move (usually to the white suburbs). Without the aggressive, large-scale, and nationwide dispersal program he champions, we "condemn a sector of the black community to suffer in perpetuity from the devastating effects of our racial history" (Fiss 2003, 6). For a similar view of the needed corrective for racial injustice, see Massey and Denton (1993). Thompson (1998 and 2003) provides an excellent critique of both of these views.

5. The Local Public Balance Sheet

1. See, for example, Smith 1979; Levine 1987; Alperovitz and Faux 1984; Luria and Russell 1981, 1982; Feagin and Parker 1990; Imbroscio 1997; Yin 2004; Williamson, Imbroscio, and Alperovitz 2002; Giloth 1988; Wyly, forthcoming; Fisher and Peters 1998.

2. For a discussion of the development of the concept in the United Kingdom, see Harte 1986.

3. See, respectively, Feagin and Parker 1990; Levine 1987; Imbroscio 1997; Fisher and Peters 1998; Williamson, Imbroscio, and Alperovitz 2002.

4. Cost-benefit analysis, conventional economics' key policymaking tool, rarely includes an assessment of the externalities arising from economic development policies in part because "[t]hese spillover effects" are "assume[d]...[to be] minimal" (Buss and Yancer 1999).

5. In this sense, the PBS is rooted in the influential ideas of economic historian Karl Polanyi, ideas Polanyi developed in his classic and masterful work, *The Great Transformation* (1957 [1944]). Explicating those ideas, planner Ernest Sternberg (1993, 104) notes that, for Polanyi, "the destructive effects of markets are not external to market transactions. On the contrary, these debilitating consequences...are inherent to the very operations of the self-regulating market" (also see Swaney and Evers 1989).

6. As Staughton Lynd (1987a, 926–27) explained in his penetrating study of Youngstown and Pittsburgh, the massive capital disinvestment occurring during this period caused the traditional distinction between public and private to become contested: "The traumatic collapse of the steel industries in those communities, with the social distress that followed, led to the appearance of new ideas. Local residents began to articulate and explore the...[idea] that *private decisions with catastrophic social consequences are really public decisions*" (emphasis added). Also see Lynd 1987b.

7. A catastrophe so poignant as to inspire great art. See Bruce Springsteen's "Youngstown"; http://www.brucespringsteen.net/songs/Youngstown.html.

8. See Williamson, Imbroscio, and Alperovitz 2002; Jakle and Wilson 1992; Dudley 1994; *New York Times* 1996; Castro 1998.

9. See Moore 1996; Wilson 1987; Bluestone and Harrison 1987.

10. Linkage policies in San Francisco and Boston date to the early 1980s; by the 1990s, at least fifteen cities had implemented linkage policies, including Seattle (WA), Santa Monica (CA), Cambridge (MA), Cherry Hill (NJ), Hartford (CT), and Palo Alto (CA) (Herrero 1991; also see Euchner and McGovern 2003; Smith 1989).

6. A Triad for Community Economic Stability

1. For a similar formulation, see the rigorous and insightful work of the geographer Gordon Clark (1983, 139), who suggests the principle of "maintaining community integrity." Also see Sundquist 1975; Imbroscio 2004a.

2. To put such an idea into practice, Shuman (2006, 170) further explains that a "sophisticated public bidding system" could be developed requiring vendors "not only to present the prices and quality of various procurement items but also calculate the different local multipliers that will flow from the deal and the resulting tax revenues."

3. These include Local Exchange Trading Systems (LETS), Time Dollar Systems, and a variety of more basic bartering schemes (see Shuman 2006; Collom 2005).

4. See chapter 8 for analysis of such a movement's political prospects.

5. Along these lines, many *value recapture* efforts are based on *resident ownership mechanisms* (see Blackwell and McCulloch 2002). Also see DeFilippis 2004.

6. For a classic statement, see the President's Commission for a National Agenda for the Eighties 1980. For an extensive critique, see Clark 1983.

7. The Folly of Liberal Politics

1. Along these lines, in another excellent article Thompson (1998, 204) explains how "liberalism privileges 'experts,' including judges and college professors who are distinguished by their supposed ability to separate higher objective and 'universal' rights and principles from particular group demands."

2. Moreover, the Louisville case also reflects how established political boundaries can promote other normatively desirable goals. In an ecological sense, Savitch and Vogel (2004, 771) reported that the old city of Louisville "was vastly different from its suburbs," given its higher densities, diverse mixed uses, pedestrian-friendly streets, and its "intricate urban fabric." The governing structure that had existed before the merger "reflected" this ecology quite "well," being

healthily balanced with the terrain governed. The merger, however, upset this ecological balance, eliminating the well-fitted governmental structure and amalgamating the territory of the old city with a suburban terrain "characterized by much lower densities, segregated land uses, and sprawled development" (Savitch and Vogel 2004, 771).

3. Weir's (2009) recent work is a notable exception and useful corrective.

4. Compare Elkin's (2006, 266) insight regarding New Deal liberalism, upon which liberal expansionism draws heavy inspiration: such liberalism "views local political life mostly as a problem—the place of backward looking, inegalitarian thinking, and administrative incompetence" (also see Hess 2009).

5. See, for example, Frug 1980, 1999; Elkin 1987; Garber 1990; Norman 1989.

6. And for liberal expansionists, the idea of state actions blocking or impeding individual mobility developed historically, especially during the mid-twentieth century. Discussing federal initiatives impacting cities from the 1930s to the 1960s, leading liberal expansionist William Julius Wilson (2009, 557) recently commented that these "policy decisions worked to *trap* blacks in... increasingly unattractive cities" (emphasis added).

7. More empirical documentation of Dagger's (1997) and Elkin's (1987) point comes from Verba, Schlozman, and Brady's (1995) large-sample statistical study. It found that the number of years one spends in a community correlates with both national and local level civic involvement (with an especially strong effect on the local level). Likewise, a similar but more recent study found such residential stability to be a strong predictor of a variety of forms of political engagement, including attending public or political meetings, belonging to a political organization, signing petitions, and possessing a greater degree of political knowledge (Williamson, forthcoming).

8. The words of Peter Bearse as quoted in Smith (1979, 4).

9. Economic journalist David Cay Johnston (2007) estimates that by 2005, the top tenth of 1 percent (three hundred thousand people) had more income than the 150 million Americans who make up the entire bottom half of the U.S. population. In contrast, in 1979, the top tenth of 1 percent received *only* about a third of the total income of those in or near the bottom half (Johnston 2006).

10. Commenting on this point, Williamson (2007, 34) perceptively writes that "the narrative of using the tools of government power to restrain the excesses of capitalism, and the vision of a society based on substantive equality of opportunity without altering the capitalist power structure, are the only narrative and vision most liberals have ever adhered to."

11. As quoted in Alperovitz (2005, 34).

12. Cf., for example, Lasch 1991; Alperovitz 2005; Elkin 2006; Lind 2007; Dahl 1985.

13. For excellent reviews of what this popular administration (or control) of the economy on the local level might look like, see DeFilippis 2004; Gunn and Gunn 1991; Alperovitz 2005.

14. See Goetz 2000.

15. This contrasts with unionization rates nearing 35 percent of the labor force in the 1950s.

16. As the economic journalist Louis Uchitelle (2008, 3) recently reported, while many leaders argue that "education and training are a route back to...[the] middle class...for those who have fallen out...the demand isn't sufficient to absorb all the workers that leaders would educate. Even now, roughly 15 percent of college-educated workers find themselves in jobs for which they are overqualified." (Also see Wolff 2006; Levy and Temin 2007; Howell 2002). Given the dynamics of economic globalization, even hardcore believers in the idea that enhancing education and skills can be the route toward a greater degree of generalized economic well-being have begun to see the folly in such a proposition (see, especially, the apostasy of Blinder 2007).

17. This trait is of course shared by liberal expansionism, which sees individual spatial mobility as a mere means toward the ultimate goal of individual social mobility.

18. Moreover, the performance of educational systems tends to very much *reflect* the broader socioeconomic environment rather than shape it. Thus, this means of improving the poor social

and economic conditions of a community seems hopeless unless broader community uplift is first achieved (as potentially brought about by the more systemic economic development efforts and attendant politics I outline in the book). Taking a political economy approach to the reform of public education systems, critical theorist and education researcher Jean Anyon (1997, 168) writes that "if we do not resuscitate our cities, we face an impossible situation regarding urban education reform: Attempting to fix inner-city schools without fixing the city in which they are embedded is like trying to clean the air on one side of a screen door" (also see Imbroscio 1998). Along similar lines, evidence strongly indicates the limitations of the Head Start program's noble but largely ineffectual efforts to provide early (pre-school) remedial education to low-income children (Besharov 2005). Such limitations also are suggestive of how difficult it is for educational efforts to overcome disadvantages rooted in broader socioeconomic conditions.

8. The Possibilities of an Alternative Politics

1. See Bruyn 1987.

2. On this last point, see the urban anarchist Murray Bookchin's (1987) explication of his concept of *municipalization*. Also see Sale (1980) and Schumacher (1975).

3. On this more nuanced sense of the commercial orientation, see Elkin's (1987 and 2006) sophisticated discussions of the United States as a *commercial republic*.

4. As quoted in Alperovitz (2005, 34).

5. See the work of political theorist John Scharr for a classic and poignant statement. Equality of opportunity, Scharr (1967, 237) writes,

is the perfect embodiment of the Liberal conception of reform. It breaks up solidaristic opposition to existing conditions of inequality by holding out to the ablest and most ambitious members of the disadvantaged groups the enticing prospect of rising from their lowly state into a more prosperous condition. The rules of the game remain the same: The fundamental character of the social-economic system is unaltered.

6. For a discussion, see Dryzek (1996).

7. See, for example, Cole 2005; Cole and Dempsey 2006; Bucklin 2002; Goldstein 1978.

8. In his recent analysis of mass prison incarceration in the United States, Loury (2007, 4) writes: "Consider the tortured racial history of the War on Drugs. Blacks were twice as likely as whites to be arrested for a drug offense in 1975 but four times as likely by 1989." Between 1980 and 1997, the number of people incarcerated for drug offenses increased elevenfold. The black-white ratio in the incarceration rate now stands at roughly eight to one.

9. For a sample, see Swanstrom (1988) and Stone (1987).

10. The last metaphor, fully expressed as "we all know what we know, it's a hard swath to mow," taken from "New Partner," written by Will Oldham and published by Palace Records/Drag City, Chicago, Illinois, copyright 1995.

11. For an earlier and fuller discussion, see Imbroscio (1999).

12. See, for example, Reed 2004; Faux 2006; Cohen and Rogers 1996; Greider 2009.

13. As the unconventional conservative writer Rod Dreher (2008, 1) recently remarked, in the context of the multiple "converging crises" faced by the United States at this historical juncture, "Wendell Berry's time is now." Explaining how and why Berry's politics transcends conventional notions of Left and Right, Dreher writes of Berry:

Though to all appearances an old-time Democrat, his faithfulness to his iconoclastic vision makes him an uncomfortable presence among the mainstream left and has won him new admirers on the dissident right. He is a moralist hostile both to big government and big business. He is a Christian who can't be understood apart from his deep religious conviction that humankind is under divine command to be good caretakers of creation—the land, its creatures and each other. . . . If you build your politics on this foundation, you will find yourself standing outside the camps of our parties. Most Republicans don't care for him because he is a harsh critic of industrialism, consumerism and the unfettered free market as a destroyer of land, community and healthy traditions. Most Democrats regard him as out of touch because he is a religious man who holds autonomous individualism, especially the sexual freedom it licenses, to be similarly destructive of families, communities and the sacredness of love.

14. http://community-wealth.org/strategies/index.html. As the preamble to this website notes, "Few Americans are aware of the steady build-up of innovative community wealth building strategies throughout the United States. Community-Wealth.org brings together, for the first time, information about the broad range of community wealth building activity."

REFERENCES

Abrams, P. 1982. *Historical Sociology*. Ithaca: Cornell University Press.

Aglietta, Michel. 1976. *A Theory of Capitalist Regulation: The U.S. Experience*. London: New Left Books.

Alexander, S. J. 2007. "Equity Policies and Practices of the Harold Washington Administration: Lessons for Progressive Cities." In *Economic Development in American Cities,* edited by M. J. Bennett and R. P. Giloth, 51–80. Albany: State University of New York Press.

Alperovitz, G. 2004. "The Coming Era of Wealth Taxation." *Dollars and Sense* (July–August): 22–24.

———. 2005. *America beyond Capitalism*. Hoboken, N.J.: Wiley.

Alperovitz, G., and J. Faux. 1979. Introduction to *Towards a Public Balance Sheet: Calculating the Costs and Benefits of Community Stabilization,* by D. Smith with P. McGuigan, i–vi. Washington, D.C.: National Center for Economic Alternatives.

———. 1984. *Rebuilding America*. New York: Pantheon.

Angotti, T. 2008. "The McCain-Obama Mismatch on Urban Policy." *Gotham Gazette* (October). http://www.gothamgazette.com/article/landuse/20081020/12/2680.

Anyon, J. 1997. *Ghetto Schooling: A Political Economy of Urban Educational Reform*. New York: Teachers College Press.

Austin, J., and A. McCaffrey. 2002. "Business Leadership Coalitions and Public-Private Partnerships in American Cities: A Business Perspective on Regime Theory." *Journal of Urban Affairs* 24, no. 1: 35–54.

Babcock, R. F. 1990. "The City as Entrepreneur: Fiscal Wisdom or Regulatory Folly." In *City Deal Making,* edited by T. Lassar, 11–43. Washington, D.C.: Urban Land Institute.

Bailey, R. W. 1999. *Gay Politics, Urban Politics: Identity and Economics in the Urban Setting.* New York: Columbia University Press.

Banfield, E. C., and M. Grodzins. 1958. *Government and Housing in Metropolitan Areas.* New York: McGraw-Hill.

Barber, B. R. 1984. *Strong Democracy: Participatory Politics for a New Age.* Berkeley: University of California Press.

Barnekov, T., and D. Rich. 1989. "Privatism and the Limits of Local Economic Development Policy." *Urban Affairs Quarterly* 25: 212–38.

Barnes, W. 2005. "Beyond Federal Urban Policy." *Urban Affairs Review* 40, no. 5: 575–89.

Bartik, T., and G. Erickcek. 2008. "The Local Economic Impact of 'Eds & Meds.'" Washington, D.C.: Brookings Institution. December. http://www.brookings.edu/reports/2008/1210_metropolitan_economies_bartik_erickcek.aspx.

Basgal, O., and J. Villarreal. 2001. "Comment on Bruce Katz and Margery Turner's 'Who Should Run the Housing Voucher Program?'" *Housing Policy Debate* 12, no. 2: 263–81.

Basolo, V., and M. T. Nguyen. 2005. "Does Mobility Matter?" *Housing Policy Debate* 16, nos. 3–4: 297–324.

Benfield, F. K., M. D. Raimi, and D. D. T. Chen. 1999. *Once There Were Greenfields.* Washington, D.C.: National Resources Defense Council.

Bennett, L., and A. Reed Jr. 1999. "The New Face of Urban Renewal: The Near North Redevelopment Initiative and the Cabrini-Green Neighborhood." In *Without Justice for All: The New Liberalism and Our Retreat from Racial Equality,* edited by A. Reed Jr., 175–211. Boulder, Colo.: Westview Press.

Bennett, L., J. L. Smith, and P. Wright, eds. 2006. *Where Are Poor People to Live? Transforming Public Housing Communities.* Armonk, N.Y.: M. E. Sharpe.

Bennett, L., and C. Spirou. 2006. "Political Leadership and Stadium Development in Chicago: Some Cautionary Notes on the Uses of Regime Analysis." *International Journal of Urban and Regional Research* 30, no. 1: 38–53.

Berger, J. 2005. "Goodbye South Bronx Blight, Hello Trendy SoBro." *New York Times,* 24 June, A1.

Berk, G., and T. Swanstrom. 1994. "Expanding the Agenda of Regime Theory." Paper presented at the annual meeting of the American Political Science Association, New York.

———. 1995. "The Power of Place: Capital (Im)mobility, Pluralism, and Regime Theory." Paper presented at the annual meeting of the American Political Science Association, Chicago.

Berliner, D. 2006. *Opening the Floodgates: Eminent Domain Abuse in the Post-Kelo World.* Arlington, Va.: Institute for Justice. June. http://www.castlecoalition.org/pdf/publications/floodgates-report.pdf.

Berliner, J. S. 1999. *The Economics of the Good Society.* Malden, Mass.: Blackwell.

Bernstein, M. 2009. "Foundation Grants Aimed to Boost University Circle." *Plain Dealer* (Cleveland), 27 March, B1.

Bernstein, R. 1976. *Restructuring of Social and Political Theory.* Philadelphia: University of Pennsylvania Press.

Berry, W. 1996. "Conserving Communities." In *The Case against the Global Economy and for a Turn toward the Local,* edited by J. Mander and E. Goldsmith, 407–17. San Francisco: Sierra Club Books.

Berube, A. 2006. "Overcoming Barriers to Mobility." In *Going Places: Neighbourhood, Ethnicity and Social Mobility,* edited by S. Delorenzi, 1–28. London: Institute for Public Policy Research.

Berube, A., and B. Katz. 2005. "Katrina's Window: Confronting Concentrated Poverty across America." *Special Analysis in Metropolitan Policy.* Washington, D.C.: Brookings Institution.

Besharov, D.J. 2005. "Head Start's Broken Promise." Washington, D.C.: American Enterprise Institute for Public Policy Research. October. http://www.aei.org/publications/pubID.23373/pub_detail.asp.

Betancur, J. J., and D. C. Gills. 1993. "Race and Class in Local Economic Development." In *Theories of Local Economic Development,* edited by R. D. Bingham and R. Mier, 191–212. Newbury Park, Calif.: Sage Publications.

Bhaskar, R. 1979. *The Possibility of Naturalism.* Atlantic Highlands, N.J.: Humanities Press.

Black, H. 1991. *Achieving Economic Development Success: Tools That Work.* Washington, D.C.: International City/County Management Association.

Blackwell, A., and H. McCulloch. 2002. "Resident Ownership Mechanisms: Low-Income Neighborhoods Take Control." *Building Blocks* 3, no. 1: 1–4.

Blakely, E. J. 1989. *Local Economic Development: Theory and Practice.* Newbury Park, Calif.: Sage Publications.

Blinder, A. S. 2007. "Free Trade's Great, but Offshoring Rattles Me." *Washington Post,* May 6, B04.

Block, F. 1977. "The Ruling Class Does Not Rule: Notes on the Marxist Theory of the State." *Socialist Review* 7, no. 3: 6–28.

Bluestone, B., and B. Harrison. 1987. "Jobs, Income, and Health." In *Deindustrialization and Plant Closure,* edited by P. D. Staudohar and H. E. Brown, 61–73. Lexington, Mass.: Lexington Books.

Bluestone, B., M. H. Stevenson, and R. Williams. 2008. *The Urban Experience.* Oxford: Oxford University Press.

Bobrow, D. B., and J. S. Dryzek. 1987. *Policy Analysis by Design.* Pittsburgh: University of Pittsburgh Press.

Bollens, S. A. 1997. "Concentrated Poverty and Metropolitan Equity Strategies." *Stanford Law and Policy Review* 8, no. 2: 11–24.

———. 2003. "In through the Back Door." *Housing Policy Debate* 13, no. 4: 631–57.

Bolton, R. 1992. "Place Prosperity vs. People Prosperity: An Old Issue with a New Angle." *Urban Studies* 29, no. 2: 185–203.

Bookchin, M. 1987. *The Rise of Urbanization and the Decline of Citizenship.* San Francisco: Sierra Club Books.

Bourassa, S. C. 2006. "The Community Land Trust as a Highway Environmental Impact Mitigation Tool." *Journal of Urban Affairs* 28, no. 4: 399–418.

Bourdieu, P. 1990. *The Logic of Practice.* Translated by R. Nice. Cambridge: Polity Press.

Bowman, A. 1987. *Tools and Targets.* Washington, D.C.: National League of Cities.

Boyte, H. 1980. *The Backyard Revolution.* Philadelphia: Temple University Press.

Bratt, R. G. 2006a. "Community Development Corporations." In *A Right to Housing,* edited by R. G. Bratt, M. E. Stone, and C. Hartman, 340–59. Philadelphia: Temple University Press.

——. 2006b. "Housing and Economic Security." In *A Right to Housing,* edited by R. G. Bratt, M. E. Stone, and C. Hartman, 399–426. Philadelphia: Temple University Press.

Briggs, X. 1997a. "Moving Up vs. Moving Out." *Housing Policy Debate* 8, no. 1: 195–234.

——. 1997b. "Comment on Sandra J. Newman and Ann B. Schnare's 'And a Suitable Living Environment': The Failure of Housing Programs to Deliver on Neighborhood Quality." *Housing Policy Debate* 8, no. 4: 743–53.

——. 2005a. "Politics and Policy: Changing the Geography of Opportunity." In *The Geography of Opportunity,* edited by X. Briggs, 310–39. Washington, D.C.: Brookings Institution.

——. 2005b. Introduction to *The Geography of Opportunity,* edited by X. Briggs, 1–16. Washington, D.C.: Brookings Institution.

——. 2005c. "Conclusion: Desegregating the City." In *Desegregating the City,* edited by D. P. Varady, 233–57. Albany: State University of New York Press.

——. 2008. "Maximum Feasible Misunderstanding: A Reply to Imbroscio." *Journal of Urban Affairs* 30, no. 2: 131–37.

Briggs, X., et al. 2005. "Moving to Opportunity in the Wake of Hurricane Katrina." 15 September. New Vision: An Institute for Policy and Progress. http://www.newvisioninstitute.org/movingOppotunityScholarsPetition.pdf.

Broder, J. M. 2008. "Obama Urges Mayors to Focus on Urban Growth, but Not Expect Increased Federal Aid." *New York Times,* 22 June.

Brookings Institution. 2002. *Beyond Merger: A Competitive Vision for the Regional City of Louisville.* Washington, D.C.: Brookings Institution.

Brown, J. 1993. "Third Sector Enterprises in the United Kingdom and Australia." In *Community-Economic Development,* edited by D. Fasenfest, 205–21. London: Macmillan.

Brown, M. 1999. "Reconceptualizing Public and Private in Urban Regime Theory: Governance in AIDS Politics." *International Journal of Urban and Regional Research* 23, no. 1: 45–69.

Browning, E. K., and J. M. Browning. 1983. *Public Finance and the Price System.* New York: Macmillan.

Bruyn, S. T. 1987. "Beyond the Market and the State." In *Beyond the Market and the State: New Directions in Community Development,* edited by S. T. Bruyn and J. Meehan, 3–27. Philadelphia: Temple University Press.

Bucklin, S. J. 2002. "To Preserve These Rights: The Constitution and National Emergencies." *South Dakota Law Review* 47: 85–98.

Burns, E., and P. Gober. 1998. "Job Linkages in Inner-City Phoenix." *Urban Geography* 19, no. 1: 12–23.

Burns, P. 2003. "Regime Theory, State Government, and a Takeover of Urban Education." *Journal of Urban Affairs* 25, no. 3: 285–303.

Buss, T. F., and L. Yancer. 1999. "Cost Benefit Analysis: A Normative Perspective." *Economic Development Quarterly* 13: 29–37.

Carr, J. H. 1999. "Community, Capital, and Markets: A New Paradigm for Community Reinvestment." *NeighborWorks Journal* 17, no. 3: 20–23.

Castro, B. 1998. "Manufacturing Jobs, Local Ownership, and the Social Health of Cities—A Research Note." *Responsive Community* 8: 63–66.

Chalkley, T. 1991. "Collision Course." *Baltimore City Paper,* 5 April: 10–19.

Charles, C. Z. 2005. "Can We Live Together?" In *The Geography of Opportunity,* edited by X. Briggs, 45–80. Washington, D.C.: Brookings Institution.

Clark, G. L. 1983. *Interregional Migration, National Policy, and Social Justice.* Totowa, N.J.: Rowman and Allanheld.

Clark, W.A.V. 2008. "Reexamining the Moving to Opportunity Study and Its Contribution to Changing the Distribution of Poverty and Ethnic Concentration." *Demography* 45, no. 3: 515–35.

———. 2009. "Residential Preferences across Income, Education, and Age." *Urban Affairs Review* 44, no. 3: 334–55.

Clarke, S. E., and G. L. Gaile. 1998. *The Work of Cities.* Minneapolis: University of Minnesota Press.

Clavel, P. 1986. *The Progressive City: Planning and Participation, 1969–1984.* New Brunswick, N.J.: Rutgers University Press.

Clavel, P., and C. Kleniewski. 1990. "Space for Progressive Local Policy: Examples from the U.S. and U.K." In *Beyond the City Limits,* edited by J. Logan and T. Swanstrom, 199–236. Philadelphia: Temple University Press.

Clavel, P., and W. Wiewel. 1991. Introduction to *Harold Washington and the Neighborhoods: Progressive City Government in Chicago, 1983–1987,* edited by P. Clavel and W. Wiewel, 1–33. New Brunswick, N.J.: Rutgers University Press.

Clawson, D. 2003. *The Next Upsurge: Labor and the New Social Movements.* Ithaca: ILR/Cornell University Press.

Cleveland Foundation. 2008. "Cleveland, OH: Blueprint for a Green Economy." Cleveland Foundation. April. http://www.community-wealth.org/_pdfs/news/recent-articles/07-08/article-cleveland-fdn08.pdf.

Cohen, J., and J. Rogers. 1996. "After Liberalism." *Good Society* 6, no. 1: 18–24.

Cole, D. 2005. *Enemy Aliens: Double Standards and Constitutional Freedoms in the War on Terrorism.* New York: New Press.

Cole, D., and J. X. Dempsey. 2006. *Terrorism and the Constitution: Sacrificing Civil Liberties in the Name of National Security.* 2nd ed. New York: W. W. Norton.

Cole, S. 1994. "A Community Accounting Matrix for Buffalo's East Side Neighborhood." *Economic Development Quarterly* 8: 107–24.

Collins, T. 2008. "Unevenness in Urban Governance: Stadium Building and Downtown Redevelopment in Phoenix, Arizona." *Environment and Planning C: Government and Policy* 26: 1177–96.

Collom, E. 2005. "Community Currency in the United States: The Social Environments in Which It Emerges and Survives." *Environment and Planning A* 37: 1565–87.

Cox, K. R. 2001. "Illusion, Reality, and the Politics of Place." *Good Society* 10, no. 2: 12–15.

Cox, K. R., and A. Mair. 1988. "Locality and Community in the Politics of Local Economic Development." *Annals of the Association of American Geographers* 78: 307–25.

Crump, J. 2002. "Deconcentration by Demolition: Public Housing, Poverty, and Urban Policy." *Environment and Planning D: Society and Space* 20: 581–96.

——. 2003. "Rejoinder." *International Journal of Urban and Regional Research* 27, no. 1: 193–95.

Cummings, S. B., C. T. Koebel, and J. A. Whitt. 1989. "Redevelopment in Downtown Louisville: Public Investments, Private Profits, and Shared Risks." In *Unequal Partnerships: The Political Economy of Urban Redevelopment in Postwar America,* edited by G. D. Squires, 202–21. New Brunswick, N.J.: Rutgers University Press.

Dagger, R. 1997. *Civic Virtues: Rights, Citizenship, and Republican Liberalism.* New York: Oxford University Press.

Dahl, R. 1961. *Who Governs?* New Haven: Yale University Press.

——. 1985. *A Preface to Economic Democracy.* Berkeley: University of California Press.

Davies, J.S. 2002. "Urban Regime Theory: A Normative-Empirical Critique." *Journal of Urban Affairs* 24, no. 1: 1–17.

——. 2003. "Partnerships versus Regimes: Why Regime Theory Cannot Explain Urban Coalitions in the UK." *Journal of Urban Affairs* 25, no. 3: 253–69.

——. 2004. "Can't Hedgehogs Be Foxes too? Reply to Clarence N. Stone." *Journal of Urban Affairs* 26, no. 1: 27–33.

——. Forthcoming. "Back to the Future: Marxism and Urban Politics." In *Critical Urban Studies: New Directions,* edited by J. Davies and D. Imbroscio. Albany: State University of New York Press.

Davies, J. S., and D. L. Imbroscio, eds. 2009. *Theories of Urban Politics, Second Edition.* London: Sage Publications.

Davis, J. E. 2006. *Shared Equity Homeownership: The Changing Landscape of Resale-Restricted, Owner-Occupied Housing.* National Housing Institute. http://www.nhi.org/pdf/SharedEquityHome.pdf.

Davis, J. E., and A. Demetrowitz. 2003. *Permanently Affordable Homeownership: Does the Community Land Trust Deliver on Its Promises?* Burlington, Vt.: Burlington Community Land Trust.

DeFilippis, J. 2004. *Unmaking Goliath: Community Control in the Face of Global Capital.* New York: Routledge.

DeLeon, R. E. 1992. *Left Coast City: Progressive Politics in San Francisco, 1975–1991.* Lawrence: University Press of Kansas.

DeLuca, S., and J. E. Rosenbaum. 2003. "If Low-Income Blacks Are Given a Chance to Live in White Neighborhoods, Will They Stay?" *Housing Policy Debate* 14, no. 3: 305–45.

De Socio, M. 2007. "Business Community Structures and Urban Regimes: A Comparative Analysis." *Journal of Urban Affairs* 29, no. 4: 339–66.

DiGaetano, A., and J. S. Klemanski. 1993. "Urban Regimes in Comparative Perspective." *Urban Affairs Quarterly* 29: 54–83.

Dionne, E. J. 1991. *Why Americans Hate Politics.* New York: Simon and Schuster.

Downs, A. 1973. *Opening Up the Suburbs: An Urban Strategy for America.* New Haven: Yale University Press.

———. 1981. *Neighborhoods and Urban Development.* Washington, D.C.: Brookings Institution.

———. 1993. "Reducing Regulatory Barriers to Affordable Housing Erected by Local Governments." In *Housing Markets and Residential Mobility,* edited by G. T. Kingsley and M. A. Turner, 255–81. Washington, D.C.: Urban Institute.

———. 1994. *New Visions for Metropolitan America.* Washington, D.C.: Brookings Institution.

Dreher, R. 2008. "Wendell Berry's Time Is Now." *Dallas Morning News,* 26 October. http://www.dallasnews.com/sharedcontent/dws/dn/opinion/points/stories/DN-dreher_26edi.State.Edition1.21c9278.html.

Dreier, P. J., J. H. Mollenkopf, and T. Swanstrom. 2001. *Place Matters: Metropolitics for the Twenty-first Century.* Lawrence: University Press of Kansas.

———. 2004. *Place Matters: Metropolitics for the Twenty-First Century.* 2nd ed. Lawrence: University Press of Kansas.

Dryzek, J. S. 1987. *Rational Ecology: Environment and Political Economy.* Oxford: Basil Blackwell.

———. 1988. "The Mismeasure of Political Man." *Journal of Politics* 50: 705–25.

———. 1996. *Democracy in Capitalist Times.* Oxford: Oxford University Press.

Dudley, K. M. 1994. *The End of the Line: Lost Jobs, New Lives in Postindustrial America.* Chicago: University of Chicago Press.

Dymski, G. A. 1997. "Business Strategy and Access to Capital in Inner-City Revitalization." In *The Inner City: Urban Poverty and Economic Development in the Next Century,* edited by T. D. Boston and C. L. Ross, 51–65. New Brunswick, N.J.: Transaction.

Edsall, T. B., and M. D. Edsall. 1991. *Chain Reaction: The Impact of Race, Rights, and Taxes on American Politics.* New York: W. W. Norton.

Eisinger, P. 1988. *The Rise of the Entrepreneurial State.* Madison: University of Wisconsin Press.

———. 2000. "The Politics of Bread and Circuses: Building the City for the Visitor Class." *Urban Affairs Review* 35, no. 3: 316–33.

Elkin, S. L. 1982. "Market and Politics in Liberal Democracy." *Ethics* 92: 720–32.

———. 1985a. "Pluralism in Its Place: State and Regime in Liberal Democracy." In *The Democratic State,* edited by R. Benjamin and S. L. Elkin, 179–211. Lawrence: University Press of Kansas.

———. 1985b. "Between Liberalism and Capitalism." In *The Democratic State,* edited by R. Benjamin and S. L. Elkin, 1–17. Lawrence: University Press of Kansas.

———. 1985c. "Twentieth Century Urban Regimes." *Journal of Urban Affairs* 7, no. 2: 11–28.

———. 1987. *City and Regime in the American Republic.* Chicago: University of Chicago Press.

———. 1993. "Beyond Policy: Good Institutions, Good Societies and the PEGS Agenda." *Newsletter of PEGS* 3: 1, 6.

——. 1994. "Business-State Relations in the Commercial Republic." *Journal of Political Philosophy* 2: 115–39.

——. 1999. "Citizen and City: Locality, Public Spiritedness, and the American Regime." In *Dilemmas of Scale in America's Federal Democracy,* edited by M. Derthick, 41–60. Cambridge: Cambridge University Press.

——. 2006. *Reconstructing the Commercial Republic: Constitutional Design after Madison.* Chicago: University of Chicago Press.

Ellen, I. G. 2000. *Sharing America's Neighborhoods: The Prospects for Stable Racial Integration.* Cambridge: Harvard University Press.

Elliott, D. S., S. Menard, B. Rankin, A. Elliot, W. J. Wilson, and D. Huizinga. 2006. *Good Kids from Bad Neighborhoods.* Cambridge: Cambridge University Press.

Etzioni, A. 1993. *The Spirit of Community: Rights, Responsibilities, and the Communitarian Agenda.* New York: Crown Publishing Group.

Euchner, C., and S. McGovern. 2003. *Urban Policy Reconsidered: Dialogues on the Problems and Prospects of American Cities.* New York: Routledge.

Fainstein, N. I., and S. S. Fainstein. 1983. "Regime Strategies, Communal Resistance, and Economic Forces." In *Restructuring the City: The Political Economy of Urban Redevelopment,* by S. S. Fainstein, N. I. Fainstein, R. Child-Hill, D. Judd, and M. P. Smith, 245–82. New York: Longman.

Fainstein, S. S., N. I. Fainstein, R. Child-Hill, D. Judd, and M. P. Smith. 1983. *Restructuring the City: The Political Economy of Urban Redevelopment.* New York: Longman.

Faux, J. 2006. "The Party of Davos." *Nation,* 13 February: 18–22.

Feagin, J. R., and R. Parker. 1990. *Building American Cities: The Urban Real Estate Game.* Englewood Cliffs, N.J.: Prentice-Hall.

Ferman, B. 1996. *Challenging the Growth Machine.* Lawrence: University Press of Kansas.

Fisher, L. M. 1987. "Cities Turn into Entrepreneurs." *New York Times,* 4 April, A33.

Fisher, P. S. 1988. "State Venture Capital Funds as an Economic Development Strategy." *Journal of the American Planning Association* 54: 166–77.

Fisher, P. S., and A. H. Peters. 1998. *Industrial Incentives: Competition among American States and Cities.* Kalamazoo, Mich.: W. E. Upjohn Institute.

——. 2004. "The Failures of Economic Development Incentives." *Journal of the American Planning Association* 70, no. 1: 27–38.

Fiss, O. 2003. "What Should Be Done for Those Who Have Been Left Behind?" In *A Way Out: America's Ghettos and the Legacy of Racism,* edited by J. Cohen, J. Decker, and J. Rogers, 3–43. Princeton: Princeton University Press.

Fitzgerald, J. 1993. "Labor Force, Education, and Work." In *Theories of Local Economic Development,* edited by R. Bingham and R. Mier, 125–46. Newbury Park, Calif.: Sage Publications.

Florida, R. 2002. *The Rise of the Creative Class.* New York: Basic Books.

Friedman, M. 1962. *Capitalism and Freedom.* Chicago: University of Chicago Press.

Friedman, R. 1986. "Entrepreneurial Renewal in the Industrial City." *Annals of the American Academy of Political and Social Science,* November: 35–44.

Frug, G. E. 1980. "The City as a Legal Concept." *Harvard Law Review* 93: 1059–1154.

——. 1999. *City Making: Building Communities without Walls.* Princeton: Princeton University Press.

Frug, G. E., and D. Barron. 2008. *City Bound*. Ithaca: Cornell University Press.

Fung, A., and E. O. Wright, eds. 2003. *Deepening Democracy: Institutional Innovations in Empowered Participatory Governance*. London: Verso.

Gainsborough, J. F. 2001. *Fenced Off: The Suburbanization of American Politics*. Washington, D.C.: Georgetown University Press.

Galster, G. C. 2005. "Consequences from the Redistribution of Urban Poverty during the 1990s: A Cautionary Tale." *Economic Development Quarterly* 19, no. 2: 119–25.

Galster, G., and A. Zobel. 1998. "Will Dispersed Housing Programmes Reduce Social Problems in the U.S.?" *Housing Studies* 13, no. 5: 605–22.

Ganz, A. 1986. "Where Has the Urban Crisis Gone?" In *Cities in Stress*, edited by M. Gottdiener, 39–58. Beverly Hills, Calif.: Sage Publications.

Garber, J. A. 1989. "The Legal Crisis of Local Land Regulations: An Evaluation." *Urban Resources* 5, no. 1: 20–26.

———. 1990. "Law and the Possibilities for a Just Political Economy." *Journal of Urban Affairs* 12: 1–15.

Gaventa, J. 1980. *Power and Powerlessness*. Urbana: University of Illinois Press.

Gendron, R. 2006. "Forging Collective Capacity for Urban Redevelopment: 'Power To,' 'Power Over,' or Both?" *City & Community* 5, no. 1: 5–22.

Gendron, R., and W. Domhoff. 2009. *The Leftmost City: Power and Progressive Politics in Santa Cruz*. Boulder, Colo.: Westview Press.

Geronimus, A. T., and J. P. Thompson. 2004. "To Denigrate, Ignore, or Disrupt: Racial Inequality in Health and the Impact of a Policy-Induced Breakdown of African-American Communities." *Du Bois Review* 1, no. 2: 247–79.

Gibson, K. J. 2007. "The Relocation of the Columbia Villa Community: Views from Residents." *Journal of Planning Education and Research* 27: 5–19.

Giddens, A. 1979. *Central Problems in Social Theory*. Berkeley: University of California Press.

Giloth, R. 1988. "Community Economic Development: Strategies and Practices of the 1980s." *Economic Development Quarterly* 2: 343–50.

———. 1991. "Making Policy with Communities: Research and Development in the Department of Economic Development." In *Harold Washington and the Neighborhoods: Progressive City Government in Chicago 1983–1987*, edited by P. Clavel and W. Wiewel, 100–120. New Brunswick, N.J.: Rutgers University Press.

———. 2007a. "Introduction: Full Employment and Local Workforce." In *Economic Development in American Cities*, edited by M. J. Bennett and R. P. Giloth, 1–21. Albany: State University of New York Press.

———. 2007b. "Investing in Equity: Targeted Economic Development for Neighborhoods and Cities." In *Economic Development in American Cities*, edited by M. J. Bennett and R. P. Giloth, 23–50. Albany: State University of New York Press.

Glaser, M., L. Parker, and H. Li. 2003. "Community of Choice or Ghetto of Last Resort: Community Development and the Viability of an African American Community." *Review of Policy Research* 20, no. 3: 525–48.

Goering, J. 2003. "Comments on Future Research and Housing Policy." In *Choosing a Better Life: Evaluating the Moving to Opportunity Social Experiment*, edited by J. Goering and J. D. Feins, 383–407. Washington, D.C.: Urban Institute.

Goering, J., and J. D. Feins, eds. 2003. *Choosing a Better Life: Evaluating the Moving to Opportunity Social Experiment.* Washington, D.C.: Urban Institute.

Goering, J., J. D. Feins, and T. M. Richardson. 2003. "What Have We Learned about Housing Mobility and Poverty Deconcentration?" In *Choosing a Better Life: Evaluating the Moving to Opportunity Social Experiment,* edited by J. Goering and J. D. Feins, 3–36. Washington, D.C.: Urban Institute.

Goetz, E. G. 1990. "Type II Policy and Mandated Benefits in Economic Development." *Urban Affairs Quarterly* 25: 170–90.

———. 2000. "The New Slum Clearance: Redevelopment of Public Housing and the Deconcentration of Poverty." Paper presented at the annual meeting of the Urban Affairs Association, Los Angeles.

———. 2003. *Clearing the Way.* Washington, D.C.: Urban Institute.

Goetz, E. G., and K. Chapple. Forthcoming. "Dispersal as Anti-Poverty Policy." In *Critical Urban Studies: New Directions,* edited by J. Davies and D. Imbroscio. Albany: State University of New York Press.

Goldsmith, W. W., and E. J. Blakely. 1992. *Separate Societies: Poverty and Inequality in U.S. Cities.* Philadelphia: Temple University Press.

Goldstein, R. J. 1978. *Political Repression in Modern America: From 1870 to the Present.* Cambridge, Mass.: Schenkman.

Goodin, R. E. 2000. "Something for Nothing? A Response to 'A Basic Income for All' by Philippe van Parijs." *Boston Review.* October/November. http://bostonreview.net/BR25.5/goodin.html.

Goodman, Robert. 1972. *After the Planners.* New York: Simon and Schuster.

Granovetter, M. 1985. "Economic Action and Social Structure: The Problem of Embeddedness." *American Journal of Sociology* 91: 481–510.

Green, D., and I. Shapiro. 1994. *Pathologies of Rational Choice.* New Haven: Yale University Press.

———. 2005. "Revisiting the Pathologies of Rational Choice." In *The Flight from Reality in the Human Sciences,* edited by I. Shapiro, 51–99. Princeton: Princeton University Press.

Greenbaum, S. 2006. "Comments on Katrina." *City & Community* 5, no. 2: 109–13.

Greenbaum, S., W. Hathaway, C. Rodriguez, A. Spalding, and B. Ward. 2008. "Deconcentration and Social Capital: Contradictions of a Poverty Alleviation Policy." *Journal of Poverty* 12, no. 2: 201–28.

Greenblatt, A. 2002. "Anatomy of a Merger." *Governing* (December): 20–25.

———. 2003. "Merger Maestro." *Governing* (November): 28.

Grieder, W. 1993. "The Temporary Miracle." *Rolling Stone,* 9 August: 32–33, 87.

———. 2005. "The New Colossus." *Nation,* 28 February: 13–18.

———. 2009. *Come Home, America: The Rise and Fall (and Redeeming Promise) of Our Country.* New York: Rodale Books.

Grover, D. 2006. "Would Local Currencies Make a Good Local Economic Development Tool? The Case of Ithaca Hours." *Environment and Planning C: Government and Policy* 24: 719–37.

Gunn, C., and H. D. Gunn. 1991. *Reclaiming Capital: Democratic Initiatives and Community Development.* Ithaca: Cornell University Press.

Gunnell, J. 2004. *Imagining the American Polity: Political Science and the Discourse of Democracy.* University Park: Pennsylvania State University Press.

Habermas, J. 1975. *Legitimation Crisis.* Translated by T. McCarthy. Boston: Beacon Press.

Hackworth, J. 2007. *The Neoliberal City: Governance, Ideology, and Development in American Urbanism.* Ithaca: Cornell University Press.

Hamel, P., and B. Jouve. 2008. "In Search of a Stable Urban Regime for Montreal: Issues and Challenges in Metropolitan Development." *Urban Research and Practice* 1, no. 1: 18–35.

Hammond, J. 1987. "Consumer Cooperatives." In *Beyond the Market and the State: New Directions in Community Development,* edited by S. T. Bruyn and J. Meehan, 97–112. Philadelphia: Temple University Press.

Harding, A. 1994. "Urban Regimes and Growth Machines: Toward a Cross-National Research Agenda." *Urban Affairs Quarterly* 29: 356–82.

Hargraves, M. 1998. "The Multiplier Effect of Local Currency." Ithaca HOURS website. http://www.ithacahours.com/archive/9812.html.

Harkavy, I., and H. Zuckerman. 1999. "Eds and Meds: Cities' Hidden Assets." Washington, D.C.: Brookings Institution. September. http://www.brookings.edu/reports/1999/09cities_ira-harkavy-and-harmon-zuckerman.aspx.

Harte, G. 1986. "Social Accounting in the Local Economy." *Local Economy* 1, no. 1: 45–56.

Hartman, C. 1984. "The Right to Stay Put." In *Land Reform, American Style,* edited by C. C. Geisler and F. J. Popper, 302–18. Totowa, N.J.: Rowman and Allanheld.

——. 1991. "Comment on Anthony Downs's 'The Advisory Commission on Regulatory Barriers to Affordable Housing.'" *Housing Policy Debate* 2, no. 4: 1161–68.

——. 2002. *Between Eminence and Notoriety: Four Decades of Radical Planning.* New Brunswick, N.J.: Center for Urban Policy Research.

Hartog, H. 1983. *Public Property and Private Power: The Corporation of the City of New York in American Law, 1730–1870.* Chapel Hill: University of North Carolina Press.

Harvey, D. 1991. "Flexibility: Threat or Opportunity." *Socialist Review* 21: 65–77.

Haveman, R. H., ed. 1977. *A Decade of Federal Antipoverty Programs.* New York: Academic Press.

Heilbroner, R. 1988. *Behind the Veil of Economics.* New York: W. W. Norton.

Henig, J. 1985. *Public Policy and Federalism: Issues in State and Local Politics.* New York: St. Martin's Press.

——. 1992. "Defining City Limits." *Urban Affairs Quarterly* 27: 375–95.

Herrero, T. 1991. "Housing Linkage: Will It Play a Role in the 1990s?" *Journal of Urban Affairs* 13: 1–19.

Herzog, D. 1989. *Happy Slaves: A Critique of Consent Theory.* Chicago: University of Chicago Press.

Hess, D. J. 2009. *Localist Movements in a Global Economy: Sustainability, Justice, and Urban Development in the United States.* Cambridge: MIT Press.

Hochschild, J. 2003. "Creating Options." In *A Way Out: America's Ghettos and the Legacy of Racism,* edited by J. Cohen, J. Decker, and J. Rogers, 68–73. Princeton: Princeton University Press.

Holman, N. 2007. "Following the Signs: Applying Urban Regime Analysis to a UK Case Study." *Journal of Urban Affairs* 29, no. 5: 435–53.

Horan, C. 1997. "Coalition, Market, and State: Postwar Development Politics in Boston." In *Reconstructing Urban Regime Theory,* edited by M. Lauria, 149–70. Thousand Oaks, Calif.: Sage Publications.

———. 2002. "Racializing Regime Politics." *Journal of Urban Affairs* 24, no. 1: 19–33.

Hornack, J. S., and S. Lynd. 1987. "The Steel Valley Authority." *Review of Law and Social Change* 15: 113–25.

Howell, D. 2002. "Skills and the Wage Collapse." In *Making Work Pay: America after Welfare,* edited by R. Kuttner, 181–96. New York: New Press.

Huber, M. S. 2000. *Community Income and Expenditures Model Implementation Manual.* Lansing: Center for Urban Affairs, Michigan State University.

Hunter, F. 1953. *Community Power Structure.* Chapel Hill: University of North Carolina Press.

———. 1980. *Community Power Succession: Atlanta's Policy-Makers Revisited.* Chapel Hill: University of North Carolina Press.

Husock, H. 2003. *America's Trillion Dollar Housing Mistake: The Failure of American Housing Policy.* Chicago: Ivan R. Dee.

Imbroscio, D. L. 1993. "Overcoming the Economic Dependence of Urban America." *Journal of Urban Affairs* 15: 173–90.

———. 1997. *Reconstructing City Politics.* Thousand Oaks, Calif.: Sage Publications.

———. 1998. "The Necessity of Regime Change." *Journal of Urban Affairs* 20: 261–68.

———. 1999. "Structure, Agency, and Democratic Theory." *Polity* 32, no. 1: 45–66.

———. 2003. "Overcoming the Neglect of Economics in Urban Regime Theory." *Journal of Urban Affairs* 25: 271–84.

———. 2004a. "Can We Grant a Right to Place?" *Politics and Society* 32: 575–609.

———. 2004b. "Fighting Poverty with Mobility: A Normative Policy Analysis." *Review of Policy Research* 21, no. 3: 447–61.

———. 2004c. "The Imperative of Economics in Urban Political Analysis." *Journal of Urban Affairs* 26: 21–26.

———. 2008. "Rebutting Non-Rebuttals: A Rejoinder to My Critics." *Journal of Urban Affairs* 30, no. 2: 149–54.

———. Forthcoming. "Keeping It Critical: Resisting the Allure of the Mainstream." In *Critical Urban Studies: New Directions,* edited by J. Davies and D. Imbroscio. Albany: State University of New York Press.

Imbroscio, D., T. Williamson, and G. Alperovitz. 2003. "Local Policy Responses to Globalization: Place-Based Ownership Models of Economic Enterprise." *Policy Studies Journal* 31: 31–52.

Isaac, J. C. 2003. *The Poverty of Progressivism.* Lanham, Md.: Rowman and Littlefield.

Jackson, K. T. 1985. *Crabgrass Frontier: The Suburbanization of America.* New York: Oxford University Press.

Jacobs, J. 1961. *The Death and Life of Great American Cities.* New York: Random House.

———. 1969. *The Economy of Cities.* New York: Random House.

———. 1984. *Cities and the Wealth of Nations: Principles of Economic Life.* New York: Random House.

Jacobus, R., and M. Brown. 2007. "City Hall Steps In." *Shelterforce,* Spring. http://www.shelterforce.org/article/675/city_hall_steps_in/.

Jakle, J. A., and D. Wilson. 1992. *Derelict Landscapes.* Savage, Md.: Rowman and Littlefield.

Jargowsky, P. 2002. "Review of *Place Matters.*" *Urban Affairs Review* 37, no. 3: 442–51.

Jencks, C., and S. Mayer. 1990. "The Social Consequences of Growing Up in a Poor Neighborhood." In *Inner-City Poverty in the United States,* edited by L. E. Lynn and M. G. H. McGeary, 111–86. Washington, D.C.: National Academy Press.

Johnston, D. C. 2006. "'04 Income in U.S. Was Below 2000 Level." *New York Times,* 28 November, C1.

———. 2007. *Free Lunch: How the Wealthiest Americans Enrich Themselves at Government Expense (and Stick You with the Bill).* New York: Penguin Books.

Jones, B., and L. Bachelor. 1986. *The Sustaining Hand.* Lawrence: University Press of Kansas.

Jost, K. 2008. "Property Rights." *Urban Issues: Selections from CQ Researcher.* 4th ed. 263–284. Washington, D.C.: CQ Press.

Judd, D. R., ed. 2003. *The Infrastructure of Play: Building the Tourist City.* Armonk, NY: M. E. Sharpe.

———. 2005. "Everything Is Always Going to Hell: Urban Scholars as End-Times Prophets." *Urban Affairs Review* 41, no. 2: 119–31.

Judd, D. R., and T. Swanstrom. 1988. "Business and Cities: The Enduring Tension." *Urban Resources* 5: 3–8, 44–46.

Kanter, R. M. 1995. *World Class: Thriving Locally in the Global Economy.* New York: Simon and Schuster.

Kantor, P. 1995. *The Dependent City Revisited.* Boulder, Colo.: Westview Press.

———. 2000. "Can Regionalism Save Poor Cities?" *Urban Affairs Review* 35, no. 6: 794–820.

Kantor, P., with S. David. 1988. *The Dependent City.* Glenview, Ill.: Scott, Foresman/ Little Brown.

Kantor, P., H. V. Savitch, and S. V. Haddock. 1997. "The Political Economy of Urban Regimes." *Urban Affairs Review* 32: 348–77.

Kasarda, J. 1992. "Urban Employment Change and Minority Skills Mismatch." In *Enduring Tensions in Urban Politics,* edited by D. Judd and P. Kantor, 616–32. New York: Macmillan.

Katz, B., ed. 2000. *Reflections on Regionalism.* Washington, D.C.: Brookings Institution.

Katz, B., and M. Muro. 2005. "Distinctive, Equitable, Competitive." *Courier-Journal* (Louisville), 23 January. http://www.brookings.edu/opinions/2005/0123metropolitan policy_katz.aspx.

Katz, B., and M. Turner. 2001. "Who Should Run the Housing Voucher Program?" *Housing Policy Debate* 12, no. 2: 239–62.

Keiser, R. A. 2009. "A Slingshot for the Urban David: How Local Referenda Alter Regime Theory Solution Sets and Provide Pluralist Representation in Sports

Stadium Policy." Paper presented at annual meeting of the Midwest Political Science Association, Chicago.

Kelly, R. M. 1977. *Community Control of Economic Development.* New York: Praeger.

Kieschnick, M. 1981. "The Role of Equity Capital in Urban Economic Development." In *Expanding the Capacity to Produce,* edited by R. Friedman and W. Schweke, 374–86. Washington, D.C.: Corporation for Enterprise Development.

King, L. A. 2004. "Democracy and City Life." *Politics, Philosophy & Economics* 3: 97–124.

Kingsley, G. T., and K. L. S. Pettit. 2005. "Comment on George C. Galster's 'Consequences from the Redistribution of Urban Poverty.'" *Economic Development Quarterly* 19, no. 2: 126–32.

Kipfer, S. 2004. "'Metropolitics' and the Quest for a New Regionalist Corporatism in the United States." *Antipode* 36, no. 4: 740–52.

Kirby, A. 2004. "Metropolitics or Retropolitics." *Antipode* 36, no. 4: 753–59.

Kleit, R. G., and L. C. Manzo. 2006. "To Move or Not to Move: Relationships to Place and Relocation Choices in HOPE VI." *Housing Policy Debate* 17, no. 2: 271–308.

Kling, J. R., J. Liebman, and L. Katz. 2007. "Experimental Analysis of Neighborhood Effects." *Econometrica* 75, no. 1: 83–119.

Kling, J. R., J. Liebman, L. Katz, and L. Sanbonmatsu. 2004. "Moving to Opportunity and Tranquility." Princeton Industrial Relations Section Working Paper #481, April.

Knopp, L. 2008. "The Role of Incubators in Cultivating Small Business." Federal Reserve Bank of San Francisco. http://www.frbsf.org/publications/community/investments/0308/article3a.html.

Kotkin, J., and D. Zimmerman. 2006. *Rebuilding America's Productive Economy: A Heartland Development Strategy.* Washington, D.C.: New America Foundation.

Kraker, D. 2000. "Keeping the Minors Home." *New Rules* 2: 13–15.

Krasner, S. D. 1978. *Defending National Interest: Raw Materials Investment and U.S. Foreign Policy.* Princeton: Princeton University Press.

Kraus, N. 2004. "The Significance of Race in Urban Politics: The Limitations of Regime Theory." *Race and Society* 7: 95–111.

Kraus, N., and T. Swanstrom. 2001. "Minority Mayors and the Hollow-Prize Problem." *PS: Political Science & Politics* 34: 99–105.

Krumholz, N. 1991. "Equity and Local Economic Development." *Economic Development Quarterly* 5: 291–300.

Kuttner, R. 1997. *Everything for Sale: The Virtues and Limits of Markets.* New York: A. A. Knopf.

———. 2007. *The Squandering of America: How the Failure of Our Politics Undermines Our Prosperity.* New York: A. A. Knopf.

Lafer, G. 2002. *The Job Training Charade.* Ithaca: Cornell University Press.

Lane, P. 1988. "Community-Based Economic Development: Our Trojan Horse." *Studies in Political Economy* 26: 177–91.

Lasch, C. 1991. *The True and Only Heaven.* New York: W. W. Norton.

———. 1995. *The Revolt of the Elites: And the Betrayal of Democracy.* New York: W. W. Norton.

Lauria, M. 1997a. Introduction to *Reconstructing Urban Regime Theory,* edited by M. Lauria, 1–9. Thousand Oaks, Calif.: Sage Publications.

——, ed. 1997b. *Reconstructing Urban Regime Theory.* Thousand Oaks, Calif.: Sage Publications.

Lees, L., T. Slater, and E. Wyly. 2008. *Gentrification.* New York: Routledge.

Leinberger, Christopher B. 2008. "The Next Slum?" *Atlantic* (March), 70–75.

Leitner, H., and M. Garner. 1993. "The Limits of Local Initiatives: A Reassessment of Urban Entrepreneurialism for Urban Development." *Urban Geography* 14: 57–77.

Lemann, N. 1991. *The Promised Land: The Great Black Migration and How It Changed America.* New York: Vintage.

——. 1994. "The Myth of Community Development." *Magazine,* 9 January: 27–31, 50, 54, 60.

Levine, J. 2006. *Zoned Out: Regulation, Markets, and Choices in Transportation and Metropolitan Land-Use.* Washington, D.C.: Resources for the Future.

Levine, M. V. 1987. "Downtown Redevelopment as an Urban Growth Strategy: A Critical Appraisal of the Baltimore Renaissance." *Journal of Urban Affairs* 9: 103–23.

——. 1988. "Economic Development in States and Cities: Toward Democratic and Strategic Planning in State and Local Government." In *The State and Democracy: Revitalizing America's Government,* edited by M. Levine, J. Faux, M. Raskin, C. Noble, and J. Kushma, 111–46. New York: Routledge.

——. 2000. "A Third World City in the First World: Social Exclusion, Racial Inequality, and Sustainable Development in Baltimore." In *The Social Sustainability of Cities,* edited by M. Polese and R. Stren, 123–56. Toronto: University of Toronto Press.

Levy, F. S., and P. Temin. 2007. "Inequality and Institutions in 20th Century America." MIT Department of Economics Working Paper No. 07–17, May.

Levy, J. M. 1992. "The US Experience with Local Economic Development." *Environment and Planning C: Government and Policy* 10: 51–60.

Lind, M. 2007. "The Smallholder Society." *Harvard Law and Policy Review* 1, no. 1: 143–60.

Lindblom, C. E. 1965. *The Intelligence of Democracy.* New York: Free Press.

——. 1977. *Politics and Markets.* New York: Basic Books.

——. 1982. "Another State of Mind." *American Political Science Review* 76: 9–21.

Lindblom, C. E., and E. J. Woodhouse. 1993. *The Policy Making Process, 3rd Edition.* Englewood Cliffs, N.J.: Prentice-Hall.

Lipietz, Alain. 1986. "New Tendencies in the International Division of Labor: Regions of Accumulation and Modes of Regulation." In *Production, Work, and Territory: The Geographical Anatomy of Industrial Capitalism,* edited by A. J. Scott and Michael Storper, 16–40. Boston: Allen and Unwin.

Logan, J. R., and H. Molotch. 1987. *Urban Fortunes.* Berkeley: University of California Press.

Long, N. E. 1987. "Labor Intensive and Capital Intensive Urban Economic Development." *Economic Development Quarterly* 1: 196–202.

Loury, G. C. 2007. "Why Are So Many Americans in Prison? Race and the Transformation of Criminal Justice." *Boston Review,* July–August. http://bostonreview.net/BR32.4/article_loury.php.

Lowndes, V. 1995. "Citizenship and Urban Politics." In *Theories of Urban Politics,* edited by D. Judge, G. Stoker, and H. Wolman, 160–80. London: Sage Publications.

Luria, D., and J. Russell. 1981. *Rational Reindustrialization: An Economic Development Agenda for Detroit.* Detroit: Widgetripper Press.

——. 1982. "Rebuilding Detroit: A Rational Reindustrialization Strategy." *Socialist Review* 12: 163–83.

Lustig, R. J. 1985. "The Politics of Shutdown: Community, Property, Corporatism." *Journal of Economic Issues* 19: 123–51.

Lynch, R. G. 1996. "Do State and Local Tax Incentives Work?" Washington, D.C.: Economic Policy Institute.

Lynd, S. 1987a. "The Genesis of the Idea of a Community Right to Industrial Property in Youngstown and Pittsburgh, 1977–1987." *Journal of American History* 74: 926–58.

——. 1987b. "Towards a Not-For-Profit Economy: Public Development Authorities for Acquisition and Use of Industrial Property." *Harvard Civil Rights–Civil Liberties Law Review* 22: 13–41.

MacDonald, H. 1997. "Comment on Sandra J. Newman and Ann B. Schnare's 'And a Suitable Living Environment': The Failure of Housing Programs to Deliver on Neighborhood Quality." *Housing Policy Debate* 8, no. 4: 755–62.

Mahtesian, C. 1996. "If You Can't Bribe the Owner, Maybe You Can Buy the Team." *Governing,* March: 42–45.

Mansbridge, J. J., ed. 1990. *Beyond Self-Interest.* Chicago: University of Chicago.

Manzo, L. C., R. G. Kleit, and D. Couch. 2008. "Moving Three Times Is Like Having Your House on Fire Once." *Urban Studies* 45, no. 9: 1855–78.

Manzo, L., and D. Perkins. 2001. "Neighborhoods as Common Ground: The Importance of Place Attachment to Community Participation and Development." Paper presented at the annual meeting of the Urban Affairs Association, Detroit.

——. 2006. "Finding Common Ground: The Importance of Place Attachment to Community Participation and Planning." *Journal of Planning Literature* 20, no. 4: 335–50.

Markusen, A. 2001. "Regions as Loci of Conflict and Change." *Economic Development Quarterly* 15, no. 4: 291–98.

Marquez, B. 1993. "Mexican American Community Development Corporations and the Limits of Directed Capitalism." *Economic Development Quarterly* 7: 287–95.

Massey, D. S., and N. A. Denton. 1993. *American Apartheid: Segregation and the Making of the Underclass.* Cambridge: Harvard University Press.

Mayer, M. 1988. "The Changing Conditions for Local Politics in the Transition to Post-Fordism." Paper prepared for the International Conference on Regulation Theory, Barcelona.

McArthur, A. A. 1993. "Community Business and Urban Regeneration." *Urban Studies* 30: 849–73.

McClure, K. 2005. "Comment on Victoria Basolo and Mai Thi Nguyen's 'Does Mobility Matter'." *Housing Policy Debate* 16, nos. 3–4: 347–59.

McCulloch, H., and B. Woo. 2008. "Expanding Asset-Building: Opportunities through Shared Ownership." Baltimore: Anne E. Casey Foundation. http://www.aecf.org/~/media/PublicationFiles/FES3622H120.pdf.

McGovern, S. 2009. "Mobilization on the Waterfront: The Ideological/Cultural Roots of Potential Regime Change in Philadelphia." *Urban Affairs Review* 44, no. 5: 663–94.

Medoff, P., and H. Sklar. 1994. *Streets of Hope: The Fall and Rise of an Urban Neighborhood.* Boston: South End Press.

Meehan, J. 1987. "Working toward Local Self-Reliance." In *Beyond the Market and the State: New Directions in Community Development,* edited by S. T. Bruyn and J. Meehan, 131–51. Philadelphia: Temple University Press.

Meeker-Lowry, S. 1996. "Community Money: The Potential of Local Currency." In *The Case against the Global Economy,* edited by J. Mander and E. Goldsmith, 446–59. San Francisco: Sierra Club Books.

Meyer, P. B. 1991. "Local Economic Development: What Is Proposed, What Is Done, and What Difference Does It Make?" *Policy Studies Review* 10: 172–80.

Mier, R., and J. Fitzgerald. 1991. "Managing Economic Development." *Economic Development Quarterly* 5: 268–79.

Miller, J. 2009. "Co-op Laundry First Up in Univ. Circle Initiative." *Crain's Cleveland Business,* 5 January: 1.

Mitchell, S. 2000. *Hometown Advantage: How to Defend Your Main Street against Chain Stores and Why It Matters.* Washington, D.C.: Institute for Local Self-Reliance.

———. 2006. *Big-Box Swindle.* Boston: Beacon Press.

Mollenkopf, J. H. 1983. *The Contested City.* Princeton: Princeton University Press.

Molotch, H. 1976. "The City as a Growth Machine." *American Journal of Sociology* 82: 309–32.

Moore, T. S. 1996. *The Disposable Work Force: Worker Displacement and Employment Instability in America.* New York: Aldine de Gruyter.

Morris, D. 1982. *The New City States.* Washington, D.C.: Institute for Local Self-Reliance.

———. 1998. "Defending Community in an Age of Globalization." *Canadian Dimension* 32, no. 3: 15–19.

Mossberger, K. 2009. "Urban Regime Analysis." In *Theories of Urban Politics, 2nd Edition,* edited by J. Davies and D. Imbroscio, 40–54. London: Sage Publications.

Mossberger, K., and G. Stoker. 2001. "The Evolution of Urban Regime Theory." *Urban Affairs Review* 6: 810–35.

New York Times. 1996. *The Downsizing of America.* New York: Times Books.

Noble, C. 2004. *The Collapse of Liberalism.* Lanham, Md.: Rowman and Littlefield.

Norman, R. T. 1989. "Empowering Cities and Citizens." In *The Gandhian Model of Development and World Peace,* edited by R. P. Misra, 223–40. New Delhi, India: Concept Publishing Company.

Nove, A. 1983. *The Economics of Feasible Socialism.* London: George Allen and Unwin.

Noyelle, T. 1986. "Economic Transformation." *Annals of the American Academy of Political and Social Science* (November): 9–17.

Nozick, R. 1974. *Anarchy, State, and Utopia.* New York: Basic Books.

O'Connor, A. 1999. "Swimming against the Tide: A Brief History of Federal Policy in Poor Communities." In *Urban Problems and Community Development,* edited by R. Ferguson and W. Dickens, 77–138. Washington, D.C.: Brookings Institution.

O'Connor, J. 1973. *The Fiscal Crisis of the State.* New York: St. Martin's Press.

Oden, M. D., and E. J. Mueller. 1999. "Distinguishing Development Incentives from Developer Give-Aways." *Policy Studies Journal* 27, no. 1: 147–64.

Offe, C. 1974. "Structural Problems of the Capitalist State: Class Rule and the Political System." In *German Political Studies Vol. 1,* edited by K. von Beyme, 31–57. Beverly Hills, Calif.: Sage Publications.

———. 1984. *Contradictions of the Welfare State.* Cambridge: MIT Press.

Office of Mayor, St. Paul. 1983. "Saint Paul's Homegrown Economy Project: A New Economic Policy and Program for a Self-Reliant City." Saint Paul, Minn.: City of Saint Paul.

Okun, A. 1975. *Equality and Efficiency: The Big Trade-off.* Washington, D.C.: Brookings Institution.

Olson, D.G. 1987. "Employee Ownership: An Economic Development Tool for Anchoring Capital in Local Communities." *Review of Law and Social Change* 15: 239–67.

Orfield, M. 1998. *Metropolitics.* Washington, D.C.: Brookings Institution.

———. 2002. *American Metropolitics.* Washington, D.C.: Brookings Institution.

Orr, M., and V. C. Johnson. 2008. "Power and Local Democracy: Clarence N. Stone and American Political Science." In *Power in the City,* edited by M. Orr and V. C. Johnson, 1–30. Lawrence: University Press of Kansas.

Orr, M., and G. Stoker. 1994. "Urban Regimes and Leadership in Detroit." *Urban Affairs Quarterly* 30: 48–73.

Osborne, D., and T. Gaebler. 1992. *Reinventing Government.* New York: Addison-Wesley.

Painter, J. 1995. "Regulation Theory, Post-Fordism, and Urban Politics." In *Theories of Urban Politics,* edited by D. Judge, G. Stoker, and H. Wolman, 276–95. London: Sage Publications.

———. 1997. "Regulation, Regime, and Practice in Urban Politics." In *Reconstructing Urban Regime Theory,* edited by M. Lauria, 122–43. Thousand Oaks, Calif.: Sage Publications.

Parzen, J. A., and M. Kieschnick. 1992. *Credit Where It's Due: Development Banking for Communities.* Philadelphia: Temple University Press.

Peirce, N. 2004. "Louisville's Metro: So Far, A Major Success." *Washington Post* Writers Group, 25 April. http://www.postwritersgroup.com/archives/peir0419.htm.

———. 2008. "Housing Policy: Turning Around the U.S. Disaster." *Washington Post* Writers Group, 20 July. http://www.postwritersgroup.com/archives/peir080720.htm.

Peretz, P. 1986. "The Market for Incentives: Where Angels Fear to Tread." *Policy Studies Journal* 5: 624–33.

Perlman, E. 1997. "Taking Mom and Pop Public." *Governing,* January: 17.

Persky, J., D. Ranney, and W. Wiewel. 1993. "Import Substitution and Local Economic Development." *Economic Development Quarterly* 7: 18–29.

Persky, J. J., and W. Wiewel. 1999. "Economic Development and Metropolitan Sprawl: Changing Who Pays and Who Benefits." In *The End of Welfare?* edited by M. B. Sawick, 27–156. Armonk, N.Y.: M. E. Sharpe.

Peterson, P. 1981. *City Limits.* Chicago: University of Chicago Press.

———. 1987. "Analyzing Development Politics: A Response to Sanders and Stone." *Urban Affairs Quarterly* 22: 540–47.

Pettit, P. 1997. *Republicanism: A Theory of Freedom and Government.* Oxford: Oxford University Press.

Pierson, P., ed. 2001. *The New Politics of the Welfare State.* Oxford: Oxford University Press.

Piore, M., and C. Sabel. 1984. *The Second Industrial Divide.* New York: Basic Books.

Polanyi, K. 1957 [1944]. *The Great Transformation.* Boston: Beacon Press.

Polikoff, A. 2006. *Waiting for Gautreaux.* Chicago: Northwestern University Press.

Polsby, N. W. 1980. *Community Power and Political Theory, 2nd Edition.* New Haven: Yale University Press.

Polsky, A. 1988. "Jane Jacobs and the Limits of Urban Capitalism." *Urban Resources* 5, no. 1: 9–14, 24.

———. 1991. *The Rise of the Therapeutic State.* Princeton: Princeton University Press.

Popkin, S., L. Buron, D. Levy, and M. Cunningham. 2000. "The Gautreaux Legacy." *Housing Policy Debate* 11, no. 4: 911–42.

Popkin, S. J., B. Katz, M. Cunningham, K. Brown, J. Gustafson, and M. A. Turner. 2004. *A Decade of Hope VI: Research Findings and Policy Challenges.* Washington, D.C.: Urban Institute.

Portz, J. 1990. *The Politics of Plant Closings.* Lawrence: University Press of Kansas.

Poulantzas, N. 1974. *Classes in Contemporary Capitalism.* Translated by D. Fernback. London: New Left Books.

Power, T. M. 1996. *Lost Landscapes and Failed Economies.* Washington, D.C.: Island Press.

President's Commission for a National Agenda for the Eighties. 1980. *Urban America in the Eighties.* Washington, D.C.: U.S. Government Printing Office.

Provo, J. 2009. "Risk-averse Regionalism: The Cautionary Tale of Portland, Oregon, and Affordable Housing." *Journal of Planning Education and Research* 28: 368–81.

Purcell, M. 2004. "Regionalism and the Liberal-Radical Divide." *Antipode* 36, no. 4: 760–65.

———. 2008. *Recapturing Democracy: Neoliberalization and the Struggle for Alternative Urban Futures.* New York: Routledge.

Purdy, M., and J. Sexton. 1995. "Facing Bank Service Shortage, Many Immigrants Improvise." *New York Times,* 11 September, C8–9.

Putnam, R. 1993. "The Prosperous Community: Social Capital and Public Life." *American Prospect,* 21 March: 35–42.

———. 2000. *Bowling Alone.* New York: Simon and Schuster.

Ramsey, M. 1996. *Community, Culture, and Economic Development.* Albany: State University of New York Press.

Rast, J. 1999. *Remaking Chicago: The Political Origins of Industrial Change.* DeKalb: Northern Illinois University Press.

Reed, A., Jr. 1988. "The Black Urban Regime: Structural Origins and Constraints." In *Power, Community, and the City: Comparative Urban and Community Research, Vol. I,* edited by M. P. Smith, 138–89. New Brunswick, N.J.: Transaction.

———. 2004. "A Lost Cause." *Boston Review,* Summer. http://bostonreview.net/BR29.3/reed.html.

Reed, A., and S. Steinberg. 2006. "Liberal Bad Faith in the Wake of Hurricane Katrina." *Black Commentator,* 4 May: 1–6.

Reese, L. A., and R. A. Rosenfeld. 2002. *The Civic Culture of Economic Development.* Thousand Oaks, Calif.: Sage Publications.

Ricker, T. 1998. *Estimating the Capital Costs of Community Destabilization.* Washington, D.C.: National Center for Economic and Security Alternatives.

Riposa, G., and G. Andranovich. 1988. "Economic Development Policy: Whose Interests Are Being Served?" *Urban Resources* 5: 25–34, 42.

Rockwell, L. H. 1994. "The Ghost of Gautreaux." *National Review,* 7 March: 57–59.

Rohter, L. 2008. "Shipping Costs Start to Crimp Globalization." *New York Times,* 3 August, A1.

Rosen, D. P. 1988. *Public Capital.* Washington, D.C.: National Center for Policy Alternatives.

Rosenbaum, J. E. 1991. "Black Pioneers: Do Their Moves to the Suburbs Increase Economic Opportunity for Mothers and Children?" *Housing Policy Debate* 2: 1179–1213.

———. 1995. "Housing Mobility Strategies for Changing the Geography of Opportunity." *Housing Policy Debate* 6: 231–70.

Rosenbaum, J. E., and S. J. Popkin. 1991. "Employment and Earnings of Low-Income Blacks Who Move to Middle-Class Suburbs." In *The Urban Underclass,* edited by C. Jencks and P. Peterson, 342–56. Washington, D.C.: Brookings Institution.

Rosenbaum, J. E., S. J. Popkin, J. E. Kaufman, and J. Rusin. 1991. "Social Integration of Low-Income Black Adults in Middle-Class White Suburbs." *Social Problems* 38, no. 4: 448–61.

Rubinowitz, L. S., and J. E. Rosenbaum. 2000. *Crossing the Class and Color Lines.* Chicago: University of Chicago Press.

Rusk, D. 1993. *Cities without Suburbs.* Washington, D.C.: Woodrow Wilson Press.

———. 1999. *Inside Game/Outside Game: Winning Strategies for Saving Urban America.* Washington, D.C.: Brookings Institution.

Sagalyn, L. B. 1990. "Public Profit Sharing: Symbol or Substance." In *City Deal Making,* edited by T. Lassar, 139–53. Washington, D.C.: Urban Land Institute.

Sale, K. 1980. *Human Scale.* New York: G. P. Putnam's Sons.

Sandel, M. 1982. *Liberalism and the Limits of Justice.* Cambridge: Cambridge University Press.

———. 1996. *Democracy's Discontent: America in Search of a Public Philosophy.* Cambridge: Harvard University Press.

Sanders, H. T. 2005. "Space Available: The Realities of Convention Centers as Economic Development Strategy." *Brookings Institution Research Brief.* Washington, D.C.: Brookings Institution.

Sanders, H. T., and C. N. Stone. 1987. "Development Politics Reconsidered." *Urban Affairs Quarterly* 22: 521–39.

Sapotichne, J., B. D. Jones, and M. Wolfe. 2007. "Is Urban Politics a 'Black Hole?' Analyzing the Boundary between Political Science and Urban Politics." *Urban Affairs Review* 43, no. 1: 76–106.

Savitch, H. V., and P. Kantor. 1993. "Can Politicians Bargain with Business: A Theoretical and Comparative Perspective on Urban Development." *Urban Affairs Quarterly* (December): 230–55.

Savitch, H. V., and J. C. Thomas. 1991. "Conclusion: End of the Millennium Big City Politics." In *Big City Politics in Transition,* edited by H. V. Savitch and J. C. Thomas, 235–51. Beverly Hills, Calif.: Sage Publications.

Savitch, H. V., and R. K. Vogel. 2000. "Metropolitan Consolidation versus Metropolitan Governance in Louisville." *State and Local Government Review* 32, no. 3: 198–212.

——. 2004. "Suburbs without a City: Power and City-County Consolidation." *Urban Affairs Review* 39, no. 6: 758–90.

Savitch, H. V., R. K. Vogel, and L. Ye. Forthcoming. "Beyond the Rhetoric: A Case Study of Louisville's Consolidation." *American Review of Public Administration.*

Scharr, J. 1967. "Equality of Opportunity and Beyond." In *NOMOS IX: Equality,* edited by J. R. Pennock and J. W. Chapman, 228–49. New York: Atherton Press.

Schumacher, E. F. 1975. *Small Is Beautiful: Economics as if People Mattered.* New York: Harper and Row.

Schweke, W. 1985. "Why Local Governments NEED an Entrepreneurial Policy." *Public Management* 67: 3–5.

Scott, A. J. 1988. "Flexible Production Systems and Regional Development: The Rise of New Industrial Spaces in North America and Western Europe." *International Journal of Urban and Regional Research* 12: 171–86.

Servon, L. J. 1999. *Bootstrap Capital: Microenterprises and the American Poor.* Washington, D.C.: Brookings Institution.

Sharp, E. 2007. "Revitalizing Urban Research: Can Cultural Explanation Bring the U.S. Back from the Periphery?" *Urban Affairs Review* 43, no. 1: 55–75.

Shavelson, J. 1990. *A Third Way, a Sourcebook: Innovations in Community-Owned Enterprise.* Washington, D.C.: National Center for Economic Alternatives.

Shefter, M. 1985. *Political Crisis/Fiscal Crisis.* New York: Basic Books.

Shipp, S. 1996. "The Road Not Taken: Alternative Strategies for Black Economic Development in the United States." *Journal of Economic Issues* 30, no. 1: 79–95.

Shuman, M. 1998. *Going Local: Creating Self-Reliant Communities in a Global Age.* New York: Free Press.

——. 1999. "Community Corporations: Engines for a New Place-Based Economics." *Responsive Community* 9, no. 3: 48–57.

——. 2006. *The Small-Mart Revolution: How Local Businesses Are Beating the Global Competition.* San Francisco: Berrett-Koehler Publishers.

Sites, W. 1997. "The Limits of Urban Regime Theory." *Urban Affairs Review* 32: 536–57.

Smith, D., with P. McGuigan. 1979. *Towards a Public Balance Sheet: Calculating the Costs and Benefits of Community Stabilization.* Washington, D.C.: National Center for Economic Alternatives.

Smith, M. P. 1989. "The Uses of Linked-Development Policies in U.S. Cities." In *Regenerating the Cities: The UK Crisis and the US Experience,* edited by M. Parkinson, B. Foley, and D. Judd, 85–99. Glenview, Ill.: Scott Foresman.

Smith, R. A. 1993. "Creating Stable Racially Integrated Communities." *Journal of Urban Affairs* 15, no. 1: 115–40.

Soifer, S. D. 1990. "The Burlington Community Land Trust." *Journal of Urban Affairs* 12, no. 3: 237–52.

Sowell, W. H. 1992. "A Theory of Structure." *American Journal of Sociology* 98: 1–29.

Spinner-Halev, J. Forthcoming. "The Trouble with Diversity." In *Critical Urban Studies: New Directions,* edited by J. Davies and D. Imbroscio. Albany: State University of New York Press.

Spirou, C., and J. Jurie. 1997. "Keep Your Eye on the Ball: Sports Ownership and Local Government." Paper presented at the annual meeting of the Urban Affairs Association, Toronto.

Squires, G. D. 1989. "Public-Private Partnerships: Who Gets What and Why." In *Unequal Partnerships: The Political Economy of Urban Redevelopment in Postwar America,* edited by G. D. Squires, 1–11. New Brunswick, N.J.: Rutgers University Press.

Squires, G. D., and C. E. Kubrin. 2005. "Privileged Places: Race, Uneven Development, and the Geography of Opportunity in Urban America." *Urban Studies* 42, no. 1: 47–68.

Staley, S. 2001. "Ground Zero in Urban Decline." *Reason* (November): 43–48.

Stanback, T., and T. Noyelle. 1982. *Cities in Transition.* Totowa, N.J.: Allanheld and Osmun.

Sternberg, E. 1993. "Justifying Public Intervention without Market Externalities: Karl Polanyi's Theory of Planning in Capitalism." *Public Administration Review* 53, no. 2: 100–109.

Stoecker, R. 1997. "The CDC Model of Urban Development: A Critique and an Alternative." *Journal of Urban Affairs* 19: 1–21.

Stoker, G. 1995. "Regime Theory and Urban Politics." In *Theories of Urban Politics,* edited by D. Judge, G. Stoker, and H. Wolman, 54–71. Thousand Oaks, Calif.: Sage Publications.

Stoker, G., and K. Mossberger. 1994. "Urban Regime Theory in Comparative Perspective." *Environment and Planning C: Government and Policy* 12, no. 2: 195–212.

Stokey, E., and R. Zeckhauser. 1978. *A Primer for Policy Analysis.* New York: W. W. Norton.

Stone, C. N. 1976. *Economic Growth and Neighborhood Discontent.* Chapel Hill: University of North Carolina Press.

——. 1980. "Systemic Power and Community Decision-Making." *American Political Science Review* 74, no. 4: 978–90.

——. 1987. "The Study of the Politics of Urban Development." In *The Politics of Urban Development,* edited by C. Stone and H. Sanders, 3–22. Lawrence: University Press of Kansas.

——. 1988a. "Political Change and Regime Continuity in Postwar Atlanta." Paper presented at the annual meeting of the American Political Science Association, Washington, D.C.

——. 1988b. "Preemptive Power: Floyd Hunter's Community Power Structure Reconsidered." *American Journal of Political Science* 32: 82–104.

——. 1989. *Regime Politics: Governing Atlanta, 1946–1988.* Lawrence: University Press of Kansas.

——. 1991. "The Hedgehog, the Fox, and the New Urban Politics." *Journal of Urban Affairs* 13, no. 3: 289–97.

———. 1993. "Urban Regimes and the Capacity to Govern." *Journal of Urban Affairs* 15, no. 1: 1–28.

———. 1997. "Urban Regime Analysis: Theory, Service Provision, and Cross-national Considerations." Paper prepared for the Workshop on Local Elites in a Comparative Perspective, Joint Sessions of the European Consortium for Political Research, Bern, Switzerland.

———. 2001. "The Atlanta Experience Reexamined." *International Journal of Urban and Regional Research* 25: 20–34.

———. 2005. "Looking Back to Look Forward: Reflections on Urban Regime Analysis." *Urban Affairs Review* 40, no. 3: 309–41.

———. 2006. "Power, Reform, and Urban Regime Analysis." *City & Community* 5, no. 1: 23–38.

———. 2008. "Urban versus American." *Urban News: Newsletter of the Urban Politics Section, APSA* 22, no. 3: 5–6.

———. 2009. "Who Is Governed? Local Citizens and the Political Order of Cities." In *Theories of Urban Politics, 2nd Edition,* edited by J. Davies and D. Imbroscio, 257–73. London: Sage Publications.

Stone, C. N., K. Doherty, C. Jones, and T. Ross. 1999. "Schools and Disadvantaged Neighborhoods." In *Urban Problems and Community Development,* edited by R. Ferguson and W. Dickens, 339–80. Washington, D.C.: Brookings Institution.

Stone, C. N., J. Henig, B. Jones, and C. Pierannunzi. 2001. *Building Civic Capacity: The Politics of Reforming Urban Schools.* Lawrence: University Press of Kansas.

Stone, C. N., M. Orr, and D. Worgs. 2006. "The Flight of the Bumblebee: Why Reform Is Difficult but Not Impossible." *Perspectives on Politics* 4, no. 3: 529–46.

Strauss, K., G. Clark, T. Hebb, and L. Hagerman. 2004. "U.S. Public Sector Pension Funds and Urban Revitalization: An Overview of Policy and Programs." School of Geography, Oxford University Centre for the Environment, working paper 05–02.

Sundquist, J. L. 1975. *Dispersing Population.* Washington, D.C.: Brookings Institution.

Swaney, J. A., and M. A. Evers. 1989. "The Social Cost Concepts of K. William Kapp and Karl Polanyi." *Journal of Economic Issues* 23, no. 1: 7–33.

Swanstrom, T. 1985. *The Crisis of Growth Politics.* Philadelphia: Temple University Press.

———. 1988. "Semisovereign Cities: The Politics of Urban Development." *Polity* 21: 83–110.

———. 1993. "Beyond Economism: Urban Political Economy and the Postmodern Challenge." *Journal of Urban Affairs* 15: 55–78.

———. 2000. "The Costs of Economic Segregation and Sprawl." Draft manuscript, Department of Political Science, State University of New York at Albany.

Swinney, D. 1998. "Building a Bridge to the High Road." Center for Labor and Community Research. http://www.clcr.org/publications/pdf/building_a_bridge.pdf.

Thompson, J. P. 1998. "Universalism and Deconcentration: Why Race Still Matters in Poverty and Economic Development." *Politics and Society* 26, no. 2: 181–219.

———. 2002. "Review of *Place Matters.*" *Urban Affairs Review* 37, no. 3: 446–48.

———. 2003. "Beyond Moralizing." In *A Way Out: America's Ghettos and the Legacy of Racism,* edited by J. Cohen, J. Decker, and J. Rogers, 60–67. Princeton: Princeton University Press.

Toups, C. 2000. "Boston's Dudley Triangle." *Building Blocks* 1, no. 2. http://www.knowl edgeplex.org/kp/text_document_summary/article/relfiles/bb_0102_toups.html.

Turner, M. A. 1998. "Moving Out of Poverty: Expanding Mobility and Choice through Tenant-Based Housing Assistance." *Housing Policy Debate* 9, no. 2: 373–94.

———. 2008. "Residential Segregation and Employment Inequality." In *Segregation: The Rising Costs for America,* edited by J. H. Carr and N. K. Kutty, 151–96. New York: Routledge.

Turney, K., S. Clampet-Lundquist, K. Edin, J. Kling, and G. Duncan. 2006. "Neighborhood Effects on Barriers to Employment." Princeton Industrial Relations Section Working Paper #511, April.

Turnham, J., and J. Khadduri. 2001. "Issues and Options for HUD's Tenant-Based Assistance Program." Report prepared for the Millennial Housing Commission's Consumer Based Assistance Task Force, Contract #MHC-2001–20. Bethesda, Md.: Abt Associates.

Uchitelle, L. 2008. "The Wage That Meant Middle Class." *New York Times,* 20 April, E3.

Unger, R. M. 1987. *False Necessity: Anti-Necessitarian Social Theory in the Service of Radical Democracy.* Cambridge: Cambridge University Press.

Vale, L. J. 2006. "Comment on Mark Joseph's 'Is Mixed-Income Development an Antidote to Urban Poverty?'" *Housing Policy Debate* 17, no. 2: 259–69.

Van Ham, M., and D. Manley. Forthcoming. "The Effect of Neighbourhood Housing Tenure Mix on Labour Market Outcomes: A Longitudinal Investigation of Neighbourhood Effects." *Journal of Economic Geography.*

Varady, D. P. 2005. Preface to *Desegregating the City,* edited by D. P. Varady, vii–xix. Albany: State University of New York Press.

Varady, D. P., and C. C. Walker. 2003. "Using Housing Vouchers to Move to the Suburbs." *Housing Policy Debate* 14, no. 3: 347–82.

Vaughan, R. J. 1988. "Economists and Economic Development." *Economic Development Quarterly* 2: 119–23.

Verba, S., K. L. Schlozman, and H. E. Brady. 1995. *Voice and Equality: Civic Voluntarism in American Politics.* Cambridge: Harvard University Press.

Vidal, A. C. 1992. *Rebuilding Communities: A National Study of Urban Community Development Corporations.* New York: Community Development Research Center, Graduate School of Management and Urban Policy, New School for Social Research.

Vogel, R. K. 1992. *Urban Political Economy.* Gainesville: University Press of Florida.

Wacquant, L. 1997. "Three Pernicious Premises in the Study of the American Ghetto." *International Journal of Urban and Regional Research* 20: 341–53.

Walzer, M. 1990. "The Communitarian Critique of Liberalism." *Political Theory* 18: 6–23.

Ward, K. 1996. "Rereading Urban Regime Theory: A Sympathetic Critique." *Geoforum* 27, no. 4: 427–38.

Warner, S. B. 1968. *The Private City.* Philadelphia: University of Pennsylvania Press.

Watkins, A. 1980. *The Practice of Urban Economics.* Beverly Hills, Calif.: Sage Publications.

Weiher, G. R. 1989. "Rumors of the Demise of the Urban Crisis Are Greatly Exaggerated." *Journal of Urban Affairs* 11: 225–42.

Weir, M. 2000. "Coalition Building for Regionalism." In *Reflections on Regionalism,* edited by B. Katz, 127–53. Washington, D.C.: Brookings Institution.

———. 2009. "Challenging Inequality in the New Metropolis." Paper presented at the Justice and the American Metropolis conference, St. Louis, Missouri.

Weir, M., H. Wolman, and T. Swanstrom. 2005. "The Calculus of Coalitions: Cities, Suburbs, and the Metropolitan Agenda." *Urban Affairs Review* 40: 730–60.

White, S. K. 1987. "Toward a Critical Political Science." In *Idioms of Inquiry: Critique and Renewal in Political Science,* edited by T. W. Ball, 113–36. Albany: State University of New York Press.

Wiewel, W., and R. Mier. 1986. "Enterprise Activities of Not-for-Profit Organizations." In *Local Economies in Transition,* edited by E. M. Bergman, 205–25. Durham: Duke University Press.

Williams, S. L. 2003. "From HOPE VI to HOPE Sick?" *Dollars and Sense* (July–August): 32–45.

Williamson, T. 2007. "There Is No Alternative to Forging an Alternative: On Gar Alperovitz's *America beyond Capitalism.*" *Good Society* 15, no. 3: 31–36.

———. Forthcoming. *Sprawl, Justice, and Citizenship: The Civic Costs of the American Way of Life.* Oxford: Oxford University Press.

Williamson, T., D. Imbroscio, and G. Alperovitz. 2002. *Making a Place for Community: Local Democracy in a Global Era.* New York: Routledge.

Wilson, W. J. 1987. *The Truly Disadvantaged.* Chicago: University of Chicago Press.

———. 1996. *When Work Disappears.* New York: Knopf.

———. 2009. "The Political and Economic Forces Shaping Concentrated Poverty." *Political Science Quarterly* 123, no. 4: 555–71.

Wolff, E. 2006. *Does Education Really Help? Skill, Work, and Inequality.* New York: Oxford University Press.

Wolman, H., with D. Spitzley. 1996. "The Politics of Local Economic Development." *Economic Development Quarterly* 10, no. 2: 115–50.

Wyly, E. Forthcoming. "√city/Radical City." In *Critical Urban Studies: New Directions,* edited by J. Davies and D. Imbroscio. Albany: State University of New York Press.

Yin, J. S. 2004. "A Review of Alternative Economic Base Methods for Community Economic Development." In *Critical Evaluations of Economic Development Policies,* edited by L. Reese and D. Fasenfest, 101–13. Detroit: Wayne State University Press.

Young, I. M. 2000. *Inclusion and Democracy.* New York: Oxford University Press.

Zaterman, S., D. Gross, and M. Kalenak. 2001. "Comment on Bruce Katz and Margery Turner's 'Who Should Run the Housing Voucher Program?'" *Housing Policy Debate* 12, no. 2: 283–90.

Zimbalist, A., and R. Noll, eds. 1997. *Sports, Jobs, and Taxes.* Washington, D.C.: Brookings Institution.

Index